HA

MORGAN   J

Hawaii

946

MORGAN   J

Hawaii

919.69   July '86

This book is due for return on or before the last date shown
above but it may be renewed by personal application, post,
or telephone, quoting this date and details of the book

**Northamptonshire
Leisure and Libraries**

Also in This Series

Arizona, Malcolm L. Comeaux

Colorado, Thomas Melvin Griffiths and Lynell Rubright

Missouri, Milton D. Rafferty

Maryland, James E. DiLisio

Texas, Terry G. Jordan, with John L. Bean, Jr., and William M. Holmes

Wyoming, Robert Harold Brown

Forthcoming Through 1984

Alaska, Robert W. Pearson and Donald F. Lynch

Michigan, Lawrence M. Sommers

Mississippi, Jesse O. McKee

New Jersey, Charles A. Stansfield

North Carolina, Ole Gade and H. Daniel Stillwell

South Carolina, Charles F. Kovacik and John J. Winberry

Utah, Clifford B. Craig

All books in this series are available in paperback and hardcover.

GEOGRAPHIES OF THE UNITED STATES

Ingolf Vogeler, Series Editor

Hawaii: A Geography

Joseph R. Morgan

Hawaii is the only one of the fifty United States that consists entirely of islands: 8 main islands and another 124 islets, rocks, shoals, and reefs stretch 1,500 miles across the tropical Pacific Ocean. The insular nature of the state, its dependence on the sea, the volcanic landscapes—including the world's most continuously active shield volcano—and a multi-ethnic population with roots in Polynesia, the Orient, and North America make for a fascinating physical and cultural geography. The landscape features Buddhist temples, Shinto shrines, and Protestant churches in both New England and Oriental architectural styles, but does not escape the freeways, traffic jams, high-rise buildings, and fast-food restaurants found on the mainland. Tourism, military bases, sugar and pineapple plantations, papaya and macadamia nut orchards, small farms, retail stores, banks, offices, and government activities are the bases of a diversifying economy that still, however, is greatly dependent on the tourist industry. Detailed treatment of the physical, cultural, and economic geography of the state, followed by a regional description of each of the main islands, makes this a comprehensive and intriguing book.

Dr. Joseph R. Morgan is assistant professor of geography at the University of Hawaii at Manoa. He has taught the geography of Hawaii for many years and is author of numerous books and articles on various aspects of the geography of the state.

HAWAII

A GEOGRAPHY

Joseph R. Morgan

Contributors:
Willard T. Chow
Brian Murton
Frank Peterson
John Street
Lyndon Wester

Westview Press / Boulder, Colorado

Geographies of the United States

Copyright © 1983 by Westview Press, Inc.

Published in 1983 in the United States of America by
  Westview Press, Inc.
  5500 Central Avenue
  Boulder, Colorado 80301
  Frederick A. Praeger, President and Publisher

Library of Congress Cataloging in Publication Data
Morgan, Joseph, 1927–
  Hawaii, a geography.
  (Geographies of the United States)
  Includes bibliographical references and index.
  1. Hawaii—Description and travel—1981–
I. Title. II. Series.
DU623.25.M67 1983   919.69   83-6713
ISBN 0-89158-942-2
ISBN 0-86531-488-8 (pbk.)

Printed and bound in the United States of America
10 9 8 7 6 5 4 3 2

To the girl on the cliffs

CONTENTS

PART 3
HUMAN ACTIVITIES AND ECONOMIC GEOGRAPHY

PART 5
CONCLUSIONS

FIGURES

TABLES

ACKNOWLEDGMENTS

Hawaii has a unique, fascinating geography, a point I have tried to make clear in this book. My interest in the geography of the fiftieth state stems both from my residence here and from my teaching duties at the University of Hawaii. At the university I have had the benefit of numerous discussions with fellow faculty members, from whom I have learned a great deal. To them I am particularly grateful. Abraham Piianaia, chairman of the Hawaiian Studies Program at the University of Hawaii and a longtime lecturer on the geography of Hawaii, has taught me the most.

In the actual preparation of the manuscript I have been helped enormously by Lori Koba and Julie Chun, who did a good deal of typing; by John David Little, who spent much time proofreading my draft, converting English units to their metric equivalents, and preparing an index of place-names; and by Everett Wingert, Dylan Hart, Karen Fukushima, Miratul Mahiuddin, Eric Roose, April Kam, George Hall, and James A. Bier, who in various ways assisted in the preparation of maps.

The authors of Chapters 7, 8, 9, 10, and 15 also deserve my gratitude for their scholarly work and cooperative attitudes. My special gratitude goes to Marian MacDorman for her contributions to Chapter 24. Although I was assisted by many people, any errors that remain in the book even after careful checking remain my responsibility.

Joseph R. Morgan
Honolulu, Hawaii

ABOUT THE CONTRIBUTORS

Dr. Willard T. Chow was associate professor of Geography and Urban Regional Planning at the University of Hawaii before becoming chief planning officer for the City and County of Honolulu. His research in the field of urbanization, particularly in Hawaii, has led to publication of articles in journals such as *Urban Geography, Town and Planning Review,* and the *Annals of Tourism.*

Dr. Joseph R. Morgan's thirteen years' residence in the Hawaiian Islands and seven years' experience in teaching the geography of Hawaii at the University of Hawaii have contributed to his interest in Hawaiian geography. His publications include a book on the island of Oahu, studies of the tsunami hazard in Hawaii and Japan, and articles on the Port of Honolulu and overseas and interisland shipping.

Brian J. Murton is interested in the cultural and historical geography of the Asian and Pacific tropics, including Hawaii. His own research in the areas of cultural adaptation and adjustment has led him to direct student research on natural hazards and hazard management in Hawaii, as well as in the South Pacific and South Asia.

Frank L. Peterson is professor of Geology at the University of Hawaii and hydrogeologist for the Hawaii Water Resources Research Center. He works mainly on problems of groundwater, engineering geology, and environmental geology, with special emphasis on the geology of the Hawaiian Islands. During the past two decades he has done hydrologic and geologic research and consulting work throughout the Hawaiian Islands and the Pacific basin.

Dr. John M. Street has observed, written about, and guided research on soil management in Hawaii for more than two decades. He has also conducted research on soil degradation in Latin America, the South Pacific, and Asia.

Dr. Lyndon L. Wester is associate professor of Geography at the University of Hawaii and a research associate in the Botany Department of the Bernice P. Bishop Museum. His main interests are the modification of natural vegetation by human activities, and his recent publications include studies of the introduction and spread of the mangrove and other problem plants in Hawaii, the weeds of taro, and changes in the composition of native grasslands of California during the nineteenth century.

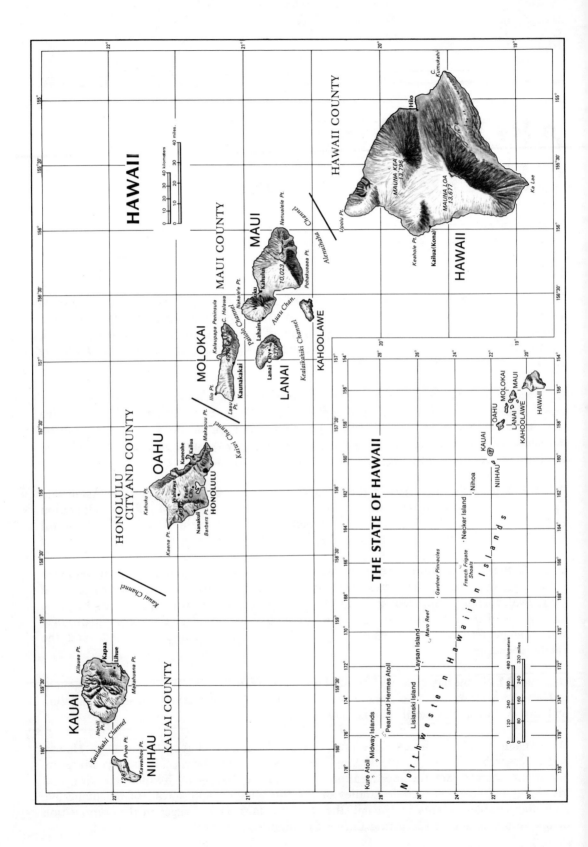

HAWAII

HONOLULU
CITY AND COUNTY

OAHU

Kahuku Pt.

Wahiawa
Pearl
City,
HONOLULU
Kaena Pt.
Barbers
Nanakuli
Pt.
Kaneohe
Kailua
Makapuu Pt.

Kauai Channel

KAUAI COUNTY

KAUAI

Kilauea Pt.
Kapaa
Lihue
Nohili
Pt.
Makahuena Pt.
Kaulakahi Channel
Puno Pt.
Kawaihoa Pt.
1281
NIIHAU

MOLOKAI

Ilio Pt.
C. Halawa
Kalaupapa Peninsula
Laau
Pt.
4970
Kaunakakai

Kaiwi Channel

Pailolo Channel

Nakalele Pt.
MAUI
Kahului
10,023
Lahaina
Auau Chan.
Lanai City
3370
LANAI
Kealaikahiki Channel
KAHOOLAWE

MAUI COUNTY

Pohakueaea Pt.
Nanualele Pt.

Alenuihaha
Channel

Upolu Pt.

HAWAII COUNTY

Hilo
C.
Kumukahi

MAUNA KEA
13,796
MAUNA LOA
13,677

Keahole Pt.
Kailua (Kona)

HAWAII

Ka Lee

0 10 20 30 40 miles
0 10 20 30 40 kilometers

THE STATE OF HAWAII

Kure Atoll
Midway Islands
Pearl and Hermes Atoll
Lisianski Island
Laysan Island
Maro Reef
Gardner Pinnacles
French Frigate
Shoals
Necker Island
Nihoa

N o r t h w e s t e r n   H a w a i i a n   I s l a n d s

KAUAI
NIIHAU

OAHU
MOLOKAI
LANAI
KAHOOLAWE
MAUI

HAWAII

0 80 160 240 320 miles
0 120 240 360 480 kilometers

PART 1

INTRODUCTION

CHAPTER 1

A UNIQUE STATE

A cursory glance at a map of the United States reveals that the fiftieth state, Hawaii, is unique. Like Alaska, it has no common boundaries with the other states, but unlike Alaska, Hawaii is not part of the great North American continental landmass. Hawaii, consisting of 132 islands, reefs, and shoals, stretches 1,523 miles (2,452 km) northwest-southeast in the tropics of the North Pacific Ocean.

Although Hawaii is certainly a small state, it is by no means the smallest. Connecticut, Delaware, and Rhode Island each is smaller—in fact, one of Hawaii's islands, Hawaii (commonly called the Big Island), is more than three times as large as Rhode Island. Eight main islands make up more than 99 percent of the state's 6,540 sq mi (16,705 sq km) (see Table 1.1). The remaining 124 are small and virtually uninhabited.

All of the state's inhabited islands are tropical. Hawaii extends from 18°54′ to 28°15′ north latitude and from 154°40′ to 178°15′ west longitude (see Figure 1.1). But the northernmost latitude of the island of Kauai, the most northerly of the main group of inhabited islands, is 22°14′ north latitude. For all practical purposes the state is completely within the tropics. This location is critical to any discussion of Hawaii's climate, vegetation, and largely tourism- and agriculture-based economy.

Hawaii's location in the North Pacific Ocean tropics makes it one of the most isolated groups of islands in the world.

The islands were settled by Polynesians who came from the Marquesas Islands, 2,400 mi (3,862 km) to the southeast, and from Tahiti, 2,800 mi (4,506 km) south of the Big Island. The closest of the mainland U.S. states is California; the distance from San Francisco to Honolulu is 2,390 mi (3,846 km). Japan's and China's mainlands are 3,850 mi (6,195 km) and 4,900 mi (7,900 km) west of Honolulu, respectively, and the Philippines, where a great many of Hawaii's recent immigrants come from, is almost 5,300 mi (8,524 km) west of the state. It is no wonder that the islands remained isolated from the non-Polynesian world until Captain James Cook, a British naval officer and explorer, "discovered" them in 1778.

The Hawaiian Islands became a Polynesian kingdom in 1795, when Kamehameha the Great, a warlike *alii* ("chief") from the Kohala district of the island of Hawaii, united most of the main islands by conquest. In 1810 the ruling *alii* of Kauai agreed to a peaceful annexation of his lands by Kamehameha, and the island became part of the Hawaiian kingdom. Increasing U.S. influence, which began with the arrival of Christian missionaries from New England in 1820, eventually resulted in the overthrow of the Hawaiian monarchy in 1893 and the establishment of first a provisional government and then a republic. In 1898, Hawaii was annexed by the United States, becoming a territory in 1900. Statehood came in 1959.

Table 1.1
Areas: State and Islands

	Total		Land		Inland water	
	Sq mi	Sq km	Sq mi	Sq km	Sq mi	Sq km
The State	6,450	16,705.5	6,425	16,640.7	25	65
Islands						
Hawaii	4,038.0	10,458.4	4,037.0	10,455.8	1.0	2.6
Kahoolawe	45.0	116.5	45.0	116.5	–	–
Molokini	0.006	0.015	0.006	0.015	–	–
Maui	728.8	1,887.6	728.2	1,886	0.6	1.6
Lanai	139.5	361.3	139.5	361.3	–	–
Molokai	261.1	676.2	260.9	675.5	0.2	0.5
Oahu	607.7	1,573.9	592.7	1,535.0	15.0	38.8
Kauai	553.3	1,433.0	548.7	1,421.1	4.6	11.9
Niihau	73.0	189.0	69.6	180.26	3.4	8.8
Lehua	0.380	0.984	0.380	0.984	–	–
Kaula	0.438	1.134	0.438	1.134	–	–
Northwestern Hawaiian Islands	3.2	8.3	3.0	7.8	0.2	0.5
Nihoa	0.298	0.771	0.298	0.771	–	–
Necker Island	0.091	0.235	0.091	0.235	–	–
French Frigate Shoals (includes La Perouse Pinnacle)	0.088	0.228	0.088	0.228	–	–
Gardner Pinnacles	0.004	0.010	0.004	0.010	–	–
Maro Reef	Awash	Awash	Awash	Awash	–	–
Laysan Island	1.533	3.970	1.312	3.398	0.220	0.570
Lisianski Island	0.675	1.748	0.675	1.748	–	–
Pearl and Hermes Reef (7 islets)	0.122	0.316	0.122	0.316	–	–
Kure Island	0.371	0.961	0.371	0.961	–	–
Green Island	0.354	0.917	0.354	0.917	–	–
Sand Island	0.017	0.044	0.017	0.044	–	–
Midway Islands	2.0	3.22	2.0	3.22	–	–

Sources: Atlas of Hawaii, 1st edition.
          State of Hawaii Data Book, 1981.

Asian cultural influences have been important in Hawaii since 1852, when a small number of Chinese came to the islands as contract laborers. Japanese and Filipinos increased the plantation labor force in the latter part of the nineteenth century and early part of the twentieth. Portuguese inmigrations in 1878 and successive years and influxes of Koreans and Puerto Ricans have also contributed to the ethnic mix of peoples now found in the islands. There has been much intermarriage, and no ethnic group can be considered to be a majority. The all-minority character of Hawaii's population is truly unique among the fifty United States.

Hawaii, with roots in both Asia and Europe, is a bridge between east and west because of its location and ethnic mix.

Hawaii is geologically part of the Pacific Ocean, not the North American continent as are the other forty-nine states. The islands are the summits of volcanoes that have been built up layer by layer from lava flows issuing from cracks in the Pacific Ocean floor. Two of these volcanoes, Mauna Loa and Kilauea on the Big Island, are active. Kilauea is the world's most active

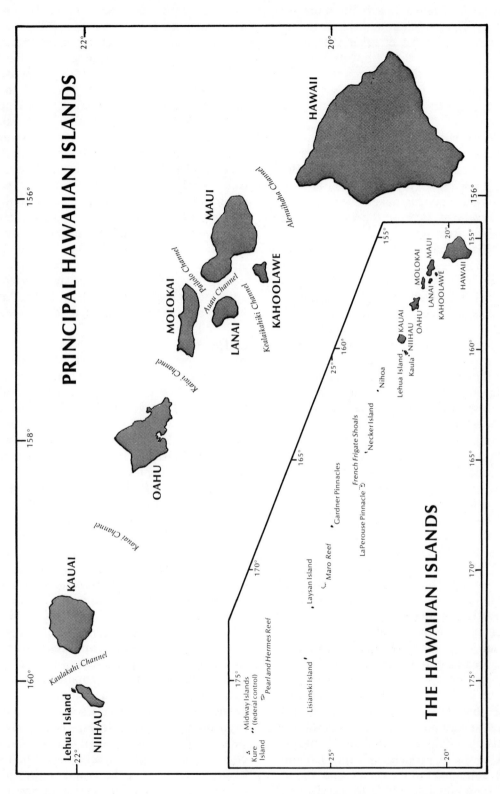

PRINCIPAL HAWAIIAN ISLANDS

THE HAWAIIAN ISLANDS

FIGURE 1.1

volcano, and Mauna Loa is, in some respects, the largest mountain on earth. Its mass far exceeds that of other volcanoes, and its height measured from its base on the Pacific Ocean floor exceeds the height of Mount Everest above sea level; truly this great shield volcano is a geological mammoth.

Volcanic activity at Kilauea is frequent but remarkably gentle by the standards of world volcanism. Tourists flock to the Big Island to witness eruptions, and the National Park Service makes viewing easy and convenient. Because the volcano is so active and its eruptions so easily observable, Kilauea has become the most useful and productive site for scientific studies of volcanic activity in all the world.

The physical landscape of the Hawaiian Islands is studded with volcanic features. There are gigantic shield volcanoes, some of which make up entire islands, as well as a variety of types of smaller cones. The world-famous Diamond Head is a tuff cone, as is the almost equally well-known Punchbowl. Both active and dormant Hawaiian volcanoes have calderas at their summits and cinder cones at the summits and on the flanks. The variety of volcanic landforms makes the state of Hawaii truly unique among the United States.

No other state is so completely dominated by the ocean, either. The ocean influences climate and creates coral reefs and coastal landforms. Hawaii's beaches are one of the foundations of the tourist industry, and the waves that break on the shores of the islands have made them a center of competitive surfing activity. Even on the largest of the islands, the Big Island, the distance from the most remote point to the shoreline is only 28.5 mi (45.9 km), and nowhere else in the state does this distance exceed 10.8 mi (17.4 km). Navigable channels lie between the various islands, and an interisland shipping service is used on a daily basis to deliver cargoes. There is no other state so dependent on ocean shipping for its needs, and in no other state is it impossible to travel over-

land to contiguous states. From Hawaii one must go either by air or sea.

The insular nature of the state makes for an interesting political geography. There are only four counties: the City and County of Honolulu (the island of Oahu and the numerous rocks, shoals, and islets making up the Northwestern Hawaiian Islands), Hawaii County (the island of Hawaii), Maui County (the islands of Maui, Molokai, Lanai, and Kahoolawe), and Kauai County (the islands of Kauai and Niihau). The government is streamlined; there are only four mayors, each governing a county, and the governor, who heads the state executive branch. There is no state police force and, since there is no extensive highway system, no highway patrol. Yet, surprisingly, there are state highways, and the island of Oahu has two interstate highways, designated H-1 and H-2.

The natural vegetation and bird and insect populations in the islands contain a very high percentage of endemic species, a consequence of Hawaii's isolation and the unusually large number of ecological environments found in the state. There are only three native mammal species, however: the Hawaiian monk seal, the hoary bat, and the Polynesian rat. The latter was inadvertently introduced by early Polynesian settlers but has since evolved into a true subspecies or geographic race.

Hawaii's soils, unlike soils on the mainland, are formed of basaltic and coral-limestone parent materials. Quartz sand does not exist in the islands, as they are basaltic rather than granitic in geological makeup. There are other features of Hawaiian soils that are unique, too, compared to soils in the mainland United States and in other tropical locales.

The climate of Hawaii is mainly tropical, and in that respect it differs from climates in the other forty-nine states. However, an even more interesting feature is the large number of micro-climates that exist, each characterized by greatly differing amounts of precipitation. On the island of Hawaii alone there are locations representative of

four of the five principal climate classifications in the Köppen system: tropical rain
forests, deserts, temperate, and tundra climates; only the "D" (snow) climates in
the Köppen system are lacking.

Hawaii's economic geography has unique
features. Tourism is the most important
industry, followed by large military bases
maintained by federal government expenditures in the islands. The success of the
islands' tourist industry is due to the fine
climate, the ocean and beaches, an exotic
multi-ethnic culture, a friendly social atmosphere called the Aloha Spirit, spectacular scenery, and live volcanoes. Hawaii's
military importance derives from its stra-
tegic location in the Pacific, midway between the continental United States and
nations in the western Pacific that are
considered crucial to the defense of the
nation.

Plantation farming of sugar and pineapple is also important in the economy of
the islands, and these crops are prominent
features of the cultural landscape. The islands are dotted with small towns that are
the outgrowth of former plantation camps;
fields of sugarcane and pineapple cover
thousands of acres. The island of Lanai is
operated as the world's largest pineapple
plantation, while Niihau is a cattle and
sheep ranch. (These two islands of the eight
main ones are privately owned.)

Place-names in the state of Hawaii are
also unique. Most are in the Hawaiian
language and are very descriptive and
meaningful to anyone who understands
their derivations. Even a slight knowledge
of the background of Hawaiian place-names
will provide insights into the physical and
cultural geography of the islands.

REFERENCES

Department of Geography, University of Hawaii. *Atlas of Hawaii*. Honolulu: University
Press of Hawaii, 1973.

State of Hawaii, Department of Planning and
Economic Development. *Data Book*. Honolulu: State of Hawaii, Department of Planning and Economic Development, 1980.

U.S. Geological Survey. *State of Hawaii* (map).
Washington, D.C.: U.S. Geological Survey,
1972.

CHAPTER 2

HAWAIIAN PLACE-NAMES

One of the unique features of the Hawaiian Islands is the exceptionally large number of place-names in the Hawaiian language. While it is not unusual to find American Indian place-names in some regions of the mainland United States, in Hawai'i* over 86 percent of the toponyms are in the original language of the native peoples—a language no longer regularly spoken, even by those of Hawaiian blood, and quite unfamiliar to island residents of mainland and Asian ancestry.

On the mainland many place-names do not have traceable meanings, particularly those of American Indian origin; most names in Hawaiian however, can be translated easily and hence are quite descriptive. As one would expect of a people living close to the land and nature, they gave names to many things: individual taro patches, house sites, valleys, streams, and sometimes even rocks that were deemed to have some particular spiritual significance. Legendary figures or demigods, such as Pele and Māui, have by their mythical feats lent names to various places. Thus, a study of toponyms in Hawai'i can be particularly interesting and instructive, and

*Hawaiian forms of words, rather than conventional forms, are used in this chapter. The list of Hawaiian Place-Names provides both conventional and Hawaiian-language spellings of place-names used in the text, as well as meanings when known.

by careful examination of the meanings of various place-names, much can be learned about Hawaiian life before the arrival of Westerners.

The original Hawaiians were immigrants from other parts of Polynesia, so their language as it was spoken in pre-1778 Hawai'i bears many similarities to other Polynesian languages. By examining cognate toponyms we can enrich our knowledge of the historical geography of Hawai'i and its relationships to other Polynesian lands and societies.

THE HAWAIIAN LANGUAGE

The Hawaiian language is particularly poor in consonants and correspondingly rich in vowel sounds. C. S. Stewart, a missionary who served in the islands during the years 1823, 1824, and 1825, described the language as consisting of seventeen letters. These were the five vowels *a, e, i, o,* and *u,* and the consonants *b, d, h, k, l, m, n, p, r, t, v,* and *w.* However, in 1826 the present orthography was adopted by the Christian missionaries, and the consonants were reduced to seven: *h, k, l, m, n, p,* and *w.* To these twelve letters (five vowels and seven consonants) have been added two additional letters: a reversed apostrophe, or glottal stop, and a macron. The glottal stop ('), which may be con-

9

sidered to be a consonant, indicates a short pause between two vowels. The macron, a short dash (-) placed over a vowel, indicates that the vowel is to be given a long, stressed pronunciation.

The glottal stop is important not only as a pronunciation aid but as a true consonant. Hence, it appears sometimes as the first letter of a word, as in *'ala* ("fragrant" or "perfumed") as contrasted with *ala* ("way," "path"). In many other cases the omission of the glottal stop changes the meaning of the word. Thus, *pau* means "finished," while *pa'u* means "soot or smudge" and *pa'ū* and *pā'ū* mean "moist or damp" and "a woman's skirt or sarong" respectively. In the latter two words the importance of both the glottal stop and the macron in the meaning of words is emphasized.

Vowel Sounds

The vowel sounds may be either stressed or unstressed. The following are examples of vowel pronunciations:

Unstressed. Unstressed vowels are pronounced like the example shown:

> *a* like *a* in *above*
> *e* like *e* in *bet*
> *i* like *y* in *city*
> *o* like *o* in *sole*
> *u* like *oo* in *moon*

Stressed. The stressed vowels are pronounced in this way:

> *a,ā* like *a* in *far*
> *e* like *e* in *bet*
> *ē* like *ay* in *play*
> *i,ī* like *ee* in *see*
> *o,ō* like *o* in *sole*
> *u,ū* like *oo* in *moon*

Some combinations of vowels are pronounced as diphthongs, that is, the sounds are run together with the stress on the first letter. These are *ei, eu, oi, ou, ai, ae, ao,* and *au.*

Consonants

The use and pronunciation of the glottal stop has already been discussed. The other consonants are pronounced about as in English, with the exception of the *w*, which is sometimes pronounced as a *v*. The *v* sound is used usually after the vowels *i* and *e*. The *w* sound is employed usually after *u* and *o*. When the word starts with the letter *w*, either the *v* or *w* pronunciation may be used. Likewise, the pronunciation is optional after the vowel *a*. The above rules have a number of exceptions and may be too complex to guide the pronunciation patterns of newcomers to the state.

HAWAIIAN PLACE-NAMES

Many names begin with an article: *ke, ka, nā,* or *he.* Place-names beginning with *ke* or *ka* are particularly numerous. With this in mind, determining the meaning of place-names is made easier, because the name can be broken up into recognizable syllables that can be translated one by one. Geographic terms that commonly find a place in toponyms in the Hawaiian language are associated with natural features of the environment, flora and fauna, colors, and sizes. Table 2.1 gives examples.

Directions

Wind directions are relatively constant in Hawai'i, with trade winds blowing more than 80 percent of the time in most regions, so the terms for *windward* and *leeward* appear as place-names for locations in the islands. Thus, *ko'olau* ("windward") is the name of the windward mountain range on the island of O'ahu, and *kona* ("leeward") is the name of a district on the west or leeward side of the island of Hawai'i.

The terms *north, south, east,* and *west* are rarely used, except on road signs for the interstate highway system on O'ahu. On O'ahu the terms *mauka* ("toward the mountains"), *makai* ("toward the sea"), *Diamond Head* ("toward Diamond Head, the prominent tuff cone in southeast O'ahu),

Table 2.1
Hawaiian Words Frequently Used in Place-Names

Geographic features

ala	path or way (commonly used to mean "street")
au	current, as an ocean current
hale	house or dwelling
hana or *hono*	bay
kai	sea
lae	cape, point, or forehead
lua	pit or crater; also the number 2
mauna	mountain
moku	island or district
pali	cliff
puna	spring
pu'u	hill or mound

Terms describing size

iki	small, little
loa	long
nui	large, big, great

Colors

kea	white
ula	red

Plants

kukui	candlenut tree
lau	leaf
ulu	grove
pua	flower
niu	coconut
hala	pandanus
hau	*Hibiscus tiliaceus*
maile	a fragrant vine
lehua	the flower of the ohi'a tree

Animals

manu	bird, insect
moa	chicken
pueo	owl
manō	shark
honu	turtle
pua'a	pig

and *Ewa* (toward the old plantation Ewa, in the southwestern part of O'ahu) are used instead of *north, south, east,* and *west.* On other islands in the state similar directions are used, with the suffix *uka* ("toward the mountains or inland") and *kai* ("toward the sea") appended to place-names. The term *waena,* meaning "middle," also is used occasionally as a direction.

Cognates

Many toponyms in Hawai'i are cognate with other parts of Polynesia. It is not difficult to trace linguistic changes in the various Polynesian languages as they evolved in Hawai'i. Certain sounds do not appear in the Hawaiian language, but do in other Polynesian tongues. Among these are the consonants *s, t, r,* and *ng.* Thus, the Samoan *Savai'i* became the Hawaiian *Hawai'i,* and *Tonga* became *Kona.* Frequently the *k* sound in other languages in Polynesia became the glottal stop in Hawaiian. An example is the island called *Tokelau* in the Tongan language, which became *Ko'olau* in Hawaiian. One of the more common sound changes is that of *t* becoming *k.* There are a number of examples, one of the most well known being the change from *Tahiti* to *Kahiki.* Thus, *Kahiki nui,* the term for a land division on the island of Maui, is cognate with *Tahiti nui,* literally "great Tahiti."

The channel between the islands of Lāna'i and Kaho'olawe is called *Kealaikahiki.* We can break down this name into its component syllables and cognate form as follows: *Te ala i tahiti*—literally, "the way to Tahiti." This translation provides linguistic evidence that there was a regular sea route between the Hawaiian Islands and Tahiti. Moreover, the path followed by a sailing canoe leaving the Kealaikahiki Channel points toward Tahiti if the vessel's stern is lined up with Kikoa Point, the easternmost point on the island of Lāna'i, and Kamakou, the highest elevation on Moloka'i.

Names of the Principal Islands

In most cases the names of the inhabited Hawaiian Islands have no translatable meanings. The island of Maui is named for the demigod Māui, and *Lāna'i* means "day of conquest," but there are no meanings for *O'ahu, Kaua'i, Moloka'i, Ni'ihau,* or *Hawai'i. Hawai'i,* however, has a number of cognates and some refer to a homeland or to the underworld of the dead. The name of the uninhabited island of Kaho'olawe translates literally to "the carrying away," as by currents.

Some Examples of Interesting Place-Names

The two largest volcanic mountains in the state are Mauna Loa ("long mountain") and Mauna Kea ("white mountain"). Mauna Kea, the Hawaiian peak with the greatest elevation above sea level (13,796ft—4,205m), is snow-capped during most winter months. Mauna Loa's oval form clearly makes it a long mountain. The giant shield volcano that forms the entire eastern half of the island of Maui, Haleakalā ("house used by the sun"), derives its name from the legend in which Māui lassoed the sun in that place in order to make the day longer so that his mother would have more time to dry her tapa. Wai'ale'ale, a Kaua'i peak that gets a mean annual rainfall of more than 470 in. (1,194 cm), is well named. The literal translation is "overflowing water."

Honolulu can be translated "protected bay," entirely appropriate as the harbor in the city of that name is well protected from winds and ocean swells. As a matter of fact, when it was discovered by Captain William Brown of the fur-trading vessel *Butterworth,* he called it Fair Haven, certainly no different in meaning from its Hawaiian name.

In the Puna district of the Big Island is the village of Kaimū, site of a famous black-sand beach. *Kaimū* means "gathering sea" and as the region is a well-known surfing area, the name presumably indicated a place where people gathered to watch surfing.

The meaning of *Kaimukī*, the name of a residential district in Honolulu, has a completely different origin, however. It can be broken down into *ka imu ki,* meaning "the ti oven." A legend tells the story of mythical people, Menehune, who cooked their ti roots in ovens there.

A city on the windward side of O'ahu, a village on the leeward side of the island of Hawai'i (in the Kona district), and a small community and land division on the north shore of Maui are named *Kailua.* Its meaning is "two seas," possibly because two strong currents flow offshore from the Big Island community. The use of *lua* as the numeral *two* is common in Hawaiian place names. Another well-known example is *Wailua*, a name that appears on the islands of Hawai'i and Kaua'i—the translation is "two waters."

The use of *lua* to mean "pit" or "crater" is equally common, particularly in the regions of recent volcanic activity. *Luamanu* ("bird pit") is the name of a pit crater in the Kīlauea volcano; *luahononu* ("deep pit") a pit crater in the caldera of Mauna Loa. Another interesting use of the word is in the place-name *luawai* ("water hole"), a land section on the island of Hawai'i and a street in the Kaimukī section of Honolulu.

Pōhakuloa ("long stone") appears seventeen times among the place-names in the state. Another very popular name is *Kukui*, which is found fourteen times in various places throughout the islands. *Waimea* ("reddish water") is one of the most famous toponyms in Hawai'i. It is the name given to a town in southwestern Kaua'i, where Captain Cook made his first landing in the islands; a small town in the Kohala district of the Big Island; a well-known bay and surfing area on the north shore of

O'ahu; and waterfalls, ditches, trails, plantations, schools, and beaches in the nearby districts of the three principal locations.

The southernmost location in the United States is South Point on the island of Hawai'i. The Hawaiian name is *Ka Lae*, which means simply "the point or cape." Cape Kumukahi ("first beginning") is the most easterly point in the state of Hawai'i. 'Upolu Point on the island of Hawai'i is cognate with 'Upolu, an island in Samoa.

Use in This Text

The importance of glottal stops and macrons notwithstanding, most readers (including many in Hawaii) are unfamiliar with this method of spelling and find the conventional spellings of Hawaiian names more to their liking. In the text that follows, conventional spellings are used.

REFERENCES

Bier, J. A. *Map of Hawai'i—The Big Island.* Honolulu: University Press of Hawaii, 1979.

——. *Map of Kaua'i—The Garden Isle.* Honolulu: University Press of Hawaii, 1979.

——. *Map of Maui—The Valley Isle.* Honolulu: University Press of Hawaii, 1979.

——. *Map of Moloka'i—The Friendly Isle and Lāna'i—The Pineapple Isle.* Honolulu: University Press of Hawaii, 1977.

——. *Map of O'ahu—The Gathering Place.* Honolulu: University Press of Hawaii, 1977.

Department of Geography, University of Hawaii. *Atlas of Hawaii.* Honolulu: University Press of Hawaii, 1973.

Pukui, M. K.; Elbert, S. H.; and Mookini, E. T. *Place Names of Hawaii.* Rev. and exp. ed. Honolulu: University Press of Hawaii, 1974.

——. *The Pocket Hawaiian Dictionary.* Honolulu: University Press of Hawaii, 1975.

Stewart, C. S. *Journal of a Residence in the Sandwich Islands During the Years 1823, 1824, and 1825.* Honolulu: University of Hawaii Press, 1970.

PART 2

PHYSICAL ENVIRONMENTS

CHAPTER 3

VOLCANIC LANDFORMS

On May 17, 1980, Mount St. Helens, in the state of Washington, erupted. Huge clouds of ash and gas rose from the summit of the volcano for thousands of feet. A state of emergency was in effect in the vicinity of the eruption, and some communities were evacuated. Sixty-five people were killed and 150 sq mi (390 sq km) of prime forest land destroyed. Inasmuch as this was the first eruption in the mainland forty-eight states in over sixty years, it is not surprising that such precautions were taken, for most of us realize that volcanic eruptions are dangerous and can cause wide-scale property damage and loss of life. In Hawaii, however, volcanic eruptions are more common and are virtually continuous in Kilauea, on the island of Hawaii. When spectacular lava fountains spew out of Kilauea or Mauna Loa, emergencies are not declared and communities are rarely evacuated. Rather, people flock to the Big Island, and the principal danger is probably the distinct possibility that two small sightseeing planes might collide as they vie for the best viewing space over the eruptive crater.

TYPES OF VOLCANISM

The Hawaiian Islands are the tops of great shield volcanoes formed from layer after layer of lava flows issuing from cracks in the floor of the Pacific Ocean. The formation of these great volcanic domes, or shields, is a characteristic of one of the six basic types of volcanic eruptions. These six types are described in order of increasing explosiveness.

Flood Eruptions. Fissures are scattered over the land. Explosive activity is completely absent as thick, basaltic lava flows flood the landscape. A volcanic plateau is formed, but no peaks or domes are evident in the flat landscape.

Hawaiian Eruptions. Numerous thin, fluid, basaltic lava flows build shield-volcanic domes. There are few or no explosions. Spatter and cinder cones are sometimes built up along the volcanic vents. Other features, such as ash or tuff cones, are occasionally formed. Hawaiian eruptions, particularly those that result in distinctive landforms, will be described in more detail.

Strombolian Eruptions. More tephra (solid volcanic material) than lava characterizes these eruptions. Composite cones are formed, such as Fuji, Vesuvius, and Mayon (in the Philippines).

Vulcanian Eruptions. Small, stubby lava flows are characteristic of this type of eruption, as well as a great amount of tephra and many violent explosions.

Peléean Eruptions. Mount Pelée, on the island of Martinique, is a classic example

FIGURE 3.1. Halemaumau, a crater within the caldera of Kilauea, has been the site of countless volcanic eruptions. It is shown here on a typical day, smoking and steaming but otherwise quiet.

of this type of very violent, explosive volcano.

Plinian Eruptions. This extremely violent eruptive type is characterized by Krakatoa; its eruption was felt worldwide.

VOLCANISM IN HAWAII

A fissure more than 1,600 mi (2,575 km) long in the floor of the Pacific Ocean has produced the Hawaiian Ridge. Along its top protrude the individual domes that are the Hawaiian Islands. The differing landscape forms of the islands are due to different stages of shield-building activity and erosion. The older islands to the northwest are more eroded, and some have become coral atolls, as erosion, sinking of the volcanic land mass, and coral growth have combined to produce the atoll landform.

It is presumed that the mass of the Hawaiian Ridge has caused the ocean-floor crust surrounding the ridge to sink and form the Hawaiian Deep, an almost continuous zone of deeper water surrounding the broad platform on which the islands sit. A bulge further out from the ridge is known as the Hawaiian Arch.

Lava Flows

The molten material within the earth is known as *magma*. When it issues from an opening in the earth's crust it is called *lava*. Hawaiian volcanism is characterized by an abundance of lava and a relative deficiency of gaseous and solid material. Eruptions sometimes are in the form of magmatic explosions, in which lava "fountains" and "curtains of fire" arise out of a volcanic vent.

There are two chief types of lava flows: *aa* and *pahoehoe*. Aa flows are rough, clinkery, viscous, and slow moving. The resultant landscape is characterized by sharp, jagged rocks that are black in color and very difficult to walk on. Volcanic gases are stirred out of solution rapidly in these flows, and this is undoubtedly the basic reason for the jagged, rough characteristic of the lava that congeals. Pahoehoe flows are much more fluid than aa. The gas content is less, and the gas comes out of solution slowly; the surface of the flow

FIGURE 3.2. Pahoehoe and aa lava flows side by side in Hawaii Volcanoes National Park. The lava is from recent eruptions of Mauna Ulu, on the East Rift Zone of Kilauea.

appears to be smooth, billowy, and sometimes ropy. Both aa and pahoehoe have the same chemical and mineral composition; it is only the physical form that differs. In a typical large lava flow there might be some intergrading of the forms, and pahoehoe sometimes changes into aa downslope from the vent. The reverse, aa into pahoehoe, has not been known to happen.

Shield Volcanoes

Thin layers of both aa and pahoehoe flows, thousands in number, combine to produce shield volcanoes: gently rounded volcanic mountains that are built with very little explosive activity. Lava issues from a summit crater and from additional vents on the flanks of the shield. These flank vents are parts of rift zones emanating from the summit crater and running downslope. There are usually two of these rift zones, frequently running at an oblique angle from the summit.

The shield volcano has a characteristic gently rounded shape, but not all shields are of the same degree of smoothness and steepness. Some are characterized by more cinder cones on their flanks, presumably as a result of a greater degree of explosiveness in their eruptive sequences. On the Big Island there are five shield volcanoes. Three of these—Mauna Loa, Kilauea, and Kohala—are of the classic smooth-shield type. The other two—Mauna Kea and Hualalai—are somewhat steeper in slope and have more cinder cones on their flanks. They are clearly shield volcanoes, differing in form quite obviously from the typical composite cone form of Fuji, but their appearance and mode of formation are sufficiently different from the classic shield volcano to perhaps be given a new classification. One author (Stearns 1966) has called them "steep domes."

Secondary Volcanic Landforms

Since all of the Hawaiian Islands are constructed of one or more shield volca-

FIGURE 3.3. The gently rounded shape of Mauna Loa as seen from the Kau Desert, Kau district, island of Hawaii.

noes, the gently rounded form of these domes, including the shape of the steep domes, constitutes the primary landform. Sometimes, however, smaller features of the physical landscape are more visible than the giant shields, which frequently cannot be recognized readily because of their extreme size. The principal secondary features will be described.

Calderas, large collapsed craters at the summits of the shields, are formed by the draining away of magma within the volcano and the consequent weakening of the entire shield. Steep slopes form the boundaries of the calderas, which have relatively flat floors. Calderas in the Mauna Loa and Kilauea volcanoes are clearly evident, while they are more difficult to find in volcanoes that have not erupted recently and have undergone considerable erosion. In some cases what appears to be a caldera is something else. For instance, at the summit of Haleakala, the giant shield volcano forming the eastern part of the island of Maui, there is a great crater within which there are a

number of cinder cones. Although often incorrectly referred to as the world's largest caldera, the feature is neither particularly large by caldera standards nor a true caldera. It is caused not by collapse of the summit of the volcano, but by erosion. Table 3.1 identifies the calderas in the Hawaiian Islands. Not all shield volcanoes have calderas—calderas have not formed in the West Molokai volcano or in the Big Island shields of Mauna Kea and Hualalai.

Pit craters are smaller collapse features found usually on the flanks of the shields, along the rift zones. Their formation is analogous to formation of calderas, and they are sometimes located within calderas.

Other forms of craters are found throughout the Hawaiian landscape. These have been classified by Stearns (1966) as "positive forms" and were the orifices of lava fountains or explosive eruptions that did not result in collapse. Some of the larger ash or tuff cones, such as Diamond Head on Oahu, were formed from quite violent explosive activity. The broad saucer-

Table 3.1
Hawaiian Calderas

Island	Mountain or Caldera Name	Length mi.	km.	Width mi.	km.	Location
Kahoolawe		3.00	4.83	2.50	4.02	
Kauai	Waialeale	13.00	20.92	11.00	17.79	Alakai swamp
Kauai	Lihue depression	11.00	17.70	6.00	9.65	
Kauai	Haupu caldera	2.50	4.02	1.00	1.61	
Lanai	Palawai basin	4.00	6.44	3.00	4.83	
Hawaii	Kilauea	2.93	4.71	1.95	3.14	
Hawaii	Mauna Loa (Mokuaweoweo)	3.70	5.95	1.74	2.80	
Maui	East Maui	2.00	3.22	1.50	2.41	Iao Valley
Molokai	East Molokai	4.50	7.24	2.00	3.22	
Oahu	Koolau	6.00	9.65	4.00	6.44	Waimanalo to Kaneohe
Oahu	Waianae	5.00	8.05	3.00	4.82	Kolekole pass, Lualualei valley

Source: Stearns (1966)

shaped depressions, found at the summits of cinder and ash cones, are also called craters.

When blobs of molten lava (*bombs* or *spatter*) fall around the volcanic vent, they form features known as *spatter cones*. The congealed lava forms asymmetric hills, sometimes in a more linear form—then known as *spatter ramparts*.

Cinder cones, which can be anywhere from 50 to 700 ft (15.2 to 213.3 m) in height and 0.75 mi (1.21 km) in diameter, are formed of light, frothy fragments of volcanic material. This may be referred to as cinder or sometimes as *scoria*.

Explosive eruptions have occasionally occurred in Hawaii as magma and water united in the form of hydromagmatic explosions. Ash fragments (less than 0.25 in. or 0.62 cm across) are showered out around the vent, sometimes to great distances, and form walls around a shallow depression. The landform that results is referred to as an *ash cone*. After the ash weathers and hardens it consolidates into tuff, and the features are called *tuff cones*. On the island of Oahu the most prominent volcanic features are tuff cones: Diamond Head, Koko Head, Koko Crater, Punchbowl, and Hanauma Bay. The bay is a tuff cone formed at the shoreline and breached by the ocean; ocean water filled the depression, and eventually a coral reef was formed in the shallow waters.

Hawaiian volcanic activity frequently forms *lava lakes,* if the eruptive activity is confined within the walls of a crater. The lake is not placid, however, as additional molten material continues to issue out of the vent at the bottom. Hence, the

FIGURE 3.4. Puu Puai, a prominent cinder cone on Kilauea, was built by an extraordinary eruption in 1959.

surface of the lake forms waves, currents, and occasionally fountains.

Lava tubes are formed in pahoehoe lava flows under certain conditions. Sometimes the surface of the flow hardens while the lava in the interior is still molten; the lava then drains out of the flow from below, leaving a tunnel or tube. Some lava tubes are of quite impressive dimensions, comparable in size to subway tunnels in large cities.

Kipukas are islands of older lava surrounded by more recent lava flows. They are common on the Big Island, where volcanic activity is still going on. The kipukas stand out in the surrounding lava fields because the older lava surfaces have weathered into soil and support vegetation.

Active volcanoes such as Kilauea are more or less continuously producing steam. The steam vents are referred to as *fumaroles*. When the fumaroles contain sulfurous gas, they are called *solfataras*.

Thus far the volcanic features described have been extrusive, caused by lava or other volcanic ejecta being extruded out from the crust of the earth. Sometimes, however, magma hardens in place within the crust, and dikes and sills are formed. *Dikes* are vertical structures of dense basalt that appear when the surrounding softer lava is weathered and eroded away. When the intrusive material is horizontal, the feature is referred to as a *sill*. Numerous dikes and sills can be seen in the Waianae Range of Oahu, and dike structures in the Koolau Range are important in the water supply of communities on the windward side of that island. Water percolates through the porous lavas, but is trapped behind the impermeable dike structures so that a fresh-water supply is available in the dike and sill swarms.

When aa lava flows reach the coast and enter the ocean, the contrast in temperature between the hot lava and the cooler ocean results in explosive activity. Sometimes a *littoral cone* is built as small particles consolidate. When sand-sized particles are formed and subsequently washed ashore, a black-sand beach may result.

A Classification
of the Stages of Hawaiian Volcanoes

Stearns (1966) described a theoretical life cycle of a typical oceanic shield volcano from birth under the surface of the water to very old age as a coral atoll. In his formulation he recognized eight separate stages. Macdonald and Abbott (1970), while generally following the Stearns scheme, had different names for the various stages and included a ninth stage. In this section the names utilized by Stearns will be followed, with the Macdonald and Abbott names in parentheses. The life cycle of a volcanic island includes both constructional processes like volcanism and coral reef growth and erosional processes. Both will be discussed in more detail in subsequent chapters, but the following is a brief list of the eight main stages in the life of a volcanic island.

1. Explosive Submarine Stage (Deep submarine stage and shallow submarine stage). A volcanic vent opens on the floor of the ocean. Fluid lavas issue from the vent in the form of pillow lavas, and a shield volcano begins to form as layer upon layer builds up. When the shield has been built up to about 5,000 ft (1,524 m) beneath the surface of the ocean, the eruptions become somewhat more explosive, with ash and pumice alternating with the more fluid lavas. When the shield reaches the surface there are hydromagmatic explosions as the hot lava and the cool seawater meet at the air surface. Ash cones are built on top of the shield at the same time as the ocean is working to erode the new island. Thus there is, in effect, a battle between the destructive forces of the ocean and the constructive forces of the volcano.

2. Lava-producing, or Dome, Stage (Subaerial shield-building stage). Once the surface of the volcano is clearly above the surface of the ocean, the volcanic activity becomes gentle again. Fluid lavas pour out and continue to build the shield. At this time the form of the shield becomes more evident, with a crater at the top and two rift zones on the flanks, intersecting in the summit crater.

Collapse, or Caldera, Stage (Caldera stage). The volcano gradually collapses at the vent areas at the summit, forming a caldera. The collapse may take place in a number of phases and may continue for a long time. The active volcanoes, Kilauea and Mauna Loa on the Big Island, are in this stage, as is the volcano that forms the island of Lanai.

4. Trachyte and Cinder Cone Stage (Postcaldera stage). Aa lava flows fill the caldera, and high lava and pumice fountains build large cinder cones. The profile of the dome changes, becoming steeper and more studded with cinder cones on the flanks. Hualalai and Mauna Kea on the island of Hawaii are examples of volcanoes in this stage.

5. Marine and Stream Erosion Stage (Erosional stage). Volcanic activity ceases, and the dome is partially destroyed by erosion. The top of the volcano is removed by the forces of stream erosion; deep valleys are cut. The ocean produces steep sea cliffs as it eats into the lava flows at the coast. Coral growth begins and fringing reefs develop.

6. Submergence and Fringing Reef Stage (Reef growth stage). The island sinks and becomes partially drowned. Coral reef growth continues, and as the island sinks, the fringing reefs become barrier reefs.

7. Secondary Eruptions and Barrier Reef Stage (Post-erosional eruptions stage). Volcanic activity begins again, and the eruptions are more explosive. In addition to lava flows there are hydromagmatic and phreatomagmatic explosions that result in the formation of ash and tuff cones. On Oahu both the Waianae and Koolau volcanoes are examples of this stage. Others are Haleakala and West Maui mountains on Maui and East Molokai, Kahoolawe, and Niihau.

8. Atoll and Resubmergence Stage (Atoll

FIGURE 3.5. Waianae Mountains as seen from Kunia Road, central Oahu. The greatly eroded shield was once the Waianae volcano, the older of the two volcanoes that formed the island of Oahu. Pineapple fields occupy the flat central plain and the lower slopes of the mountains.

stage). Submergence of the volcano continues, and stream and ocean erosion plane off the island. As coral reef growth continues, an atoll is formed. Midway and Kure atolls are examples.

Examples of the Stages

While there are examples of all but the first two of these stages among the volcanoes that make up the Hawaiian Islands, not all volcanoes follow the complete sequence. Apparently some volcanoes have skipped the caldera stage, and others have not been through the secondary eruptions and barrier reef stage.

The presence of a number of atolls in the Northwestern Hawaiian Islands indicates that these volcanoes are older than the main group of islands. Ages in the main group, as determined by the potassium-argon method, increase from southeast to northwest. Stearns (1966) has given

the following order of extinction for the volcanoes: Kauai, Waianae, Koolau, West Molokai, East Molokai, West Maui and Lanai, Kahoolawe, Haleakala, Kohala, and Mauna Kea. Hualalai, Mauna Loa, and Kilauea are either currently active or have erupted in historic time. All of these facts are consistent with the scheme of stages previously described. It seems apparent that the Pacific plate, on which the Hawaiian chain sits, has drifted northwestward over a volcanic vent, or "hot spot," and the volcanic islands have formed, grown to maturity, and reached the atoll stage in order from northwest to southeast.

REFERENCES

Macdonald, G. A., and Abbott, A. T. *Volcanoes in the Sea.* Honolulu: University of Hawaii Press, 1970.

Stearns, H. T. *Geology of the State of Hawaii.* Palo Alto, Calif.: Pacific Books, 1966.

CHAPTER **4**

EROSIONAL LANDFORMS

Certainly one of Hawaii's most attractive features is the state's spectacular scenery. The huge volcanic domes, such as Mauna Loa, are often too large and gentle in slope to give the appearance of great mountains, but once erosion of these giant shields takes place, slopes become steeper and unique landscapes form. These unique landforms are the result of the powerful effects of streams, the ocean, wind, and even ice. Other tropical islands may rival the Hawaiian Islands in their beautiful scenery, but there is not another of the fifty United States that has such magnificent amphitheater-headed valleys and palis. These are features common only to tropical volcanic islands.

Hawaii is an island state, so the work of the ocean in sculpturing the land is everywhere evident. There are great sea cliffs, thousands of feet high in places, and wide, white sand beaches. The ocean gnaws into the lava and tuff that form the basic bedrock of the islands and creates arches, stacks, and blowholes. And eventually it will be the ocean that erodes the islands down to sea level and reduces the once giant shield volcanoes to atolls.

Wind, too, is a factor in creating landforms in the fiftieth state. While less important than streams and the ocean, strong winds on sometimes dry, unvegetated slopes can move large quantities of soil and vol-

canic ash, forming dunes. Even ice has been effective in changing the appearance of the land in Hawaii, although it is not currently an important agent.

EROSIONAL PROCESSES

Weathering

Before the various forces can produce large-scale erosion, some preparation of the hard rock forming the islands is needed. Mechanical and chemical weathering provide this preparation—chemical weathering is the more important in Hawaii.

Mechanical weathering is effective where there are daily changes of temperature sufficient to cause alternate freezing and thawing, such as at the summits of the high mountains. This is limited, however, to a few specific locales: Mauna Kea and Mauna Loa on the island of Hawaii and Haleakala on Maui. At lower elevations tree roots provide sufficient wedging action to produce mechanical weathering, but the effects are generally masked by chemical weathering in regions of warm temperature and high humidity.

Conditions for rapid chemical weathering of rocks are almost ideal in Hawaii. The climate is tropical with ample rainfall, and the rocks are composed of minerals that are easily decomposed.

Mass Wasting

While erosion by the forces of wind and water can be thought of as a gradual but continuous process, there are times when huge quantities of material are dislodged from a slope. The effectiveness of a landslide in changing the shape of the land can be many times greater than that of the slower but more continuous action by a stream. In the Hawaiian Islands mass transfer occurs in both the wet and dry regions. The chief processes in the dry regions are gravity fall and sliding of fragments of rock, rain wash, and soil creep.

In the wetter areas of the islands another process is most important: a landslide type known as a soil avalanche. When the rainfall is heavy and the slopes are steep, the soil dislodges itself from the underlying bedrock and slides down the slope. Bright reddish brown scars of bare soil appear in the hillsides, surrounded by vegetation. After several months the soil-avalanche scars tend to disappear as the vegetative cover grows over the area. Not only does the soil avalanche result in mass movement of material itself; but it also prepares the denuded land for further assault by running water and wind.

Changing Shorelines

During the course of geologic history of the Hawaiian Islands, the level of the ocean relative to the islands has risen and fallen many times. Sea-level changes can be caused in several ways. When glaciers and ice caps thaw during interglacial periods, the sea level increases. The lowering of sea levels occurs during ice ages as more of the earth's water is removed from the ocean to fall on the land in the form of snow. Yet another cause for the changing sea level is the sinking of the islands due to the excess weight of volcanic material as volcanoes grow.

Evidence for at least thirty-three ancient shorelines in the islands has been described and summarized by Stearns (1978).

When the level of the sea falls, streams increase their grades and run more swiftly; when sea level is higher, the converse takes place. Elevated sea levels permit ocean waves to attack at higher levels along a coast and thereby cause a greater degree of coastal erosion.

Stream Erosion

The Hawaiian Islands receive copious amounts of rain, most of it falling at high elevations. The characteristic volcanic landform, the shield volcano, causes the drainage to be radial as the streams run downslope from the summits of the volcanic domes. Eventually the drainage is channeled into rivulets and streams.

Despite the great amounts of precipitation, most streams in Hawaii are not perennial. The new lava flows are exceptionally porous in many cases, and the water percolates into the ground after run-

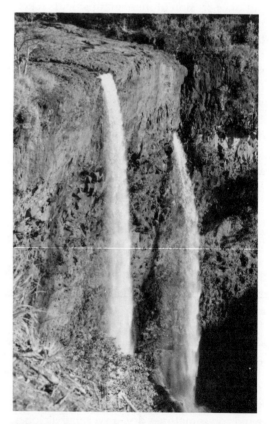

FIGURE 4.1. Wailua Falls, Kauai.

ning a short distance. On the older islands the streams tend to become perennial, as the soil particles clog the pores in the lava and prevent water from seeping into the rock.

The islands are geologically young; hence the streams are young, characterized by waterfalls and steep grades. A number of waterfalls are spectacular for both beauty and size. Hiilawe, the highest free-fall waterfall in the state (and one of the highest in the world), is not shown in Table 4.1 because it is now usually dry, the stream that fed it having been diverted to provide irrigation for nearby cane fields!

When streams are young, they cut vertically, creating characteristic steep-walled, V-shaped deep valleys. As the streams get older, grades decrease, vertical cutting power is reduced, and the horizontal erosional effects are increased. The floors of the valleys are widened and flattened; the shape becomes a wide V. Kaluanui Stream on Oahu has cut an exceptionally deep, narrow-V-shaped gorge, while Waipio Valley on the Big Island typifies the wide-V type. An unusual feature of valley formation in the Hawaiian Islands is that even though the valley floor may widen as the stream begins to age and cut horizontally, the valley walls remain exceptionally steep.

Streams are short; the longest, on the island of Oahu, is 30.0 mi (48.3 km) (Table 4.2). Generally the length of the streams is controlled by the size of the islands. Yet the largest island, Hawaii, has as its longest stream the Wailuku River, which is shorter than the Kaukonahua Stream on the much smaller island of Oahu. Undoubtedly the porous nature of the young lavas on the

Table 4.1
Major Named Waterfalls

Island	Waterfall[a]	Height					
		Sheer Drop		Cascade		Horizontal Distance	
		feet	meters	feet	meters	feet	meters
Hawaii	Kaluahine			620	189	400	122
	Akaka	442	134				
	Waiilikahi	320	98				
	Rainbow			80	24	150	46
Maui	Honokohau			1,120	341	500	152
	Wailiumalu			400	122	150	46
	Waimoku			40	12	50	15
Molokai	Kahiwa			1,750	533	1,000	305
	Papalaua			1,200	366	500	152
	Wailele			500	152	150	46
	Haloku			500	152	200	61
	Hipuapua			500	152	300	91
	Olupena			300	91	150	46
	Moaula			250	76	200	61
Oahu	Kaliuwaa (Sacred)	80	24	1,520	463	3,000	914
	Waihee (Waimea)	80	24				
	Manoa			200	61	250	76
Kauai	Waipoo (2 falls)			800	244	600	183
	Awini			480	146	500	152
	Hialele	280	85				
	Kapakanui	280	85				
	Manawaiopuna	280	85				
	Wailua	80	24				
	Opaekaa	40	12				
	Puwainui	20	6				

Source: Adapted from Atlas of Hawaii, 1973

[a]Includes the largest named waterfall on each major island, all other named waterfalls 250 ft (75 m) high or higher, and well-known smaller falls.

FIGURE 4.2.   A V-shaped valley in Iao Valley State Park, west Maui.

Big Island accounts for the lack of longer perennial streams.

Amphitheater-headed Valleys. Although these valleys are caused mainly by stream erosion, they are so unique among landforms in the United States and so characteristic of Hawaiian scenery that they deserve special mention. They have precipitous (virtually vertical) valley walls and semicircular heads; their similarity to amphitheaters is obvious.

The very steep valley heads are formed when streams plunge over the steep head wall in the form of waterfalls. The plunge pools at the base of the valley walls cause erosion at the bottom of the walls, thus steepening the slope. Another important reason for the steepness of the valley walls is that they consist of alternating beds of lava with differing degrees of resistance to erosion. Some easily eroded material, such as aa clinkers, is rapidly removed, and the

more resistant layers are undercut. According to Macdonald and Abbott (1970, 174) "The latter, broken by innumerable, nearly vertical joints, cave away as undercutting reaches a critical amount, producing nearly vertical cliffs."

The semicircular shape of the valley heads results from the general nature of the radial drainage characteristic of stream development on volcanic shields. The major streams are close together near their beginnings, and stream capture occurs frequently. The valleys of the coalescing streams join in a semicircular form.

Some additional landforms appear along the side walls and head walls of the amphitheater-headed valleys. Vertical notches or valleys are located high up on the face of the cliff, cut by small tributary streams that have not eroded a valley down to sea level. Giant grooves, referred to sometimes as organ pipe fluting, are found on the

Table 4.2
Rivers in Hawaii

Island	Feature or Stream	Length	
		Miles	Kilometers
Hawaii	Wailuku River	22.7	36.5
Maui	Palikea Stream	7.8	12.6
	Honokohau Stream	9.4	15.1
Molokai	Wailau-Pulena Stream	6.5	10.5
	Halawa Stream	6.4	10.3
	Waikolu Stream	4.7	7.6
	Pelekunu	2.3	3.7
Oahu	Kaukonahua Stream	30.0	48.3
	Waikele Stream	15.3	24.6
	Kipapa Stream	12.8	20.6
	Waikakalaua Stream	11.8	19.0
Kauai	Waimea River	19.7	31.7
	Makaweli River	15.1	24.3
	Wainiha River	13.8	22.2
	Hanapepe River	13.3	19.0

Source: Adapted from Atlas of Hawaii, 1973.

FIGURE 4.3.   Amphitheater-headed valleys in the Waianae Range, leeward Oahu.

valley walls. While the grooves are usually dry, after heavy rains they become the sites of spectacular waterfalls.

Palis. *Pali* is a Hawaiian word meaning "cliff," but in the physical geography of the Hawaiian Islands these are cliffs of a special type—their formation follows sequentially the formation of amphitheater-headed valleys. The valleys frequently form in a series along a stretch of terrain with intervening ridges separating the individual valleys. With continued erosion the ridges are reduced to mere knife edges, and eventually they disappear completely. The semicircular valley head walls then coalesce into a scalloped ridge, a pali. The Nuuanu Pali, on the windward side of Oahu, is perhaps the best example in the islands, but there are numerous other palis on all the Hawaiian Islands. In some cases the force of the ocean may play a part in eroding the bottom of the cliffs, thus serving the same purpose as the waterfalls and their plunge pools.

Erosional Remnants. Stream erosion is very effective in changing the shape of the land; the forms left by running water are frequently intricate, detailed, and picturesque. These erosional remnants attract the attention not only of visitors to the islands but also of resident geologists and geographers anxious to find explanations for what they see. The lava flows, tuff, cinder, and other volcanic eruptive material have varying degrees of hardness and resistance to erosion. Hence material might be easily eroded all around a particularly resistant structure that is left as a remnant.

Two of the most interesting and easily observed erosional remnants are Iao Needle on the island of Maui and Olomana Peak, Oahu. The latter bears striking resemblance

FIGURE 4.4.   Iao Needle, an erosional remnant in the ancient caldera of the West Maui volcano, Iao Valley State Park, West Maui.

to a glacial horn (Macdonald and Abbott 1970, 233), but, of course, it was formed not by the erosional work of glaciers but by the power of running water.

Erosion by the Ocean

The ocean surrounds the Hawaiian Islands and causes coastlines to erode, beaches to form, and coral reefs to grow. The ocean has profound effects on the land; it rivals stream erosion as the most important force in creating physical landscapes. In the stages of growth and decay of a volcanic island, streams start the destructive process, but the ocean concludes it. When the land has been reduced to a surface without much slope, running water loses its effectiveness, but the ocean can still gnaw away at the land, eventually reducing it to the level of the surrounding seas.

The force of the ocean is mainly in its waves and surf, which can attack a coastline with tremendous force, eroding the base of the coast and tending to form sea cliffs. Sea cliffs on the north shore of Molokai are thousands of feet high and virtually vertical; the Na Pali coast on Kauai is equally spectacular. Sea cliffs are more prevalent on the younger islands of the chain; the ocean has created coral reefs and beaches around the shores of the older islands.

After the formation of a sea cliff, a joint consequence of the effects of volcanism and erosion by the sea, continued erosion can produce a cave at the base of the cliff. Subsequent lowering of the sea level can result in such a cave being found on dry land: Kaheana Cave on the leeward coast of Oahu is a good example.

If the ocean continues to attack the land in the vicinity of the cave, eventually the lava or tuff will be worn completely through, and a bridgelike structure called an arch results. Further erosion may cause the top of the arch to collapse, leaving an offshore rock, or stack. There are a great many examples of arches and stacks in the islands. On the Big Island arches are cut into the Kilauea lava flows on the south

coast, and Onomea Arch, on the Hamakua coast north of Hilo, has changed from an arch to a stack during recent history (Macdonald and Abbott 1970, 205). The leeward coast of Oahu near Kaena Point has two fine examples of arches and numerous stacks.

Occasionally a lava flow that has entered the water will have one or more holes or cracks in it through which water may enter when the approach and force of breaking waves is just right. The result is a blowhole, or spouting horn. The latter name is appropriate, because frequently the spouting of sea water and spray causes a moaning sound reminiscent of a fog horn. The Spouting Horn on the south coast of Kauai and the Halona blowhole on the windward side of Oahu are excellent examples. Both are tourist attractions of some importance.

Erosion by Wind

Despite wind velocities in Hawaii that are generally moderate to high, wind erosion is not a factor of great importance. Generally, running water is a far more important force than is wind in sculpturing landscapes on the Hawaiian Islands. However, in areas where vegetation has been removed or where rainfall is light, the force of the wind can become consequential.

In describing the geology of the islands of Kahoolawe and Lanai, Stearns (1966, 2) wrote, "In windy seasons ribbon-shaped dust clouds from these two islands commonly extend many miles over the ocean." Dunes of red soil were formed on these two islands as a consequence of overgrazing by animals, the resultant deforestation, and strong winds. On the island of Molokai the same effect was noted by Stearns (1966, 177). He wrote, "Introduction of livestock and agricultural development caused great quantities of red soil to be eroded from the uplands, partly filling 53 fishponds along the south coast now being invaded by mangrove trees."

The principal erosional feature caused by the wind is the dune. There are examples in the islands of dunes of volcanic ash, of

FIGURE 4.5. The Na Pali coast, Kauai. The upper view is looking southwest, the lower view northeast.

FIGURE 4.6. Arches on the Waianae coast, Oahu, near Kaena Point. In the foreground *below,* the erosive power of the ocean is most evident, as the arch is well on its way to becoming a stack.

FIGURE 4.7. The Spouting Horn, on the southeast coast of Kauai, in action. Blowholes, called spouting horns when they combine a moaning sound with the fountain of spray, are not uncommon along lava coasts. Wave action offshore forces seawater through small openings in the porous lava.

red soil, and of sand. Dune areas behind (mauka of) beaches are usually kept in place by hardy species of plants that grow well in the sandy soil and the salt air. In many areas, however, dunes have been removed to build highways and to make room for other coastal development.

On Oahu the best examples of sand dunes are found at Kaena Point, where the lighthouse sits on an extensive dune area.

Erosion by Ice

At present the least important erosional agent in Hawaii is ice, but in the past alpine glaciation was of some importance, at least in limited areas. The summit of Mauna Kea, usually snowcapped for a por-

tion of each winter, was once the site of a glacier, estimated to cover 28 sq mi (72 sq km). Glacial striations and moraines are found here.

Neither Mauna Loa nor Haleakala seems to have had glaciers, although the summit of the former is high enough. Apparently the nature of the volcanic rock at the summit or Mauna Loa's continued activity prevented the formation of a permanent ice cap.

REFERENCES

Department of Geography, University of Hawaii. *Atlas of Hawaii.* Honolulu: University Press of Hawaii, 1973.

Macdonald, G. A., and Abbott, A. T. *Volcanoes in the Sea.* Honolulu: University of Hawaii Press, 1970.

Stearns, H. T. *Geology of the State of Hawaii.* Palo Alto, Calif.: Pacific Books, 1966.

————. *Quaternary Shorelines in the Hawaiian Islands.* Honolulu: Bishop Museum Press, 1978.

CHAPTER 5

THE SURROUNDING OCEAN

On the island of Hawaii no point is more than 28.5 mi (45.9 km) from the ocean, and on the other islands in the chain the greatest distance is 10.8 mi (17.4 km) from the surrounding seas. The influence of the Pacific Ocean on the Hawaiian Islands is therefore great. It controls climate, creates the state's beaches, erodes coasts, and causes some of the islands' most disastrous natural hazards.

THE NORTH PACIFIC OCEAN AND HAWAII

Hawaii's location in the tropics of the North Pacific subjects it to influences of the ocean's currents, waves, sea surface temperatures, tides, and salinities.

Ocean Currents in the Islands

The Hawaiian Islands are under the influence of the northern portion of the North Equatorial Current, which flows past and through the various island channels in a westerly direction. Current speeds in both winter and summer are generally 0.3 to 0.5 knots (15 to 25 cm/sec) in the basic flow of the current, but the speeds and directions vary greatly in the channels between the islands under the influence of strong trade winds. A further complication is the presence of sometimes strong tidal currents that are, of course, reversing. Thus there are occasions when the tidal current and the North Equatorial Current flows reinforce each other, and times when the effects tend to cancel. Trade-wind velocities are high in the island channels and the resultant wind-driven currents can influence both the speed and direction of the basic flow.

Sea Surface Temperatures

In the vicinity of the islands, sea surface temperatures are between 72.5°F and 77°F (22.5°C and 25°C) in the winter and between 77°F and 81.5°F (25°C and 27.5°C) in the summer. Seawater has a high heat capacity, changing little in temperature with increased absorption of solar heat, so these ocean temperatures are influential in the temperature regime of the land. The surrounding ocean tends to keep land temperatures within a relatively narrow range.

Surface Salinities

In the vicinity of the islands, surface salinities range between 34.6 percent and 35.4 percent during the year. These salinities are somewhat higher than those in the North Pacific generally, due to the higher than average amount of evaporation of ocean waters in the trade-wind zone. Winter salinities are slightly higher because of higher winter evaporation rates.

Wind Waves

The spectacular surf that sometimes breaks on Hawaii's beaches is caused by wind-driven waves from storms that may be located thousands of miles from the islands. These waves, referred to as "sea" while under the influence of the wind, are transformed first into swells and eventually into breakers or surf. The most impressive breakers, found on the north coasts of the islands (particularly Oahu), are caused by winter storms traveling across the Pacific north of the islands. The swells travel with little loss of energy until they reach the shallow coastal waters, where they are transformed into spilling and plunging breakers. The plunging breakers, called "tubes" by surfers, are the most challenging to those on surfboards or riding the breakers without boards (body surfing).

In the summer months the north shores of the islands have only small breakers, since storms north of the islands are infrequent and of little consequence. But on the south shores there are sometimes good surfing waves. Storms occurring during the Southern Hemisphere's winter can generate waves and swell of sufficient energy to reach the islands, and the south-shore beaches are then visited by breakers that provide a challenge to surfers. These summer waves are smaller than the winter waves on the north shores, because the storms are located much farther from the islands and there is more loss of energy.

On the windward sides of the islands there are almost always waves and small surf due to the presence of trade winds. These trade-wind waves can reach moderate heights, but they are usually not of the spectacular nature of the north-shore waves.

When severe cyclonic storms strike the islands, waves and surf are generated that can be damaging to affected shores. Sometimes these occasional storms result in considerable erosion of beaches and damage to coastal structures.

When strong trade winds have been blowing for several days, wave heights in the channels between the islands can reach dangerous proportions. It is not uncommon for seas in the channels to reach heights of 15 ft (4.57 m) or more. Crossing from island to island in a small boat is a notoriously adventurous trip at times.

Tides

While waves and surf in the islands are impressive, tides are not. The tidal range is small and rarely presents a navigational problem. Tides are of the mixed type with large inequalities in the heights of daily high waters at the same location and lesser differences in low water heights. Tidal currents in the navigable channels and harbors are usually not bothersome, but around some island promontories they can be strong enough to create problems for swimmers and snorkelers.

TSUNAMIS

Although most of the characteristics of the Pacific Ocean are beneficial to residents of Hawaii, *tsunamis* are not. These are destructive, impulsively generated waves that spread out from the source and travel with little loss of energy. The impulse can be a landslide (either underwater or subaerial), a volcanic eruption, or faulting of the crust of the earth underwater. The faulting produces earthquakes; consequently there is an association between underwater earthquakes and tsunamis.

A tsunami-producing earthquake must be of large magnitude, usually measured at 7 or greater on the Richter scale; must be shallow focus; and, of course, must occur underwater or close to a coast. Although some of the largest tsunamis in the world have been a consequence of landslides and volcanic activity, those that have affected the Hawaiian Islands have been associated with earthquakes.

A somewhat arbitrary distinction is made between tsunamis generated at considerable distance from the affected coast and those generated in faults near the coast. The former are called "distant tsunamis," the latter "local tsunamis." In Hawaii, most destructive tsunamis have been distant, but there have been six local tsunamis in the known history of the islands—two of them very destructive.

Tsunamis cause flooding of coastal areas, sometimes extending thousands of feet inland. Strong currents are associated with the flooding, particularly as the water ebbs. Occasionally the tsunami wave is translated into a bore, a steep "wall of water" that crashes into the waterfront with tremendous destructive force. Both of these effects have occurred in Hawaii.

Tsunami Characteristics

Tsunamis have very long wave lengths (sometimes 100 mi [161 km] or greater) in the open sea. Wave heights, on the other hand, in the deep ocean probably do not exceed a few feet. Wave periods are anywhere from fifteen minutes to one hour. These very long waves travel at a speed proportional to the depth of water, according to equation 5.1:

$$C = \sqrt{gD} \qquad (5.1)$$

where g is the acceleration of gravity and D is the water depth. Since the wave length is so long, the forward part of the wave may be in much shallower water than successive wave crests as the wave approaches a coast: consequently the forward crest travels at a much slower speed. The wave length shortens and the wave height increases as a result of this "catch-up" effect. A number of other effects can play a part in increasing the height of a tsunami wave in shallow water: resonance, refraction, diffraction, funneling, and reflection to name but a few.

Tsunami Warning System

The association with earthquakes and the equation permitting accurate determination of tsunami wave speed are the basis for a tsunami warning system. This system has its headquarters at Ewa Beach, Oahu, and provides warnings to the Hawaiian Islands and to other Pacific locations as well. A number of seismographs at the headquarters and throughout the Pacific serve to detect earthquakes and to determine their locations and magnitudes. If the earthquake is of sufficient magnitude and in the proper location to generate a tsunami, a large number of tide stations in the system can be queried to determine whether or not an actual tsunami has been generated. If one has, the arrival time of the tsunami can be calculated for a number of Pacific coastal locations and warnings can be promulgated. At present, the system does not attempt to forecast the height of a tsunami at any coastal location; it merely reports the estimated arrival time. Research to enable the accurate forecasting of tsunami wave heights is underway.

Tsunamis travel at great speeds in the deep ocean. An average of seventeen distant tsunamis, arriving at various locations in the islands and approaching from several different directions, indicates a speed of 460 mph (740 km/hr). Thus, unless the tsunami is generated far from Hawaiian shores, there may not be enough time for the warning system to make the required calculations and promulgate a warning. Improvements are being made in the system, but the problem of providing a warning for local tsunamis remains a difficult one.

History of Tsunamis in Hawaii

The number of tsunamis cannot be determined for Hawaii because written records only exist from the early nineteenth century. The earliest tsunami of record occurred in 1813 or 1814 (available historical information does not permit fixing the date more accurately). The most recent in the islands was November 29, 1975. Tsunamis causing severe damage occurred in 1837, 1868, 1877, 1946, 1960, and 1975. The year 1868 was undoubtedly the worst in Hawaiian history for tsunami damage— there were two in that year, a local tsunami

40

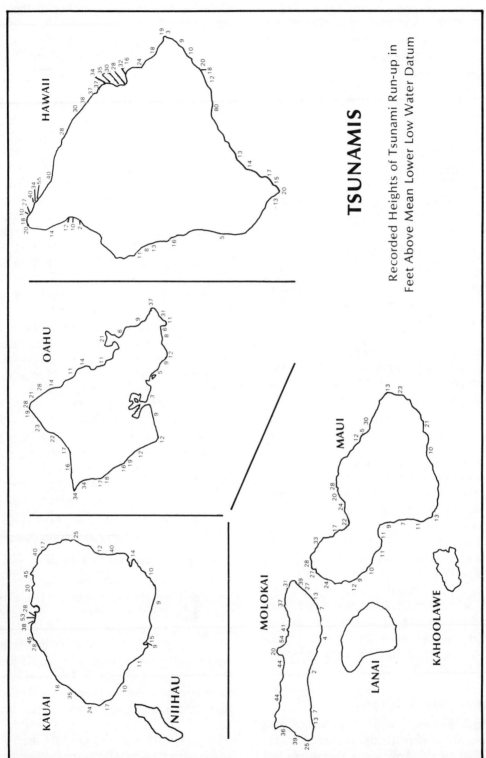

TSUNAMIS

Recorded Heights of Tsunami Run-up in
Feet Above Mean Lower Low Water Datum

FIGURE 5.1

on April 2 and a distant tsunami on August 13.

There were five tsunamis during the eighteen-year period from 1946 to 1964. The 1946 and 1960 tsunamis were devastating, particularly to the city of Hilo; the 1957 tsunami caused damage to the island of Kauai; the tsunamis in 1952 and 1964 had very noticeable wave heights in the islands, but caused little property damage and no loss of life.

The most detailed and accurate information regarding tsunami wave heights in the Hawaiian Islands is for the tsunamis of 1946, 1952, 1957, 1960, and 1964. Figure 5.1 shows the highest recorded wave height for these tsunamis for a number of coastal locations. At most of the locations more than one of the tsunamis was detected, and at some locales there appears to be a degree of vulnerability to tsunamis approaching from a number of different directions.

The north coasts of Kauai and Molokai have suffered the greatest wave heights, followed by the northeast coast of the Big Island. Property damage and loss of life have been concentrated on the island of Hawaii, particularly the city of Hilo and the small settlement at Laupahoehoe Point that existed prior to the 1946 tsunami. Clearly, it is not just the presence of high waves that makes a region vulnerable; population clusters, buildings, industry, and other factors also play an important role.

CORAL REEFS

The Hawaiian Islands are in the northern portion of the main reef-building zone in the North Pacific. Consequently, the waters are a trifle too cool for the most productive coral assemblages. The main reef-producing coral species in the Pacific, those of the genus *Acropora*, are lacking in the reefs around the islands. *Porites* and *Pocillopora* are the principal reef builders in the state.

Coral reefs are complex environments, supporting a great many different species of marine plants and animals. Reef fish,

including butterfly fishes, parrot fishes, wrasses, surgeon fishes, and squirrel fishes, are numbered in the thousands in some of the more productive reef areas. Their vivid colors provide a considerable attraction for snorkelers and scuba divers. The shallow reef at Hanauma Bay, Oahu, has been designated as a marine conservation area. Because the fish cannot be speared or otherwise harmed in the area, they are extremely numerous and even novice snorkelers can see and identify most of the common species that abound in quite shallow waters.

Distribution of Reefs

In general the younger islands at the eastern end of the Hawaiian chain have only scanty reef development, while those that are geologically older have more extensive reefs. On the Big Island only the small area on the leeward coast north of Keahole Point has reefs, and on Maui there are reef areas only in the western part of the island. There are no reefs on the north coast of Molokai, the site of giant sea cliffs, but reefs are extensive on the shallower south coast. On Lanai it is the north coast that has the reefs, while the south coast, which is much steeper, is a cliffed coast. Of the main group of islands the best reef development is on Oahu, almost completely surrounded by reefs except for prominent cliffs at the southeastern and northwestern extremities. Kauai's reef areas generally extend all around the island with the exception of the Na Pali coast in the northwest, which is the site of giant, spectacular sea cliffs. There are coral reefs on both the east and west coasts of Niihau, and the entire group of leeward islands has reefs in various stages of development, ranging from fringing reefs to barrier reefs to atolls.

OCEAN RESOURCES

The surrounding ocean provides the residents of Hawaii with biological, mineral, recreational, and energy resources. Biolog-

FIGURE 5.2. Tsunamis are a menace on the north and northwest coasts of Kauai. Campers and hikers on the Na Pali coast are provided with warnings, as shown in these two views.

ical resources, in the form of a commercial fishing industry, are discussed in Chapter 14. The recreational values of the ocean form the basis of the state's tourist industry; Chapter 11 is devoted to that subject. Mineral and energy resources are discussed here.

Mineral Resources

The Pacific Ocean in the general vicinity of the Hawaiian Islands is rich in manganese nodules. Hawaii could become the site for the extraction and processing of the nodules, as the islands are well placed for the harboring of mining ships and the ores could be treated within the state. The possibility has been considered of a manganese-nodule processing plant on the Big Island, which has the potential for development of a number of sources of energy other than imported petroleum. For example, if either geothermal steam or ocean thermal energy could be produced in sufficient quantities, excess electrical power could support a processing plant for manganese nodules.

However, manganese nodules can only be considered a potential ocean resource. First, there are some important problems concerning ownership of the nodules, which are on the ocean bottom in an area not under U.S. control. Until the ownership question is settled, it is unlikely that any company would chance the considerable financial investment needed to locate, mine, process, and transport the minerals. Second, there is the problem of waste disposal of the tailings, something that people in Hawaii may be reluctant to undertake, as the wastes would be unsightly and would reduce the scenic beauty of the island environment. And finally, any processing plant would have to be in the nature of a "smokestack industry," with the attendant problems of air pollution.

For the time being mineral resources obtained from the ocean bottom around Hawaii will continue to be of a more prosaic nature. The most valuable resource is sand and gravel, mined from shallow areas off-shore of the southwest coast of Molokai and barged to Honolulu for use in manufacturing concrete. The only other ocean-floor resource of consequence is precious coral, both black and pink, the raw material for a small but thriving jewelry industry.

Energy Resources

The only energy resource of the oceans seriously considered for use in Hawaii is ocean thermal energy. Utilizing this energy source involves a relatively simple principle. The ocean's waters are warm at the surface and much cooler at depth; the depth of the thermocline, the zone in which the change of temperature with depth is most rapid, is relatively shallow in the tropical oceans. Therefore the warm surface water can be used to vaporize a liquid, such as ammonia, and the cooler deep water can be pumped to the surface to condense the vapor. In this way a closed-cycle engine can be set up, analogous to a steam turbine.

The area currently being considered for the development of ocean thermal energy is the Kona coast of the Big Island. Here the surface waters are warm and calm, and the deep, cold water is found close to the shore. In the vicinity of Keahole Point an experimental ocean-thermal-energy conversion plant has been set up on a small barge moored offshore. The system has demonstrated that the production of electrical energy is feasible; energy in excess of that needed to pump the cold water and run other equipment on the barge already has been produced. Further development of the process and technical engineering studies are needed before electrical power generated by the ocean can become available to the island's residents at a cost competitive with energy produced by burning petroleum. But as oil continues to increase in price and the engineering problems associated with the ocean process are solved one by one, the price of ocean thermal energy will become competitive with electrical energy produced by more conventional methods.

REFERENCES

Cox, D. C., and Mink, J. F. "The Tsunami of 23 May 1960 in the Hawaiian Islands." *Bulletin of the Seismological Society of America* 53, no. 6 (1963):1191–1209.

Cox, D. C., and Morgan, J. *Local Tsunamis and Possible Local Tsunamis in Hawaii.* Honolulu: Hawaii Institute of Geophysics, Report HIG-77-14, 1977.

Department of Geography, University of Hawaii. *Atlas of Hawaii.* Honolulu: University Press of Hawaii, 1973.

Shepard, F. P.; Macdonald, G. A.; and Cox, D. C. "The Tsunami of April 1, 1946." *Bulletin of the Scripps Institution of Oceanography of the University of California* 5, no. 6 (1950):391–528.

CHAPTER 6

A TROPICAL CLIMATE

It is no surprise that Hawaii's climate differs considerably from that of the other forty-nine states—Hawaii is the only state that is completely tropical in location. Actually a number of features of the climate of the fiftieth state make it unique. There are extreme variations in rainfall over small distances; tropical rain forests and deserts exist almost side by side; and the presence of high mountains makes the temperature distribution even on a single island quite varied. Most small-scale climatic maps appearing in geography texts show the islands as having a single climate type; however, when the islands are examined in more detail it becomes evident that their climates are much more complex.

CLIMATIC CONTROLS

Despite notable variations in some of the climatic elements, three basic controls provide some consistency to the climate of Hawaii: a tropical location, the presence of the Pacific Ocean surrounding the islands, and the greatly varied topography from island to island and within a single island.

Tropical Location

Characteristic of the tropics, the islands have only small variation in lengths of day and night throughout the year. The longest day in Honolulu at the time of the summer solstice is thirteen hours and twenty minutes, while the shortest day is ten hours and fifty minutes. Los Angeles and Atlanta, at about 34° north latitude, have days fourteen hours and thirty minutes and nine hours and fifty minutes for the longest and shortest day respectively. Cities like Seattle, at approximately 48° north latitude, and Anchorage, at about 61° north latitude, have far longer summer days and much shorter winter days than does Honolulu. Also, the sun is high in the sky at noon throughout the year in the tropics and is overhead twice a year. The small variation in length of day and night throughout the year and the generally high sun elevation account for the small variation of average temperatures during the change of seasons. Winter maximum temperatures differ by only a small amount from summer maximums.

Oceanic Influences

Seawater has a high heat capacity, that is, it changes little in temperature even with great changes in incoming solar radiation. Consequently it exercises a pronounced thermostatic effect over the Hawaiian Islands, which are under the influence of the surrounding ocean to an exceptional degree—no matter what the direction of the wind, the air that influences

45

the temperature and humidity of the islands comes from the ocean. This ocean-influenced air is mild in temperature throughout the year and is generally high in humidity. The islands have a marine climate to a marked degree, with none of the continental influences that characterize the climates of the other states. Small variation of temperature from winter to summer is characteristic of marine climates, and Hawaii's annual temperature regime clearly shows this. Thus, both the tropical location and the presence of the ocean contribute to the uniform temperatures throughout the year.

Varied Topography

Volcanic and erosional landforms create a variety of climatic environments in the islands. Plains and mountains, deep valleys and palis are almost side by side. Tremendous variations in rainfall occur over small distances, as rain shadows are created by the intervening higher elevations. For instance, the windward and leeward sides of islands, when there are higher elevations in between, display very great differences in annual precipitation. Differences in temperature are much less extreme, but are noticeable. Wind directions, quite constant over the surrounding ocean, show considerable variations—variations clearly influenced by the intricate topography prevalent on some of the islands.

CLIMATIC ELEMENTS

Climates usually are described by indexes based on the two primary climatic elements, temperature and precipitation. The Hawaiian Islands are somewhat different, however, because of the importance of a third element, wind. An understanding of the wind regime is essential, and it, in turn, influences both temperature and precipitation to a considerable degree.

Wind

The Hawaiian Islands' location in the Pacific Ocean is south of the prevailing subtropical high pressure zone and north of the intertropical convergence zone. The air flow from north to south is influenced by the Coriolis effect, so northeasterly winds are produced. These are the northeasterly trades so influential in controlling the climate in Hawaii.

The positions of both the subtropical high and the intertropical convergence zone move with the seasons, north during the summer and south in the winter. In the summer months the subtropical high is north of the islands and is strong; trade winds are then very constant, blowing more than 90 percent of the time. In addition to the constancy of wind direction, velocities are high, and the effect of the trades in moderating the high summer temperatures is one of the most important factors in Hawaii's salubrious climate.

The constancy of the trade winds has influenced the geographic nomenclature of the islands. Hawaiians speak of windward and leeward sides, both referring to prevailing wind directions, and "Kona winds" are winds that blow from southerly quadrants. Recall that *kona* means "leeward," hence Kona winds are those that do not follow the prevailing, or windward, wind pattern.

While the trades are remarkably constant in direction over the Pacific Ocean, their direction over land is greatly influenced by topography, and trades blow from a variety of directions as they are funneled through valleys and around slopes.

During the winter months the trade winds are far less constant, as the subtropical high moves south and weakens. Sometimes the trades are replaced by land and sea breezes as the land alternately heats and cools during the course of the day. With the weakening of the subtropical high, low pressure systems can move through the islands, and the associated fronts create a variety of wind directions in winter as compared to summer (Table 6.1).

There are other winds in the islands; notable are the downslope winds on the lee side of Haleakala, referred to as "Kula winds" after the Kula district of Maui.

Table 6.1
Summer and Winter Winds - Hawaii

Wind Directions	Wind Direction Frequencies (%)		Wind Speeds		Wind Speed Frequencies (%)	
	January	August	(m.p.h.)	(km/hr)	January	August
NNE to E	50	92	0-12	0-20	69	39
ESE to S	18	4	13-24	21-39	29	58
SSW to W	10	< 1	25 and over	40 and over	2	3
WNW to N	20	3				
CALM	2	1				

Source: Adapted from Blumenstock and Price, 1967.

Temperature

The most notable characteristic of the temperature regime in the islands is the narrow range of winter and summer conditions. Average temperatures for the warmest and coolest months differ by less than 9°F (5°C) for all locations below 5,000 ft (1,524 m). Nighttime and daytime maximums and minimums vary by a greater amount—the change from day to night produces a greater cooling effect than does the change from summer to winter.

The greatest temperature variations are those controlled by elevation. Mauna Loa observatory's low August and January temperatures are due to its 11,150 ft (3,399 m) elevation (Table 6.2).

The effects of the Pacific Ocean and the constancy of solar radiation throughout the year produce generally mild temperatures in the islands. Extreme temperatures are rare; the highest ever recorded was 100°F (37.7°C) at Pahala, Hawaii, and the lowest 9°F (−12.7°C) at the summit of Mauna Kea. However, temperatures in the summer months at most locations close to sea level do not exceed 90°F (32.2°C) except on rare occasions.

Windward locations show the least variation of temperature from day to night, usually around 10°F (5.5°C). Day-to-night temperature differences in leeward areas and at higher elevations may be twice as great.

Precipitation

Mount Waialeale on Kauai gets 486 in. (1,234 cm) of rain per year, while Puako on the Kona coast of the Big Island receives about 7 in. (17 cm). This extreme variability of rainfall in the islands is one of the most remarkable characteristics of the climate of the state.

Precipitation, virtually all in the form of rain except at the extreme elevations, results from orographic, convectional, and cyclonic effects. The effects of the topography are most pronounced: windward locations at moderately high elevations receive high rainfall (Figure 6.1).

Moisture-laden air that sweeps in from

Table 6.2
Temperatures at Selected Big Island Stations

Station	Elevation Above Sea Level (feet)	(m)	Mean January Temperature °F	°C	Mean August Temperature °F	°C
Hilo	40	12	71	22	76	24
Olaa	280	85	70	21	75	24
Mountain View	1,530	466	65	18	70	21
Hawaii National Park	3,971	1,210	58	14	64	18
Kulani Camp	5,190	1,582	53	12	58	14
Mauna Loa Observatory	11,150	3,399	41	5	47	8

Source: Adapted from Blumenstock and Price, 1967.

the Pacific Ocean is forced to rise over windward slopes, and this orographic effect results in cloudiness and rain. Hence, windward locations receive rain throughout the year, whenever trade winds blow. The greatest amount of rain falls not at the summits of the high mountains, but at elevations of 2,000 to 4,000 ft (610 to 1,219 m) on the slopes of Mauna Kea and Mauna Loa on the Big Island and Haleakala on Maui. On the other islands the maximum elevations are 6,000 ft (1,829 m) or less, and the highest annual rainfall generally coincides with the highest elevations.

Leeward locations are in a rain shadow and are shielded from these orographic effects. The bulk of their annual rain is from winter storms, which generally affect all the islands. Hence, leeward locations get far less rain than do the much wetter windward areas.

The heating of the land masses of the islands during hot summer afternoons sometimes results in towering cumulus clouds and contributes to the annual rainfall. This convectional effect is important on the island of Hawaii, with its much greater land mass than the other islands.

In all areas of the islands except the Kona coast of the Big Island, winter rainfall exceeds summer rain. However, winter rain, which comes from storms, is much more variable than the summertime orographic conditions, which depend on the strength and constancy of the trade winds.

Rainfall can be very intense. In March 1980 a total of 120.04 in. (304.9 cm) of rain fell at Kaumana, a station six miles north of Hilo on the windward side of Hawaii. Ookala Mauka, on the coast of the North Hilo district, had 103.17 in. (262.05 cm). Although Honolulu has an average annual rainfall of only 24 in. (61 cm), more than 17 in. (43 cm) has fallen in a single day. More than 11 in. (26 cm) has fallen in a single hour on the island

49

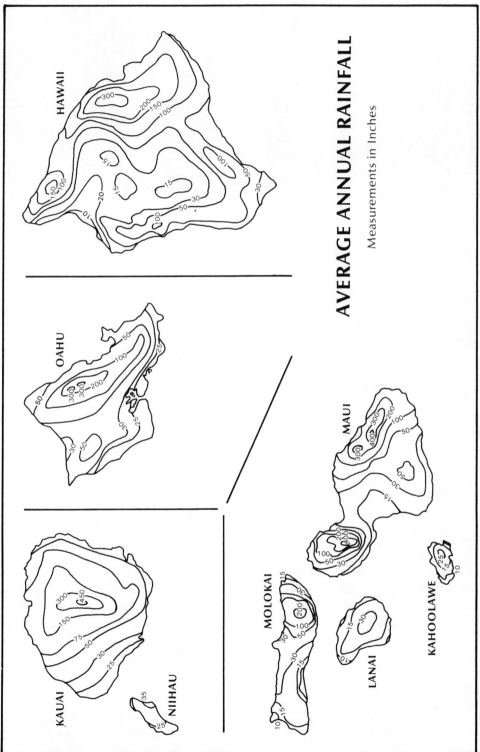

AVERAGE ANNUAL RAINFALL

Measurements in Inches

FIGURE 6.1.

FIGURE 6.2.   Makapuu Beach on the southeast shore of Oahu is in a rain shadow. It is famous not only for its abundant sunshine but also for its body-surfing waves.

of Kauai (Blumenstock and Price 1967).

In contrast to the intensity of rainfall in some regions, other areas in the islands experience droughts. In leeward locations, which depend on winter storms for most of their rain, a winter or two of lower than normal storm frequency coupled with the predictable very low summer rain can become a serious problem.

SEASONS

Hawaii has but two seasons, winter and summer, as might be expected because of its tropical location. Ancient Hawaiians referred to the seasons as *kau*, "summer" and *hooilo*, "winter" (Blumenstock and Price 1967).

Kau

Summer in the islands generally runs from May through September. It is the warmer and dryer of the seasons at most places; only the Kona coast of the island of Hawaii has a summer rainfall maximum. During the kau season the trade winds are more constant and blow at higher velocities, ameliorating the warmer temperatures and producing pleasant, comfortable conditions.

Hooilo

The rainier winter season was recognized by the Hawaiians. From October through April there are cooler temperatures, more variable winds, and more rain. This is the season of storms, which on occasion can be very severe. Heavy rain and wind can have serious effects on agricultural productivity, and the ancient Hawaiians, dependent as they were on the produce of the land, recognized the hooilo season as the less desirable of the two seasons.

The Change of Seasons

Although the differences between summer and winter in the islands are slight compared to seasonal variations on the mainland, the change of seasons can sometimes be recognized quite readily. In early May 1980 a windier, rainier, and stormier than average winter suddenly gave way to summer. Although maximum daily temperatures rose only a few degrees, the change was quite noticeable. The most pronounced change was in surf conditions along the shores of Oahu. Winter surf is high on the island's north shore, the result of Northern Hemisphere storms, waves, and swells. When summer comes—sometimes quite abruptly—north-shore surf diminishes and surf on the south shore increases in height, sometimes to 8 or 10 ft (2.4 or 3.04 m). As already noted, the summer surf is due to storms in the Southern Hemisphere, and does not reach the gigantic heights that the surf on the north shore sometimes does. But Oahu residents know that summer has arrived when surfers shift their operations from Sunset Beach and Pipeline to popular south-shore surfing spots.

STORMS

Climatic conditions described thus far in this chapter are those associated with the trade winds. As the trades are present a great majority of the time, the associated weather might be considered to be representative of Hawaii's climate. But there are occasions when the subtropical high in the Northern Hemisphere breaks down, and the islands are subjected to weather conditions not normally present during the more prevalent northeast trades. Several types of storms visit the Hawaiian Islands, not frequently, but often enough to merit discussion. Three of the four storm types are associated with non-trade-wind conditions; the fourth occurs even when the trades are blowing (Blumenstock and Price 1967).

Cold-front Storms

During the winter season, when the trades are weak or nonexistent, a number of cold-front storms might sweep through the islands. They are characterized by winds from the northwest and north. Heavy but spotty rains accompany the winds, and on rare occasions the intense rain and wind can cause damage. The passage of the cold front brings cool, dry air, and the temperatures in the islands drop markedly. The cold-front storms are really the southern portions of cyclonic storms that cross the Pacific Ocean north of the islands, so the islands of Kauai and Oahu are the ones most frequently affected. It is not rare for Kauai to have more of these storms than the other islands.

Kona Storms

Also a feature of winter in the islands are Kona storms, which bring winds from the leeward, or kona, direction and sometimes result in considerable damage. Rains can be torrential and winds quite strong. The leeward sides of the islands bear the brunt of the heavy rains and seas caused by the strong Kona winds. Kona storms are less frequent than cold-front storms; usually there are one or two a year and in some years none. While less frequent, Kona storms are longer lasting and produce more rain.

Hurricanes and Tropical Storms

Tropical cyclones in the eastern Pacific are called hurricanes if they produce winds equalling or exceeding 75 miles per hour (121 km/hr.). Most eastern-Pacific hurricanes are spawned over the ocean off the Mexican coast and proceed in a general

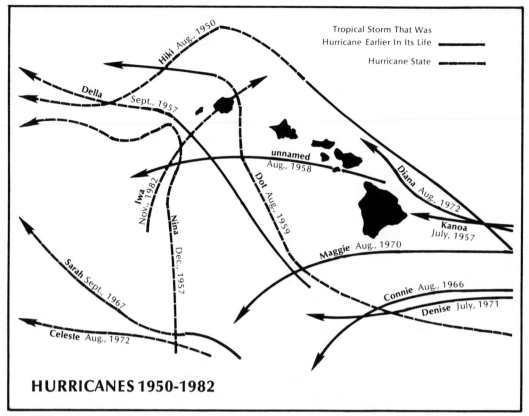

FIGURE 6.3.

westerly direction. A few, however, including two damaging ones, originated in the ocean south of the islands and proceeded north. True hurricanes are rare in the islands, but Hurricane Iwa, in November 1982, struck the islands of Kauai and Niihau with great force, and hurricane-force winds were felt on Oahu as well. A number of other hurricanes have come close and have caused some damage.

While cold front storms and Kona storms are features of the winter season, hurricanes are most prevalent from July through December. Some true tropical storms have been misnamed Kona storms, since their characteristics are similar. Although hurricanes are a relative rarity in the islands, the considerable damage caused by Iwa and the number of hurricane tracks that have passed close to Hawaii are indicative

of the ever present danger these severe storms can represent. Some hurricane tracks are shown in Figure 6.3.

Storms Associated with Upper-level Lows

Occasionally the trade winds are blowing but the expected trade-wind weather is lacking. A well-developed low pressure system in the upper atmosphere causes this unusual phenomenon, and the result can be towering cumulus clouds and torrential rains. When the upper-level low occurs in the presence of trade winds, the most intense rain may fall in windward areas. At other times upper-level lows are present under other than trade-wind conditions, and the storm winds can be from any direction and are frequently not strong.

THE CLIMATES OF HAWAII

Although all the inhabited Hawaiian Islands are within the tropics and all are under the same general climatic influences, seven basic climates in the various island regions can be identified.* In actuality a number of microclimates are present in the intricate topography of the islands. The extreme variability of rainfall from place to place reflects this intricacy.

Windward Lowlands. At elevations less than about 2,000 ft (610 m) on windward coasts, the land is generally perpendicular to the direction of the prevailing winds, and an orographic rainfall effect is present. These areas are moderately rainy with most of the precipitation being of the typical trade-wind variety. Cloudy and partly cloudy days are common. Temperatures are more uniform than in other areas, with less difference between day and night readings. Daytime summer temperatures are milder than in other regions.

Leeward Lowlands. Because of the shielding effect of intervening mountains, these regions receive far less trade-wind rain. Hence, they are distinctly drier than windward regions. Temperatures are a bit more extreme, with summertime highs frequently reaching or exceeding 90°F (32.2°C). Nighttime temperatures are lower, however, than in windward locations. Dry weather is common except when winter storms visit the islands. Occasional trade-wind rain sometimes occurs when the winds are strong and blow the moisture over the tops of intervening ridges. In summer it is not uncommon for the trades to be supplanted by an afternoon sea breeze.

Interior Lowlands. On the islands of Oahu and Maui there are central plains between large volcanic shields. The northern parts of the central lowlands have the general characteristics of windward locations at low elevations. The southern parts

*Climate descriptions and classifications are according to Blumenstock and Price 1967.

of the interior lowlands are similar in climate to leeward lowlands, with the central portions of the plains having conditions in between windward and leeward conditions. On Oahu it is not uncommon for the central lowland plain to receive heavy local showers in the afternoons, as intense heating of the land produces convection and towering clouds.

The Kona Coast of Hawaii. In this region there are some distinct climatic features. There is more rain in the summer than in the winter: nowhere else in the islands is this condition found. Land and sea breezes, rather than trade winds, are the rule. In the summer, late afternoon and early evening showers are frequent, typical of rain due to convectional effects.

Rainy Mountain Slopes on the Windward Side. The highest rainfalls in the islands occur in these regions. Humidities are generally high, and temperatures are relatively constant both seasonally and diurnally. Rain falls in copious amounts throughout the year.

Lower Mountain Slopes on the Leeward Side. Here conditions are between those in the leeward lowlands and similar elevations on windward sides. Temperature extremes exceed those on windward sides. There is a good deal of cloudiness.

High Mountains. On the slopes of Mauna Kea, Mauna Loa, and Haleakala rainfall drops off rapidly with increasing elevation beyond 2,000 to 3,000 ft (609.6 m to 914.4 m). The summits of the high mountains are very dry, with humidities sometimes as low as 5 percent. Skies are clear and temperatures are low. Snow falls in some winters, and below-freezing temperatures are common.

KÖPPEN CLIMATE CLASSIFICATIONS IN THE ISLANDS

In the widely used Köppen system for classifying climates, the Hawaiian Islands are usually classed as "Af" (tropical rain forest) on small-scale maps appearing in elementary geography texts. In truth, four of the five main Köppen classifications are found in Hawaii—only the "D," or snow, climates are missing. While it is true that many places have the tropical, or "A," climate, there are numerous examples of "B" (dry) climates, and there are even some places that have temperate, "C," climates. It should be no surprise that the mountain summits, with their winter snow-caps, have an "ET" (Tundra climate) classification.

The greatest variety of climates occurs on the Big Island, with its great range of elevations and windward/leeward characteristics. Figure 6.4 has been prepared from temperature and precipitation data from a number of stations on the island of Hawaii. On the other islands the lack of low temperatures associated with high elevations makes climate classifications less varied. For most of the islands only the "A" and "B" climates are significant. However, most places have a winter rainfall maximum and are classified "As" (tropical dry summer), rather than the "Af" that most world climatic maps show for the Hawaiian Island chain.

CLIMATE MISCELLANY

Other features of the islands' climate are not of prime importance perhaps, but nevertheless are worthy of mention. Some are aspects of the climate itself; others are interesting activities in the islands that take place primarily because of certain features of the climate.

Rainbows

One of the features of Hawaii's climate is the prevalence of rainbows—it is not unusual to see spectacular examples of double rainbows arching across the sky. Even when the sky seems clear and blue there are rainbows, and fine examples are also seen when there are dark clouds. Rainbows are such a familiar phenomenon in the islands that the University of Hawaii teams are nicknamed the Rainbows.

Atmospheric Clarity

Hawaii's air is generally free of atmospheric pollutants. True smog is virtually unknown in the islands, and only under conditions of very light, variable winds—known in the islands as Kona weather—does haze appear. Skies are generally clear blue. On some days the dark blue sky contrasted with fair-weather cumulus clouds provides a spectacular scenic view—the islands are a photographer's paradise. The clarity of the air is due to the prevalence of winds and the natural orographic and convectional effects. The air is lifted and the pollutants dispersed by the prevailing trade winds.

Wind Sports

The steadiness and force of the prevailing trade winds make the waters around the various islands ideal for sailing and wind surfing. The latter sport uses a sail on an oversized surf board and has become very popular in the islands. Regular competitions are held, and, as might be expected, local wind surfers take their share of the titles.

Hang gliding is another very popular sport that depends to an exceptional degree on the steadiness of the wind. The natural orographic effects on some of the windward coasts provide ideal launching sites. The strength and consistency of the trades provide the needed force to keep the gliders aloft for long periods of time. Consequently, records for time aloft have been set by hang-glider enthusiasts locally.

Sail planes take off and land regularly at Dillingham Field on Oahu's north shore. Small, single-engined airplanes are employed to tow the sail planes aloft, but it is the constancy of the winds that keeps them there.

Wind Energy

Hawaii has some of the highest electrical-power rates in the nation, and almost all

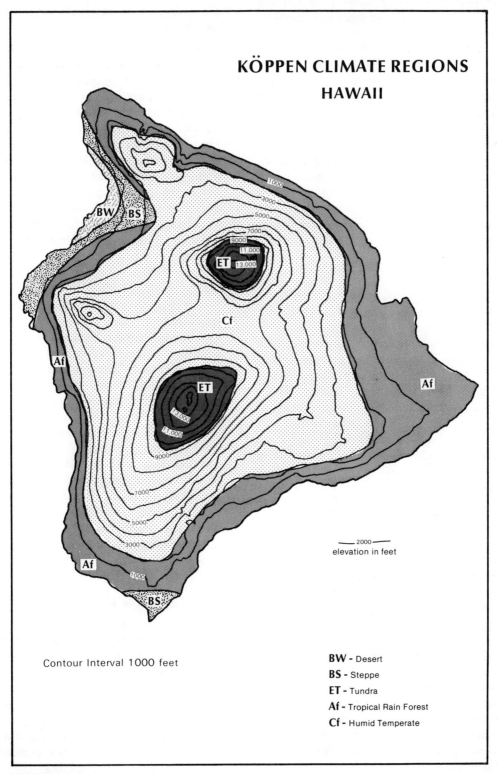

FIGURE 6.4.

electrical power is generated by burning oil. The oil has to be shipped into the state over long distances, and is even more expensive than petroleum in the other forty-nine states. The strength and consistency of the trade winds makes them an attractive alternative source of wind energy. Huge windmills have been erected in particularly windy sites, and experiments are being made to determine the economic feasibility of generating electricity by wind generators. If electrical power can be produced at competitive rates, large "wind farms" at a number of locations are planned. The generated power would then be fed into the electrical-power grids of the islands.

Solar Energy

The sun is available to Hawaii's residents throughout the year and can be used with existing technology to provide energy to heat water. Solar panels and other necessary equipment to provide hot water independent of electrical power or gas are a feature of many houses and some business structures, and the use of solar energy is increasing. Obviously, solar hot water systems work best where there is less cloudiness and rain, and leeward areas are particularly attractive.

Insects and Hawaii's Climate

Not all aspects of the climate of the Hawaiian Islands are salubrious. In most areas temperatures are warm throughout the year, and humidities are somewhat high: ideal conditions for insects. Flying and crawling insects thrive in the islands, and it is an extremely rare house that does not have a roach or two to plague the residents. The most serious of the insect pests are the termites, a decided menace to wooden buildings in the islands. As a consequence of the ever present termite menace, a number of "tented" houses are always to be seen, each covered with brightly colored cloth within which poisonous gases kill these destructive creatures.

AN ANCIENT HAWAIIAN VIEW OF CLIMATE

Before the arrival of western civilization to the islands, Hawaiians lived close to the land, and they were naturally quite aware of climatic phenomena. This is expressed in their language, which has an extraordinarily large number of words to express various types of climatic elements. We have already mentioned the Hawaiian words for winter and summer seasons and their concept of the changing patterns of wind, rain, and temperature as hooilo gave way to kau. The principal climatic elements, wind and rain, were described in the Hawaiian language quite expressively.

Hawaiian Words for Wind

The basic term for wind in the Hawaiian language is *makani,* and there are numerous variations of this basic word. A variable wind is a *makani palua,* and a fair wind a *makani oluolu.* There were several words for the northeast trade wind: *moae, ae, ae-loa, moae lehua,* and *moae pehu* to name but a few. The wind from the leeward direction was, of course, known as the Kona wind. There were a number of winds associated with specific places: *ala honua* (Hilo), *apaapaa* (Kohala, Hawaii), *ala-hou* (Molokai), *kaua-ula* (Lahaina, Maui), and *ahiu* (Kahana, Oahu), for example. There are dozens of other words for winds, some referring to local areas, others defining winds with specific characteristics. (Pukui and Elbert 1971).

Hawaiian Words for Rain

Ua means rain in Hawaiian, and, as in the case of winds, there are many variations. A continuous rain is an *ua hookina,* and a downpour is an *ua lani pili.* Examples of names of rains associated with various places are *ua kuahine* (Manoa, Oahu) and *ua lani haa haa* (Hana, Maui). *Anuenue* means rainbow, and it was thought that the rainbow symbolized the presence of *alii* or gods (Pukui and Elbert 1971).

REFERENCES

Blumenstock, D. I., and Price, S. *Climates of the States: Hawaii, Climatography of the United States No. 60-51*. Washington, D.C.: U.S. Department of Commerce, 1967.

Department of Geography, University of Hawaii. *Atlas of Hawaii*. Honolulu: University Press of Hawaii, 1973.

Morgan, J., and Street, J. *Oahu Environments*. Honolulu: Oriental Publishing Co., 1978.

Pukui, M. K., and Elbert, S. H. *Hawaiian Dictionary*. Honolulu: University of Hawaii Press, 1971.

CHAPTER 7

THE NATURAL HAZARDS OF AN ISLAND PARADISE

Brian Murton

Although the Hawaiian Islands have a reputation for having a benign, unchanging environment, natural events can, and do, interact with human activities to create natural hazards. Even though social and technological hazards are often allocated more news space, statistics indicate the extent of natural hazards: the islands can expect one damaging tsunami every 7.7 years; on the average during the 1970s there were five severe weather events each year; there have been over eighty volcanic eruptions on the island of Hawaii since 1800; since 1950 there have been six earthquakes of magnitude over 6 on the Richter scale with epicenters on the island of Hawaii, plus several hundred others that have been felt. The natural processes involved in these happenings can be called *events.* They may have no immediate human implications, or they may kill people and destroy property. These and other impacts on humans and what they value we call *consequences.* The division of hazards into events and consequences has implications for *hazard management,* the choosing of adjustments to cope with hazards.

HAZARDOUS EVENTS IN THE HAWAIIAN ISLANDS

The major natural hazards of Hawaii are the product of extreme geophysical events of either a meteorological or geomorphic nature (Table 7.1). Lesser geophysical events, such as beach and soil erosion and normal surf conditions, also can be hazardous. For instance, numerous drownings and injuries occur each year as the result of surfing and boating mishaps in the waters around the islands. Biological hazards of both a floral nature (for example, pollen in the air) and faunal nature (for example, goats) are also present in the islands. While these are all hazardous events and should be included in a comprehensive survey of natural hazards, only major events of a geophysical nature are considered in this chapter.

Natural Processes

One way of describing the extreme natural events that are hazardous to life and property in the Hawaiian Islands is to focus upon the natural processes characterizing

Table 7.1
Examples of Major Natural Hazards in the Hawaiian Islands

Hazard	Date	Area Affected	Property Damage and/or Loss of Life
Tsunami	May 22, 1960	Hilo, Hamakua, Kohala, and Kona Coasts of island of Hawaii	Total damages $23.5 million, 61 killed, 282 injured.
Volcanic eruption	Jan.-Feb., 1960	Puna District on island of Hawaii	Village of Kapoho destroyed, total damages $5 million.
Earthquake	Jan. 23, 1938	Maui	Considerable damage.
High Wind	Jan. 13-14, 1970	Oahu	Peak gusts of 96 mph at Kaneohe MCAS and Schofield Barracks. Total damages $4.5 million.
High Surf	Dec. 1-2, 1969	Oahu	30 to 50 foot waves. Total damages $1.2 million. One person drowned.
Flash Flood	April 19, 1974	Oahu	Total damage $3.2 million, four persons drowned.
Waterspout-tornado	Jan. 28, 1971	Kailua-Kona, island of Hawaii	Waterspout moved inland destroying buildings, four injured, total damages $1 million.
Hurricane	Aug. 4-7, 1959	Kauai	Hurricane DOT passed directly over eastern Kauai from the south. Total damages $5 million.
Tropical Storm	Aug. 6-7, 1958	Maui, Hawaii, and Oahu	Total damages $552,000.

Source: "Catalog of Natural and Man-Caused Incidents and Disasters in the Hawaiian Islands," State Civil Defense Division, December 1978.

them. Major extreme natural events of a geomorphic nature include volcanic eruptions, earthquakes, and tsunamis. Expansive soil and beach, sheet, and gully erosion appear of lesser significance, because they are not as spectacular, yet they cause damage.

The island of Hawaii has the distinction of containing the only currently active volcanoes in the state. Today it is Mauna Loa and Kilauea that are highly active. Between 1830 and 1950 Mauna Loa erupted on the average of once every three and one-half years; it was then quiet until 1975. Kilauea is believed to have been continuously active during most of the century from 1823 to 1924. Twenty-one separate eruptions were recorded between 1924 and 1965, and since that time Kilauea has been active about 80 percent of the time.

Strong earthquakes have caused damage in the recent past on all islands but Kauai. The Hawaiian Islands are located in a seismically active area known as the Molokai Fracture Zone: major earthquakes, here as elsewhere, are the result of faulting. Some of the faults are on, and probably genetically associated with, the volcanoes; others are on the ocean floor near the islands. Since 1925, ten earthquakes with magnitudes greater than 5.3 Richter have occurred; of these, six originated on the island of Hawaii and four on faults on the ocean floor. In 1951 an earthquake of magnitude 6.8 Richter originated on the Kealakekua fault, just off the west coast of Hawaii. The 1938 Maui earthquake (magnitude 6.75) had its epicenter about 25 mi (40 km) north of the island, probably on one of ten strands of the Molokai Fracture Zone. The greatest Hawaiian earthquake of historic time occurred in April 1868. It was accompanied, and probably was caused, by movements on faults both onshore and offshore near the south end of the island of Hawaii. Of late, the greatest number of earthquakes have occurred on or near Kilauea volcano, but there have also been concentrations on the southeast flank of Mauna Loa, to the north of Hilo on the Hamakua coast, and offshore to the south.

Tsunamis are perhaps Hawaii's best-known natural hazard. Based upon a careful search of the records, it is estimated that between 1813 and 1975 there have been twenty-one destructive tsunamis.

Beach erosion is a problem on heavily urbanized Oahu. Sheet and gully erosion have long led to considerable soil loss on sloping agricultural land on many of the islands; urban development on Oahu has also been a prime contributor to soil wash, especially from ridge lines. Expansive soil is scattered over considerable areas in urban Oahu, and there have been a number of instances of property damage when construction has taken place there.

Extreme events of a meteorological nature have persistently posed threats to human life and property. High winds, heavy rain, storm surf, flash floods, waterspouts, tornadoes, drought, mudslides, and lightning strikes occur frequently (Haraguchi 1979). In addition to affecting land activities, severe weather also strikes at marine activities.

Types of strong winds that are the sources of most severe weather problems are those associated with Kona storms, thunderstorm downdraft, waterspouts and/or tornadoes, and hurricanes and tropical storms. When reinforced by topography such as a mountain mass or downslope flow over a mountain ridge, winds associated with Kona storms can gust to over 100 mph (161 km/hr). On Oahu the Wahiawa area below Kolekole Pass in the Waianae Mountains and the Kaneohe-Kahaluu area below the Koolau Mountains have suffered from extensive wind damage during these storms, which also can bring very heavy rainfall. Fortunately, Kona storms are not common. Before 1970 they averaged one every two to three years, but since then there have been only three occurrences.

Thunderstorms are not common; the frequency of thunderstorm days is low, averaging one to three per month in the winter and none to one per month in summer. Waterspouts and tornadoes, which develop from the base of heavy cumulonimbus clouds or thunderstorms, occur predominantly during the winter. About thirty to forty funnels aloft are sighted annually, but very few touch water or land.

Hawaii is unfortunately not free of hurricanes and tropical storms. Most weaken before they reach the islands or pass harmlessly to the south, but over the last thirty years at least nineteen hurricanes or tropical storms have come within 300 mi (483 km) (Table 7.2). Hurricane Iwa caused more than $200 million damage to property and farm crops on the islands of Kauai and Oahu. It passed almost directly over Kauai with winds as high as 110 miles per hour.

Swells from all directions reach the shores of the islands. During the past ten years high surf from northerly and northwesterly swells has occurred four times (Table 7.3).

Table 7.2
Selected Damaging Tropical Storms and Hurricanes 1950-1982

Name	Date	Characteristics	Damage
HIKI	Aug. 1950	Passed 15 miles NW of Kauai, heavy rains flooded Waimea Valley, windspeed 68 mph.	
DELLA	Sept. 1957	High surf along south Kauai.	
NINA	Dec. 1957	High Surf along Kauai's coast, windspeed 92 mph.	$100,000
--	Aug. 1958	Unnamed tropical storm impacted island of Hawaii.	$500,000
DOT	Aug. 1959	Impacted Kauai, high winds, heavy rains, windspeed 103 mph.	$5.5 million Kauai $150,000 Oahu
MAGGIE	Aug. 1970	Came within 100 miles of island of Hawaii, but weakened, heavy rains only.	
CELESTE	Aug. 1972	Came within 380 miles of island of Hawaii, 15 foot waves pounded southern coast.	
DIANA	Aug. 1972	A tropical storm that passed within 60 miles of the Puna coast, 30 foot waves struck the coast.	
KATE	Sept. 1976	Veered northwest about a day's distance from Hawaii. Generated 8 foot surf along northern coasts of all islands.	
FICO	July 1978	Passed 200 miles south of the island of Hawaii. Wave heights of 20 feet damaged 12 houses.	$140,000
IWA	Nov. 1982	Passed over Niihau and Kauai with winds of 110 miles per hour. Widespread damage to structures and crops. Great damage on Oahu as well.	More than $200 million

Source: State of Hawaii, State Civil Defense Division 1978.

Hurricanes also cause high surf when they come within 300 mi (483 km) of the islands.

Human Dimensions of Hazards

The common measures of hazardous events found to be significant in human terms are listed in Table 7.4. The significance of these seven dimensions is measured in terms of the type of response each requires or allows.

Volcanic eruptions are moderately frequent, of medium duration, somewhat limited in their areal extent, moderate in their speed of onset, concentrated in terms of their spatial dispersion, and random in regard to their temporal spacing. Major

Table 7.3
High Surf During the Winter

Date	Maximum Height/Shores Affected	Fatalities/$ Damage
Dec. 1, 1969	50 ft., west-north	1 drowned, 15 injured, $1.5 million
Jan. 7, 1974	30 ft., west-north	none, $200,000
Mar. 23, 1974	30 ft., west-north	5 drowned, $130,000
Nov. 11, 1976	30 ft., northwest-north	none, $15,000

Source: State of Hawaii, State Civil Defense Division 1978.

Table 7.4
Definitions of Human Parameters of Extreme Events

Magnitude:	the maximum height, force, or strength reached by the event.
Frequency:	how often an event of a given magnitude may be expected to occur in the long-run average. Range: frequent to rare.
Duration:	the length of time over which a hazard event persists. Range: long to short.
Areal extent:	the space covered by a hazard event. Range: widespread to limited.
Speed of onset:	the length of time between the first appearance of an event and its peak. Range: slow to fast.
Spatial dispersion:	the pattern of distribution over space in which an event can occur. Range: diffuse to concentrated.
Temporal spacing:	the pattern of distribution over time, the sequence of events. Range: regular to random.

Source: Burton, I.; Kates, R. W.; and White, G. F. The Environment as Hazard. New York: Oxford University Press, 1978, pp. 22-23.

earthquakes are infrequent, of short duration, and relatively concentrated. Speed of onset is usually very high, and the event occurs in a more or less random fashion. Tsunamis are somewhat similar to earthquakes in their dimensions, except that the arrival time of distant tsunamis is known several hours in advance.

The various kinds of severe weather events are of much greater frequency, apart from hurricanes, which are rare. Duration is usually short, areal concentrations can either be limited (as in a flash flood or tornado) or widespread (heavy rain), and the speed of onset varies, although most events are predictable in advance. Most events are concentrated into certain seasons, but are random in occurrence.

Hazardousness of Places

Public attention and scientific activity focused on natural hazards is most often directed toward individual natural events. However, most places and communities are affected by a variety of hazards: floods, hurricanes, tornadoes, high winds, high surf, and even volcanic eruptions.

Over the period of historic record, the island of Hawaii has been affected by the greatest number of damaging events, followed by Oahu, Maui, Kauai, Molokai, and Lanai (Table 7.5). Each island has its own blend of hazards, although severe weather events are the most common everywhere. Hawaii is the only island on which volcanic eruptions occur. Tsunamis also have visited Hawaii more frequently than any other island, drought is common there, and the island leads in damaging earthquakes. The hazardousness of this island gives it a unique set of hazard management problems.

On Oahu, in addition to severe weather, threats to life and property are tsunamis, earthquakes, and drought. Droughts, earthquakes, and tsunamis are relatively more significant hazards on Maui than they are on Oahu. Kauai has never recorded a damaging earthquake, but tsunamis, drought, and especially severe weather events have

Table 7.5
The Hazardousness of Islands

| | Number of Recorded Events, 1835–1978 | | | | | |
	Hawaii	Lanai	Maui	Molokai	Oahu	Kauai
Tsunami	19	3	10	3	6	5
Severe Weather	67	3	57	10	88	38
Earthquakes	5	1	2	1	3	0
Volcanic Eruption	10	0	0	0	0	0
Drought	29	5	21	6	7	8
Total	130	12	90	20	104	51

Source: State of Hawaii, State Civil Defense Division 1978, Mimeo, pp. 1–39.

struck. In fact, on Oahu and Kauai severe weather, of one type or another, makes for the greatest degree of hazardousness.

CONSEQUENCES OF HAZARDOUS EVENTS

The consequences of hazardous events depend as much upon the nature and extent of human occupance as they do upon the characteristics of the natural events involved. On this basis we expect Oahu, the major population center, to have experienced loss of life and property. On the other hand the island of Hawaii, even with fewer people, has also suffered much damage and loss of life.

On Hawaii considerable damage to property has resulted from volcanic eruptions. However, apart from a party of Hawaiians killed by falling rocks and volcanic gas from Kilauea caldera about 1790, loss of life has been small, because evacuation is possible. The 1926 and 1950 eruptions of Mauna Loa disrupted communications and destroyed property when lava flowed to the sea in South Kona, but the most damaging eruptions of recent times have been on the East Rift Zone of Kilauea, where nearly $1 million in losses occurred in 1955 and over $5 million in 1960. This latter eruption destroyed eighty buildings in the village of Kapoho, and lava covered 2,500 acres (1,000 ha), several hundred of which had been cultivated.

The earthquake of 1868 caused severe damage on the island of Hawaii, and others in 1957, 1973, and 1975 also damaged much property on this island. In 1871 buildings, walls, and chimneys were damaged on Maui, Oahu, Lanai, and Molokai. The 1938 earthquake caused considerable damage on Maui; Oahu's last damaging earthquake was in 1948.

As noted in Chapter 5, the most destructive tsunamis were in 1837, 1868, 1877, 1946, 1960, and 1975. The tsunami of local origin in 1868 resulted in 81 deaths, all in the Puna and Kau districts of Hawaii. But the worst natural disaster ever to strike the Hawaiian Islands was the tsunami of April 1, 1946: property damage was great, particularly at Hilo on the island of Hawaii; 159 people were killed and 165 injured, most in Hilo. Again, on May 22, 1960, a tsunami devastated Hilo and other parts of the state. Extreme wave heights resulted in 61 deaths and 282 injuries in Hilo, and property damage of nearly $24 million. A local tsunami in 1975 killed two persons.

The most common severe weather hazards are related to wintertime Kona storms and winds and to swells created far to the north and northwest by winter storms. Indeed, of the 208 "Severe Weather Incidents" between 1881 and 1978 that are listed in the Hawaiian Civil Defense Division's "Catalog of Natural and Man-Caused Incidents and Disasters in the Hawaiian Islands," 185 occurred between October and April, during the so-called winter months. Ninety of these incidents were flash floods, which are particularly severe in areas with small, steep-sided valleys where streams can flood in thirty minutes when heavy rain falls. Damages from flash flooding since 1881 total over $20 million and at least eighty people have been killed. Until flood-protection works were completed in the 1960s on Oahu, death and damage were particularly severe in urban Honolulu. Regular flooding adds another $5 million to the flood-damage figure. Twenty-seven high-wind episodes since 1881 have caused damages totaling almost $10 million—the high winds from the southwest on January 13 to 14, 1970, caused more damage than any other single event apart from the 1946 and 1960 tsunamis. High surf has been particularly bad on sixteen occasions since 1881 and has caused about $5 million damage and killed at least thirteen people. For instance, high surf on December 2, 1969, struck Kauai, Oahu, Molokai, and Hawaii, causing over $1.5 million in losses, one death, and fifteen injuries.

But most often severe weather involves a combination of effects—high winds, heavy rain, flooding, and high waves. There have been at least twenty-four such events over the past century, each causing very considerable damage, totaling nearly $16 million. Hurricane Dot of 1959, which devastated Kauai, made a large contribution to this total.

Waterspouts and/or tornadoes have been recorded on fifteen occasions since 1881. The tornado of December 17, 1967, on Kauai destroyed five homes, damaged twenty-nine, and left 126 persons homeless at Kaumakani. A bad year for tornadoes was 1971 when seven occurred: three on Hawaii causing $1.7 million damage in the Kona area; two on Oahu; and two on Kauai.

THE ASSESSMENT OF RISK

Risk assessment involves not only the identification of hazards and the allocation of cause, but also the estimation of the probability of events of a dangerous nature occurring. Judgments about risk generally are made for specific hazards by scientists who specialize in the study of the physical processes involved. In the islands risks have been assessed for volcanic hazard, earthquake hazard, and flood hazard on many streams, and a tsunami-inundation zone has been estimated.

On the island of Hawaii, based on the location and frequency of past eruptions, five volcanic-hazards zones have been designated (U.S. Geological Survey 1976). Zones of highest risk include the summit areas and major rift zones of the two active volcanoes. The flanks of Kilauea and Mauna Loa that lie downslope from the calderas and rifts are areas of moderately high risk. Risk on Hualalai is rather poorly defined, but all of Mauna Kea is an area of very low hazard, as are the Kohala Mountains, where there has not been an eruption for about 60,000 years. The area of relatively high risk includes the city of Hilo and areas of recent development in the Kona, Kau, and Puna districts.

Seismic-risk maps, which show zones of approximately equal seismic risk, were calculated for Hawaii in the early 1950s. The island of Hawaii was placed in risk zone 3, where major damage could occur; Maui and Kahoolawe in zone 2, that of potentially moderate damage; Oahu, Molokai, and Lanai in zone 1, that of potentially minor damage; and Kauai in zone 0, where no damage should be expected to occur. However, as Furamoto et al. (1972) point out, this seismic-risk scheme for Hawaii was based solely on damage reported from the 1868 earthquake, and earthquakes centered on the Molokai Fracture Zone could cause much heavier damage on Maui and Oahu. They suggested increasing the zoning for the Hawaiian Islands so that zone 3 would include Maui and Molokai as well as Hawaii, Oahu would fall into zone 2, and Kauai zone 1. A State Senate Resolution in 1979 highlighted the need for the state to reassess seismic-risk zoning in Hawaii.

Stream-gauging stations have long been in existence in Hawaii, but a data collection network of crest-gauging for flood studies only dates to 1957 for Oahu, 1962 for Hawaii and Kauai, and 1963 for Maui and Molokai. These records were used to calculate flood frequencies, especially for streams on Oahu, in order to facilitate flood control and adjustments (State of Hawaii, Department of Land and Natural Resources 1970). Flood frequency, or the recurrence interval of a flood, is the average time interval within which a flood of a given magnitude will be equaled or exceeded once. Today it is known how often a flood of a certain size can be expected, but it should be remembered that such designations do not imply a regular frequency. Rather, they indicate an average interval within which a flood of that magnitude will occur. Such floods may recur at any time, as witnessed by the recurrence of three so-called 100-year floods on streams on the Hamakua coast in early 1981.

While not involving estimations of probability, the tsunami-inundation zones established by the Hawaii Institute of Geophysics, University of Hawaii (under the direction of Doak C. Cox, who was then in charge of the tsunami research program), provide an indication of potential hazardous areas (Cox 1961). Recently these zones have been modified and stream flood-hazard areas of different frequency-magnitude added, as part of the requirements of the National Flood Insurance Program.

HAZARD MANAGEMENT

Hazard management involves the choice of options to be used in controlling and reducing consequences of extreme events. While all the people of Hawaii are hazard managers in the sense that each person in his own way has to cope with hazards, individuals operate within limits set by their communities. In Hawaii collective decisions dominate hazard management. This type of management involves a growing bureaucracy, a series of seemingly irresolvable political battles, and an interplay between science and social values that often confounds rational discussion. Major institutional categories of hazard management include the development of hazard warning systems (including education), relief and rehabilitation, technological aids, regulatory adjustments (including zoning and building codes), and insurance.

Hazard Warning Systems

The purpose of a hazard warning system is to inform as many people as possible in an area at risk that a damaging event is imminent and to alert them to actions that can be taken to avoid losses. Earthquake prediction has not yet reached a level of reliability that enables quake forecasting to be done with confidence in the islands, but warning systems exist for all other major hazards. The responsibility for providing forecasts of an impending extreme event rests primarily with two federal agencies, the U.S. Geological Survey in the case of volcanic hazard and the National Weather Service (NWS) in the cases of tsunamis and severe weather. These organizations communicate with civil defense authorities, who issue watches and warn-

ings and set emergency procedures in operation.

Civil defense in Hawaii is organized first at the county level. The Civil Defense Division, State Department of Defense, coordinates plans, programs, and actions for the entire state and is responsible for dealing with major emergencies of disaster proportions. However, most civil defense actions are initiated at the county level for local emergencies such as flood, earthquake, or volcanic eruption. Warnings received by the Civil Defense Division are transmitted over the Hawaii Warning System simultaneously to the State Warning Point and to county warning points located in county police headquarters; these warning points alert the public through siren signals and radio broadcasts over Civ-Alert, the State's emergency broadcast system. Emergency Operating Centers (EOCs) are activated at state and county levels. EOCs, of course, can be activated by county Civil Defense directors for local calamities.

The volcanic-hazard warning system is limited to the island of Hawaii. Here the U.S. Geological Survey notifies Civil Defense headquarters in Hilo when its instruments indicate the likelihood of an eruption (Sorensen and Gershmehl 1980, 125–136). When the eruption is confirmed, the county Civil Defense director issues a warning. County fire, police, public works, and parks departments; the county administration; the National Guard; and the Red Cross are all contacted; the EOC is activated. The EOC then notifies the leaders of local community organizations in the threatened area, and each agency moves to carry out its specified duties and responsibilities. Most of the plans are geared for typical slow flows that warrant careful monitoring, crowd control, and an occasional orderly evacuation, carried out according to a detailed master plan. Taken alone, the formal warning arrangements might not be particularly effective, but official efforts mesh well with informal mechanisms developed by local community leaders.

Today Hawaii participates in the Pacific Tsunami Warning System (described in Chapter 5), and there is local warning capacity as well (Morgan 1978). Once a warning has been declared, civil defense authorities sound the attention/alert signal on the warning sirens. At this time the emergency broadcast system will direct evacuation of threatened areas, under police supervision.

The National Weather Service has the responsibility of issuing advisories, watches, and warnings about severe weather in and around the islands. A *watch* means that the possibility of severe weather exists, whereas a *warning* means that the possibility has been transformed into a probability or a certainty. In Hawaii watches and warnings are issued by the Weather Service Forecasting Office at Honolulu Airport, whose staff use all the tools available to modern meteorologists to help them in their task.

In Hawaii a major problem in predicting severe, "short-fused" weather and issuing warnings is caused by a lack of reporting stations in surrounding areas. Especially with regard to rainfall, the NWS can tell that a Kona storm is forming, but cannot predict how much rain will fall. Flash-flood warnings are problematical because of this and because of difficult terrain. A flash flood can occur in thirty minutes, and residents of low-lying areas have to be prepared to evacuate at a moment's notice.

Hurricanes, tropical storms, and high surf, on the other hand, do not spring suddenly upon Hawaii, for with today's satellite weather coverage there is ample warning. Winter storms to the north and summer hurricanes and tropical storms to the south are closely monitored, and on several occasions a hurricane watch has been issued for the island of Hawaii. A warning would only be issued when hurricane conditions would be expected within twenty-four hours.

In addition to providing severe-weather forecasts, the NWS provides continuous broadcasts of the latest weather information designed especially for mariners. When severe-weather warnings are in order, routine transmissions are interrupted and the broadcast is devoted to emergency warnings.

Hazard Education

Education is a critical component of hazard warning systems and of hazard management. Students in Hawaii's schools participate in civil defense drills, usually involving building evacuation procedures. Schools in areas of flash floods, or in potential tsunami-inundation zones, also hold drills oriented to these specific events. The public school system maintains a Civil Defense coordinator; on request, state and county Civil Defense and NWS officials will visit schools and give talks on appropriate procedures and responses concerning disasters.

Hazard education of the general public can be divided into four areas. First, the major mechanism to provide information is in a section of the telephone book. Several pages cover general civil defense procedures, while part of another page contains very general information on the four major recognized hazards—tsunami, flash flooding, earthquake, and hurricane. Tsunami run-up maps are also printed in the telephone book. Second, the public is informed in newspaper stories, television broadcasts, and radio announcements. The extent to which the popular media actually educate the public on preparedness and response is difficult to measure. A tally of published newspaper articles for the year 1978 reveals that only fifty-four stories dealt with some aspect of the four major local hazards. Most articles concerned disasters in far distant parts of the world.

A third category of public education is carried out by designated public agencies that prepare and distribute pamphlets about various hazards and procedures to combat them. For instance, the U.S. Geological Survey (U.S. Department of Interior) has a publication entitled *Natural Hazards on the Island of Hawaii,* which deals with the major geomorphic hazards. The NWS has pamphlets available on tsunamis and all possible types of severe weather. These describe in detail the nature of the events, the meanings of watches and warnings, and the kinds of behavior appropriate to each situation. Other agencies, such as the Red Cross, police and fire departments, and public utilities companies, also have material available.

Finally, some information reaches a small section of the public, including administrators and officials, through legislative hearings, neighborhood board meetings, community meetings, and civic-group activities. The NWS has also held seminars for public and private agency officials, the news media, and other concerned groups on severe weather problems and hurricane preparedness.

Efficacy of Hazard Warning Systems and Hazard Education

The efficacy of any warning system and of hazard education depends partly on how people perceive hazards and partly on their awareness of possible adjustments.

Information on perception of hazards is at best fragmentary for Hawaii. Several studies have been carried out concerning the perception of hazard from volcanic eruptions and of appropriate responses (Murton and Shimabukuro 1974, 151–159; Hodge et al. 1978, 110–138). What emerges from these may be indicative of more generally held views about natural events and how to cope with them. On the island of Hawaii residents in areas of high volcanic risk generally perceive the behavior of the volcano very much as do the scientists. They are also well aware of warning-system procedures and of the major adjustment, evacuation. Certainly of late there is every indication that the volcanic-hazard warning system has operated efficiently, though with changing social and demographic structures, this may not be the case in the future (Sorensen and Gershmehl 1980, 126–136).

However, differences do emerge in per-ception of hazards and what can be done. Hawaiians are much more fatalistic than other ethnic groups, probably through continuing beliefs in the volcano goddess, Pele. In the past, when threatened by lava, Hawaiians would continue their daily activities, trusting all to Pele. Today, such belief is manifest in a reluctance to evacuate in the face of advancing lava flows, as was the case in Kalapana during the 1977 eruption. On the other hand, Japanese and Filipinos believe that people should trust their elected officials to make decisions for them, while Caucasians feel that individuals should make their own decisions.

In the face of overwhelming geomorphic hazards, most people understand that evacuation is the only possible adjustment. However, many appeal to the supernatural. In volcanic-hazard areas this is mainly to Pele. Many people, especially elderly Hawaiians, make offerings of liquor, candy, tobacco, flowers, food, and ti leaves. Further, some pray to dead relatives to intercede with Pele to direct lava away from a piece of land.

A critical point about hazard perception in the islands is the curiosity displayed by residents when a volcano erupts, a tsunami is predicted, or there is high surf. In Hawaii, people flock to the place where the event is occurring.

This is particularly alarming in regard to the tsunami warning system. There has not been a major distant tsunami since 1960, and based on past behavior, there is a real question of whether the people in threatened areas will respond in an appropriate manner when one occurs again. In 1957, for example, after a warning the coastal residents evacuated, but thousands flocked to the beaches to see the "big event." Even worse was the behavior of many residents in Hilo in 1960. The tsunami arrival time was accurately forecast, and the warnings were conveyed to the public in ample time to permit orderly evacuation from endangered areas. Yet many did not heed the warnings. A study of Hilo residents who survived the tsunami was made by Bonk, Leachman, and Tatsuoka (1960). It revealed that the warning signal was sounded for a twenty-minute period more than four hours prior to arrival of the first wave, yet only 40 percent of the endangered public moved to safety. Ninety-five percent of those questioned admitted to hearing the signal, and almost all claimed to know what the signal meant, although closer questioning revealed that there were differing interpretations and some confusion. Some thought that the sirens signaled an alert, which would be followed by an additional signal to evacuate the area. Others thought that the signal meant to immediately evacuate the danger area. In short, the public was unable to assess the degree of danger and to take proper action from the information provided.

Somewhat similar conclusions were reached in a recent study of hazard preparedness on Oahu (Sorensen and Murton 1979). It was found that the telephone book is not widely perceived to be a useful source for learning about hazard response; that other channels of communication, especially the popular news media, are seen as having more utility; and that the formal education process contains little on hazard education. A general implication is that hazard education is at best a hit-or-miss process in need of greater coordination and careful planning.

Relief and Rehabilitation

Relief and rehabilitation following major natural disasters have been routinely provided in Hawaii. After the 1946 and 1960 tsunamis in Hilo, state and federal assistance was provided immediately after the event and during the rehabilitation phase. In addition other relief organizations, such as the Red Cross, were intimately involved. Various kinds of relief activities were necessary during the volcanic eruptions of 1955, 1960, and 1977. In all these cases shelter, food, food stamps, clothing, personal loans, transportation, and housing loans were provided. Furthermore, as a consequence of the 1960 tsunami and various volcanic eruptions, the state of Hawaii passed Act 1973, which permits property taxes and income taxes to be remitted, refunded, or forgiven equal to losses due to natural disasters.

Flash floods, earthquakes, and droughts have also led to either the state or federal governments, or both, declaring places to be major disaster areas. In all these examples, government (in addition to the Red Cross) has taken the responsibility for relief and rehabilitation, thus spreading the financial burden among all citizens. Such a routine provision of relief and rehabilitation funds can create a feeling of complacency and can encourage the continued occupance or reoccupance of hazardous areas.

Technological Aids

Technological aids consist of various protective works ranging from planting trees to construction of elaborate structures such as seawalls and dams. A number have been adopted in Hawaii to combat different hazards.

Various experiments, including bombing the flows and watering the edges of flows, have been attempted to divert or stop lava and thus protect property. Barriers also have been constructed, and a permanent diversion barrier has been proposed a number of times (1937, 1950, and 1975) to protect Hilo from Mauna Loa lava flows. The last proposal met with considerable community resistance on social, economic, legal, and religious grounds.

At different times technological adjustments have been suggested as the solution to the tsunami hazard in Hilo. After the 1960 tsunami, extensive hydraulic-modeling experiments were carried out with twenty possible configurations of breakwaters and seawalls. Although protective barriers were found feasible, economic analyses demonstrated that the benefit-cost ratio was unfavorable; the cost of the proposed structures would have exceeded the value of the property to be protected. Some tree plantings have been made along the Hilo waterfront, but they are probably inadequate to serve as a tsunami break.

Flood control since 1950, especially on Oahu, has involved decreasing flood runoff through reforestation, improving channel capacity by excavating and clearing, providing more uniform cross-sections, eliminating unnecessary bends, lining the channel with concrete or rubble masonry, and building debris traps. On Oahu the lower courses of most streams flowing through Honolulu have concrete-lined channels; on the windward side, in 1980 the Corps of Engineers completed a reservoir (plus park) in the headwaters of the hazardous Kaneohe Stream.

Regulatory Adjustments

Land-use management is a legal device, instituted by government, to preclude certain uses of land in areas subject to natural hazards. As yet there has been no attempt to zone land in relationship to volcanic hazard, but zoning has been used to combat the tsunami hazard in Hilo and the threat of flash flooding on all islands.

In Hilo, after the 1960 tsunami, it was decided that zoning was the best solution to the problem of tsunami damage (Morgan 1979, 149–159). The plan adopted was called Project Kaikoo ("strong sea"), and it set aside 353 acres (143 ha) of the most vulnerable area as open space, providing for a few nonconforming uses and commercial uses on about 40 acres (16 ha) of filled area above 22 ft (6.7 m) in elevation. Zoning against floods has involved the establishment of buffer zones defined by encroachment lines and the revision of ordinances in some places to permit only recreational and agricultural uses.

Seismic risk and—along the coast—tsunami risk are taken into account in the building codes. After the 1960 tsunami, new design standards were developed for hotels and large buildings constructed in the tsunami-inundation zone. In actual practice many engineers use higher standards than mandated by the seismic-risk

codes, and all buildings funded by the state meet zone 3 requirements.

Insurance

Insurance against earthquakes is available, but relatively few property owners have policies. Since 1973 residents have been able to participate in a coastal and riverine flood-insurance program under the Flood Disaster Protection act, which provided subsidized insurance under the National Flood Insurance Program (NFIP). One of the key items of this act was that pending completion of floodplain flood-risk mapping studies, communities could enter an emergency phase of NFIP by satisfying very simple requirements, thus deferring the unpopular subject of floodplain zoning.

Since 1973 flood-risk maps of the islands have been under preparation, so that each county could enter the regular NFIP. However, no county has yet entered the scheme, because of disagreements relating to future construction and development. Without entering the regular program, low-cost flood insurance is no longer available, and future federal flood-disaster relief money and funds for construction of projects in flood-risk areas will not be forthcoming.

THE STATE OF HAZARD MANAGEMENT IN HAWAII

Hawaii, while not one of the parts of the world most prone to natural disasters, is threatened by a range of geomorphic and climatological hazards. Slow to be aroused, the people of Hawaii have begun to respond with vigor to the more extreme events. Considerable money has been spent on research and scientific assessment of the risks from nature in the islands. But still the major individual and institutional adjustment to hazards remains loss acceptance, either bearing losses or sharing losses through relief, rehabilitation, and insurance. However, attempts have been made to reduce losses, usually through engineering adjustments: concrete-lined stream beds, seawalls, and the like. In one case, that of Hilo, losses have been so great as to be intolerable, and legal action has been used to change land use. In Hawaii there is a mix of adjustments to any single extreme event and in any specific place. The factors that contribute to the particular mix reflect the characteristics of the events themselves, the local experience with hazard and success of adjustment, and variation in intensity of occupance. A comprehensive hazard management plan does not exist for Hawaii. Damaging events will occur again, and it is to be hoped that the present system of adjustments is capable of coping with their effects.

REFERENCES

Bonk, W. J.; Leachman, R.; and Tatsuoka, M. *A Report of Human Behavior During the Tsunami of May 23, 1960.* Hilo: Hawaii Division of the Hawaiian Academy of Science, 1960.

Cox, D. C. *Potential Tsunami Inundation Areas in Hawaii.* Honolulu: Hawaii Institute of Geophysics, Report No. 14, 1961.

Furamoto, A. et al. "A Study of Past Earthquakes, Isoseismic Zones of Intensity and Recommended Zones for Structural Design for Hawaii." Honolulu: University of Hawaii, Center for Engineering Research, Engineering Bulletin Pace 72033, 1972.

Haraguchi, P. *Weather in Hawaiian Waters.* Honolulu: Pacific Weather, Inc., 1979.

Hodge, D. C. et al. "Social Implications of Volcano Hazard. Case Studies in the Washington Cascades and Hawaii." Final Report to the National Science Foundation-RANN Program, Project No. ENV-76-20735. Seattle: Department of Geography, University of Washington, 1978.

Morgan, J. "The Tsunami Hazard in the Pacific: Institutional Responses in Japan and the United States." Ph.D. dissertation, Department of Geography, University of Hawaii, 1978.

_____. "The Tsunami Hazard in Tohoku and the Hawaiian Islands." *Science Reports of the Tohoku University,* 7th Series (Geography), 29 (1979): 149–159.

Murton, B. J., and Shimabukuro, S. "Human Adjustment to Volcanic Hazard in Puna District, Hawaii." In *Natural Hazards, Local, National, Global,* edited by Gilbert F. White, pp. 151–159. New York: Oxford University Press, 1974.

Sorensen, J. H., and Gershmehl, P. J. "Volcanic Hazard Warning System: Persistence and Transferability." *Environmental Management* 4 (1980): 125–136.

Sorensen, J. H., and Murton, B. J. "Natural Hazard Education in Hawaii." Paper presented at National Council for Geographic Education Meeting, 1979, Mexico City.

State of Hawaii, Department of Land and Natural Resources, Division of Water and Land Development. "Flood Frequencies for Selected Streams in Hawaii." Report R36. Honolulu: State of Hawaii, 1970.

State of Hawaii, State Civil Defense Division. "Catalog of Natural and Man-Caused Incidents and Disasters in the Hawaiian Islands." Mimeographed. Honolulu: State of Hawaii, 1978.

U.S. Geological Survey. *Natural Hazards on the Island of Hawaii.* Washington, D.C.: U.S. Government Printing Office, 1976.

CHAPTER 8

WATER RESOURCES

Frank Peterson

Hawaii's water resources are extremely diversified, both from island to island as well as within islands, and in many respects appear anomalous. For example, the Hawaiian Islands enjoy abundant rainfall, with the precipitation averaging over 70 in. (178 cm) per year for the islands as a whole, but the rainfall is not evenly distributed in either space or time. Furthermore, despite the generally abundant precipitation, there are few large perennial streams in the Hawaiian Islands; most of these are quite flashy. In fact, in some areas covered with young volcanic rocks, virtually no surface runoff occurs even though rainfall may exceed 100 in. (254 cm) per year. At the same time, however, one of the most pressing water-resource problems in Hawaii is flooding, especially flash flooding. Finally, groundwater rather than surface water provides the most abundant and dependable source of fresh water in the Hawaiian Islands. This is in spite of the fact that groundwater bodies in Hawaii are both underlain and surrounded by saline waters that pose the ever constant threat of contamination by salt water intrusion.

The diverse and seemingly anomalous nature of Hawaii's water resources can best

be understood by consideration of the local geology and its effect on the water budget in the Hawaiian Islands.

GEOLOGY

Basalts are among the most permeable rocks on earth. Those that make up the Hawaiian Islands are especially permeable because of their young ages and because the individual lava flows vary in thickness from a few inches to several hundred feet, but are mostly twenty ft (6 m) or less. This is especially important as many of the water-bearing and water-transmitting structures in lavas are associated with surface and near-surface portions of flows. The physical characteristics of aa and pahoehoe, including water-bearing and water-transmitting properties, may be quite varied.

The high permeability of Hawaiian lavas results primarily from major flow structures such as clinker layers in aa, lava tubes in pahoehoe, gas vesicles, vertical contraction joints formed by cooling of lavas, and irregular openings associated with the surface between flows. Figure 8.1 illustrates some of these features. Generally the lateral components of permeability exceed the vertical by at least one or two orders of magnitude; however, permeability in all directions is very large and is subject to extreme local variations. Consider, for example, the permeability contrast between a massive portion of an aa flow and a lava

Some material in this chapter has been adapted from "Ground Water," in Gordon A. Macdonald, Agatin T. Abbot, and Frank L. Peterson, *Volcanoes in the Sea* second edition (Honolulu: University Press of Hawaii, 1983).

74

FIGURE 8.1.   Aa and pahoehoe lava flows.

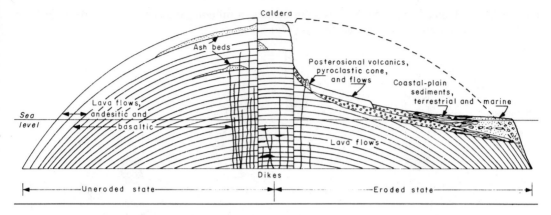

FIGURE 8.2.   Geologic structure of an idealized Hawaiian volcano (after Cox 1954).

tube. Although most Hawaiian lava flows are very thin and hence quite permeable, on occasion the lavas become ponded and are not able to spread out to form thin flows. The thick, ponded flows that result are generally quite massive and are much less permeable than the more typical, thinner lava flows. Such flows often form barriers that greatly retard or even block the flow of water in the subsurface. The Sugarloaf flow that occupies much of the lower part of Manoa Valley on Oahu is an example of a thick, ponded flow.

Lavas that were extruded above sea level are generally thin bedded, highly clinkery, and very permeable. In contrast, the lavas extruded below sea level were quickly chilled and generally are more massive and much less permeable. Since all of the Hawaiian Islands have sunk many hundred feet in response to the loading caused by the tremendous mass of volcanic material on the earth's crust, the highly permeable lavas that were originally formed above sea level now extend well below sea level, greatly enhancing the occurrence and development of groundwater.

Calderas and rift zones contain many vertical or steeply dipping dikes that intrude into the lava flows. Within the caldera region and central portions of the rift zones, the dikes are more widely spaced and often form large compartments that enclose permeable lavas. Because the dikes cooled

very quickly they are massive and generally have low permeabilities, often impounding groundwater within the compartments.

On the older Hawaiian Islands, such as Kauai and Oahu, the margins of the volcanic mountains are covered by coastal-plain sediments of marine and alluvial origin, deposited during periods of volcanic quiescence. The sediments reach a maximum thickness of more than 1,000 ft (300 m) beneath the Honolulu and Pearl Harbor areas on southern Oahu. The coastal-plain sediments contain significant quantities of water that varies in salinity from fresh to saline. Compared to the basaltic lava aquifers, however, the storage and transmission capacity of the sediments is small. Consequently the sediments act as a caprock retarding the seaward movement of fresh groundwater from the more permeable underlying lava aquifers. Figure 8.2 shows the geologic structure of an idealized Hawaiian volcanic island.

RAINFALL

Because Hawaii is an insular state, the precipitation that falls on each island is the sole source of the fresh-water resource for that island. The amount and distribution of Hawaii's surface-water and groundwater resources are a direct function of the spatial and time distribution of precipitation.

FIGURE 8.3.   Water budget for the Hawaiian Islands in million gallons per day (mgd) (after State of Hawaii, Water Resources Regional Study 1979).

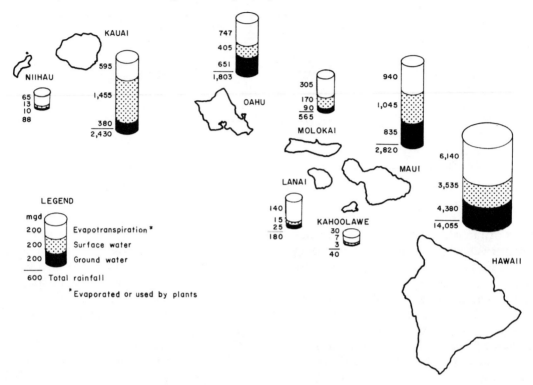

The average annual rainfall over the Hawaiian Islands of approximately 75 in. (190 cm) provides nearly 7 trillion gal (26 trillion l) of water a year to Hawaiian land surfaces (Ekern et al. 1971, 187). However, there are great differences in the amount of annual precipitation at places only a short distance apart, and there are also large differences in rainfall from year to year at the same locality, especially in the winter months.

WATER BUDGET

The disposition of precipitation that falls on the Hawaiian Islands can be represented by the usual water budget equation:

$$P = ET + I + RO \qquad (8.1)$$

where P is precipitation, ET is evapotranspiration (a combination of surface evaporation plus transpiration by plants), I is

infiltration to the subsurface, and RO is surface runoff. Figure 8.3 illustrates the average water budget for each of the Hawaiian Islands.

Evapotranspiration

Evapotranspiration is the loss of water from the surface and near-surface zones, both by direct evaporation and by plant usage or transpiration. Thus evapotranspiration is a net-loss term in the water budget and represents that portion of the precipitation that is not available for infiltration or surface runoff.

Evapotranspiration is primarily influenced by such factors as temperature, humidity, rainfall, and winds. In Hawaii, evapotranspiration varies widely both in time and space, although annual variations at any one place tend to be small. Maximum evapotranspiration occurs generally in the dry summer months. On the large islands potential evapotranspiration (the

FIGURE 8.4.   Surface water and groundwater usage in Hawaii in 1975 in millions of gallons per day for municipal, agricultural, and industrial purposes (after State of Hawaii, Water Resources Regional Study 1979).

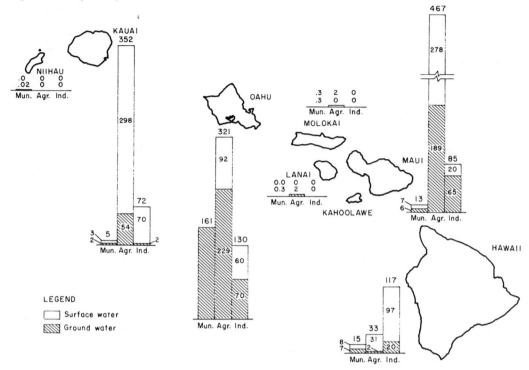

evapotranspiration that would occur if water were continuously available for evaporation and plant use) ranges from less than 20 in. (50 cm) to more than 80 in. (200 cm) per year, and in windy areas may exceed 90 in. (230 cm) per year. In areas of heavy rainfall, evapotranspiration losses may be only a small percentage of total precipitation; however, in areas with low rainfall, all or most of the rainfall may be lost to evapotranspiration.

Surface Runoff Versus Infiltration

The portion of precipitation not lost through evapotranspiration becomes either surface runoff or groundwater infiltration, which together constitute the fresh-water resources in the Hawaiian Islands. Because Hawaiian streams are generally short and steep, stream flow quickly discharges into the ocean. However, Hawaiian streams do provide large quantities of water for agricultural and industrial use, and much

lesser amounts for domestic usage. In addition, surface waters provide an invaluable aquatic environment and recreational and aesthetic resources in Hawaii.

Groundwater also flows through the subsurface and discharges into coastal waters; however, it moves much more slowly than surface runoff and hence is easier to capture for domestic water supply. Figure 8.4 illustrates surface water and groundwater usage in Hawaii.

SURFACE RUNOFF

Even though rainfall may exceed 300 in. (780 km) in the wet, mountainous portions of the major Hawaiian Islands, most streams are very flashy and only a few contain water throughout the year. This is the result primarily of two opposing effects commonly observed in the Hawaiian hydrologic cycle: high rainfall and watershed characteristics favoring high rates of surface

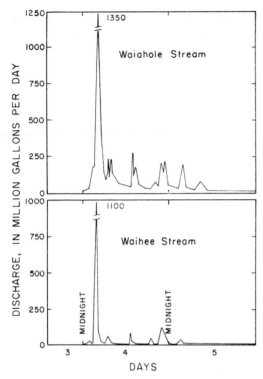

FIGURE 8.5. Flood hydrographs for Station 2838 in Waihee Stream and Station 2910 in Waiahole Stream, Oahu, during the period February 3–5, 1965 (after Hoffard 1965).

runoff, and high permeabilities of the rocks and soil cover favoring high infiltration rates and low runoff (Peterson 1972).

Most of Hawaii's drainage basins are very small compared with those in other parts of the world; their areas average only about 1 sq mi (2.6 sq km). Furthermore, watersheds in Hawaii are characterized by steep slopes and steep valley walls with little channel storage. As a result, storm hydrographs characteristically have high peak flows with a sharp rise and recession, but with low total flow volumes (Figure 8.5). Concentration times (time required for water to flow through the drainage basin) and time to flood peak generally are less than one to two hours. One of Hawaii's most serious hydrologic problems is flash flooding caused by intense rainfall.

Conversely, the permeability of surface rocks and soils is extremely high; thus,

infiltration capacities are also very high, often exceeding 10 in. (25 cm) per hour in some areas. Therefore, even though intense rainfall usually produces momentary high peak discharges, most small- and moderate-sized storms produce relatively small amounts of runoff and disproportionately large amounts of infiltration. This relation is well illustrated by the water budgets shown in Figure 8.3. Of all the Hawaiian Islands, only Kauai shows high surface runoff relative to infiltration. This is to be expected because Kauai is the wettest and also the oldest and most intensely weathered of all the major Hawaiian islands.

In 1975 approximately 54 percent of the fresh water used in the Hawaiian Islands was diverted from stream flow (Takasaki 1978); however, except for the perennial streams that drain high rainfall areas along windward slopes and coasts and spring-fed streams in mountainous areas, surface runoff is generally unreliable as a source of year-round water supply. As a result surface water is used primarily for industrial and agricultural purposes, and even then extensive ditch and tunnel systems are required to collect and convey the water from wet mountainous areas to irrigated fields at lower elevations.

Collection and storage of large quantities of surface runoff from high flows is difficult because of the very flashy nature of Hawaiian stream runoff and the high permeability of surface rocks and soil that allows extensive leakage from unlined reservoirs.

GROUNDWATER

Because the permeability of the rocks and soils that make up the bulk of the Hawaiian Islands is exceedingly high, the ratio of infiltration to runoff is unusually high. As a result, groundwater plays a very important role in the Hawaiian water budget (see Figure 8.3). Almost all the domestic water supply, and slightly less than half of the industrial and agricultural water supplies, comes from groundwater sources (see Figure 8.4).

FIGURE 8.6. Occurrence and development of groundwater in an idealized Hawaiian volcano (modified after Cox 1954).

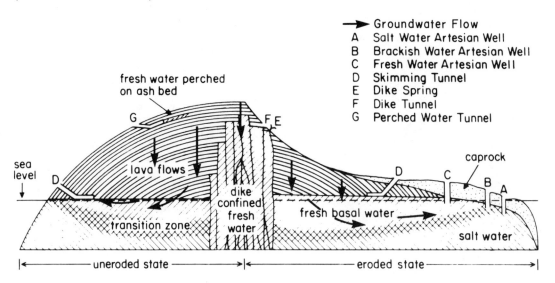

Two principal modes of groundwater occurrence are commonly found in Hawaii. The first of these is high-level groundwater either impounded within compartments formed by relatively impermeable dikes that have intruded into the lava flows, or, to a much lesser extent, perched on low-permeability layers such as ash beds, buried soil horizons, unconformities, or other relatively impervious lava flows (for example, the dense cores of aa flows). The second and principal groundwater occurrence is fresh basal water floating on and displacing salt water. Figure 8.6 shows the occurrence and development of these groundwater bodies on an idealized Hawaiian island, and Figure 8.7 shows the generalized groundwater occurrence for each of the Hawaiian Islands.

High-level Groundwater

High-level perched aquifers commonly have been identified by the presence of springs. The areal extent of perching beds and structures usually is quite limited, hence storage in these aquifers is small and the flow from perched aquifers tends to be relatively unstable. Perched groundwater

has been developed primarily by means of tunnels that follow the perching layers and serve mainly to collect or divert flow to perched springs, rarely increasing either the storage or the natural spring discharge. As a result, perched water is important mainly because of its high elevation; it constitutes only a very small part of all high-level groundwater developed.

Dike-confined water bodies, like perched water bodies, generally are identified by natural spring discharges. Although not usually found at the very high elevations at which perched water may occur, dike-confined water often occurs several hundred feet above sea level, and thus constitutes a very significant high-level groundwater source. The volume of water stored in dike-confined aquifers is large compared to other high-level water sources; equally important, dike aquifers provide a relatively stable source of water supply. Compared to basal groundwater bodies, however, the amount of dike-confined water is small.

Development of dike water has been mainly by horizontal and inclined tunnels that penetrate several dike compartments. In some instances, dike water has been

80

FIGURE 8.7. Generalized groundwater occurrence in the Hawaiian Islands (after State of Hawaii, Water Resources Regional Study 1979).

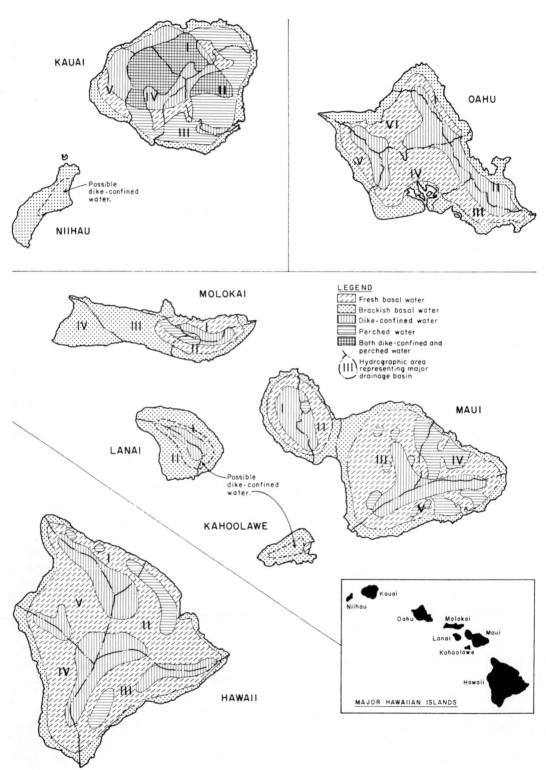

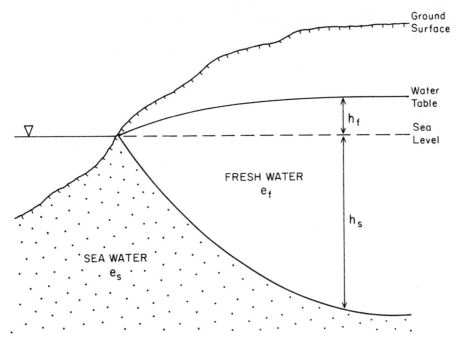

FIGURE 8.8.   Fresh Ghyben-Herzberg lens overlying saltwater.

developed by vertical wells, which have the disadvantage of usually penetrating only a single dike compartment. Generally, when a dike-confined aquifer is first developed, initial flows are very high in response to depletion of the underground dike storage, and it is only when water levels in dike compartments are lowered to the tunnel level that a more permanent equilibrium flow is achieved. In recent years bulkheads have been used in some tunnels to maintain or replenish the storage capacities within the dike compartments.

Basal Groundwater

The principal source of fresh groundwater in Hawaii is the basal or Ghyben-Herzberg lens that floats on and displaces the underlying salt water. The extent to which the fresh-water lens displaces salt water is a function of the relative densities of the two liquids and is described by the following simple mass balance equation:

$$h_s = \frac{h_f}{e_s - e_f} \qquad (8.2)$$

where h_s is the thickness of fresh water below sea level, h_f is the head of fresh water above sea level, and e_f and e_s are, respectively, densities of fresh water and saltwater (Figure 8.8). Thus, for the usual densities of fresh water and saltwater, the familiar condition applies that every foot (0.3 m) of fresh water above sea level will be balanced by an additional 40 ft (12 m) of fresh water below sea level. This mass balance, commonly called the Ghyben-Herzberg relationship, assumes that steady-state conditions apply and, hence, that a sharp interface separates the fresh water and underlying saltwater. In reality, however, steady-state conditions are never fully achieved because of constant movement of the interface between the fresh water and saltwater resulting from disturbances such as tidal fluctuations, seasonal fluctuation in recharge and discharge, and discharge caused by aquifer development. As a result, mixing of the fresh water and saltwater occurs, and a zone of transition separates the two. The existence of the mixed or transition zone does not mean, however, that the Ghyben-Herzberg relationship has no value in Hawaii; in fact, this relationship provides a very good estimate of the depth to the center of the transition zone (Figure 8.6).

In Hawaii, the thickness of the freshwater lens normally is a few tens to several hundred feet and the thickness of the transition zone varies from only a few tens of feet in relatively undisturbed groundwater bodies to as great as 1,000 ft (300 m) in parts of southern Oahu where extensive groundwater development has occurred. In some of the drier leeward coastal areas in Hawaii where heads may be very close to sea level, tidal fluctuations rapidly mix all the fresh rain water with the underlying saltwater so that only brackish water occurs.

Because rainfall generally tends to be greatest in the interior mountainous areas, recharge to the basal groundwater bodies is also greatest in these regions. As a result, groundwater levels are high in these areas, which causes groundwater to flow generally from the interior to the coastal portions of the islands (Figure 8.6). If low-permeability coastal-plain sediments are not present to impede its seaward flow, fresh and brackish groundwater freely discharges into the coastal water. Generally, the groundwater discharge is dispersed and difficult to detect readily. In some areas, however, local geological and structural features sufficiently channelize flow to cause freshwater springs along the shoreline and in the shallow coastal water. The presence of such fresh, coastal groundwater discharge provides a good indication of potential sites for basal groundwater development in dry, low-recharge areas that may otherwise appear unpromising for potable water development. In fact, such sites along the dry leeward coasts were often used by the early Hawaiians.

Basal groundwater bodies may be either confined or unconfined. They occur principally in the lava flows, but are found also in lesser amounts in the alluvial and marine sediments that occupy stream-valley and coastal-plain areas. In coastal regions where the basaltic aquifers are directly overlain by less permeable sedimentary caprock, the basal groundwater bodies are confined, and artesian heads of a few feet to over 20 ft (6 m) above sea level may occur. In portions of the aquifers behind the caprock and in aquifers that extend to the coast without a cover of sediments, unconfined or water-table groundwater conditions prevail. In the unconfined aquifers there are generally no low-permeability barriers to impede either the seaward flow of fresh water or the landward intrusion of saltwater; groundwater heads in the unconfined aquifers tend to be lower and the groundwater more brackish than for confined basal aquifers.

As described previously, significant quantities of basal groundwater also occur in coastal-plain and valley sedimentary deposits. In the past, groundwater from the sedimentary aquifers has not been extensively developed, primarily as a result of two factors. Compared to basaltic lava aquifers, the storage capacity and permeability of the sediments is small, so groundwater has always been much easier to develop from the lavas than from sedimentary aquifers. Furthermore, because of the close proximity of the coastal-plain sedimentary aquifers to the sea, much of the water in these deposits tends to be brackish. In future years, however, increasing demands for fresh-water supplies will necessitate increasing development of many of the more promising sedimentary aquifers, especially those occupying stream valleys on the windward coast of Oahu.

Basal groundwater bodies in Hawaii have been mainly developed by drilled wells in both artesian and unconfined aquifers and by skimming tunnels in unconfined aquifers. The skimming tunnels (sometimes called Maui tunnels) generally consist of one or more horizontal, or nearly horizontal, tunnels constructed at or just below the water table. The basic advantage the skimming tunnels have over conventional wells is their capability of producing fresh water from basal lenses so thin that vertical wells would recover only brackish water. In addition, in thick, basal groundwater bodies, Maui tunnels are capable of producing extremely large discharges. For example, the Navy's Waiawa tunnel near Pearl Harbor is capable of developing 45 million gal (169 million l) of water a day from about 1,700 ft (520 m) of tunnel, and the Waikapu tunnel (Shaft 16) on Maui can develop up to 40 million gal (150 million l) per day from only 600 ft (180 m) of tunnel (Peterson 1972). Because of excessive tunnel construction costs and the greater flexibility of modern deep-well pumping stations, construction of new skimming tunnels in Hawaii has largely ceased, and only a single tunnel, one for domestic supply near Kona, Hawaii, has been constructed during the past decade. However, the city of Honolulu still relies on several large Maui tunnels for significant quantities of domestic water, and many other skimming tunnels throughout the state are utilized for large quantities of domestic and agricultural water.

WATER PROBLEMS

Although the Hawaiian Islands are blessed with annual rainfalls much greater than many other parts of the world, the most serious water problem today is supply, both of groundwater and surface water. Other important problems include groundwater and surface-water quality and surface-water flooding, erosion, and siltation.

Water Supply

The single most pressing water problem in the Hawaiian Islands is one of inadequate supply, especially on Oahu and parts of Maui, Hawaii, and Molokai. However, the water-supply problems are not caused primarily by lack of rainfall, but rather by the extremely uneven distribution of rainfall. Also contributing to water-supply problems in many parts of the outer islands is the tendency for population centers, especially in resort areas, to be concentrated in the dry coastal areas where the climate is most favorable, but where rainfall and hence recharge are at a minimum.

On an island-wide basis, rainfall is sufficient to supply the present and foreseeable future water requirements of all the major islands, with the possible exception of Oahu, where continued usage under present trends almost certainly will result in a shortage of developable fresh-water supplies before the end of the century. Comparison of water-supply and water-use data (Figure 8.9) shows that total water resources on each island generally are adequate to meet present needs. However, local problems of varying intensity on nearly all the islands include "Shortages resulting from poor distribution of supplies, limited capital to fund development projects, instream-offstream water use conflicts, competition among various users, ground water overdraft, quality degradation of both surface water and ground water, and institutional conflicts that prevent a unified approach to water management" (State of Hawaii, Department of Land and Natural Resources 1980, 48).

The water-supply problems are of particular concern because over the next one to two decades it is anticipated that water demand will approach, or possibly even exceed, island-wide supplies. Because of their flashy and relatively uncertain nature, surface waters cannot be counted on to provide substantially greater supplies than are presently being developed. Hence, groundwater sources must provide the bulk of additional water supplies. Table 8.1 shows the 1975 and the projected year 2000 groundwater demand, and Figure 8.10 illustrates the estimated sustainable yield from the various groundwater basins on Oahu. It can be seen that the projected groundwater demand of 570 million gal (2.1 billion l) per day for the year 2000 exceeds the lower limit (480 million gal or 1.8 billion l per day) for total island-wide groundwater sustainable yield. Even at the present time, the major groundwater aquifers in the Honolulu, Pearl Harbor, and Waialua areas are being pumped at rates

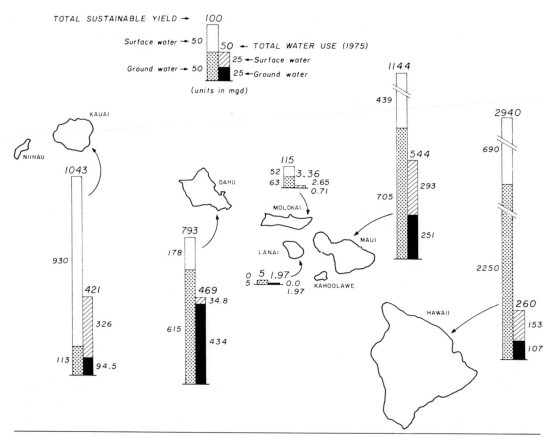

FIGURE 8.9. Water supply and water use, 1975 (after State of Hawaii, Department of Land and Natural Resources 1980).

Table 8.1 Present and Projected Water Demand for Oahu
(After Hawaii State Water Commission, 1979)
(Unit: mgd)

WATER USE	1975	2000
MUNICIPAL		
Board of Water Supply	130	220
Others	5	5
INDUSTRIAL (self-supplied)	50	50
AGRICULTURAL		
Sugarcane	240	240
Diversified Crops	5	10
MILITARY (includes municipal use)	40	45
Total	470	570

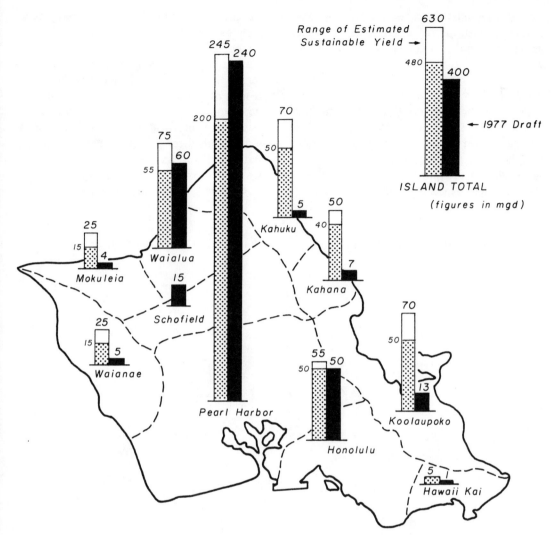

FIGURE 8.10. Estimated sustainable yield of groundwater on Oahu (after State of Hawaii, State Water Commission 1979).

approaching (or possibly exceeding) their estimated sustainable yields. The data in Figure 8.10 also indicate that additional groundwater supplies should be available on windward Oahu from about Kahuku to Waimanalo, and lesser supplies should be available from the Waianae and Mokuleia areas of western Oahu. Indeed, much of the future groundwater development by the Honolulu Board of Water Supply probably will be centered in these areas.

To offset the water-supply problems on Oahu and water-deficient areas on the outer

islands, several courses of action must be pursued: (1) increased water-conservation practices and policies; (2) more efficient development of groundwater by more judicious well-spacing and pumping practices; (3) increased use of treated waste water for irrigation purposes; (4) blending of fresh water with brackish waters; (5) use of dual water systems that utilize fresh water only for drinking and cooking purposes in especially water-deficient coastal areas on the outer islands and use brackish water for all other purposes; and (6) continued research on technologies for extending the supply of potable water, such as desalination of brackish water and saltwater.

Water Quality

As described previously, the principal groundwater supplies in Hawaii are developed from basal groundwater bodies that float on and displace the underlying saltwater. Overexploitation of the fresh groundwater resources results in intrusion of saltwater from the coastal margins as well as upconing of the underlying saltwater. Hence, the most serious groundwater-quality problems involve contamination by saline waters and are the direct result of overdevelopment or inefficient development of groundwater aquifers.

Other groundwater-contamination problems result locally from recharge by return irrigation waters, cesspool seepage, and waste disposal by injection wells.

Generally the quality of Hawaii's surface

FIGURE 8.11.   Mean annual stream discharge from the coast of Oahu (after State of Hawaii, State Water Commission 1979).

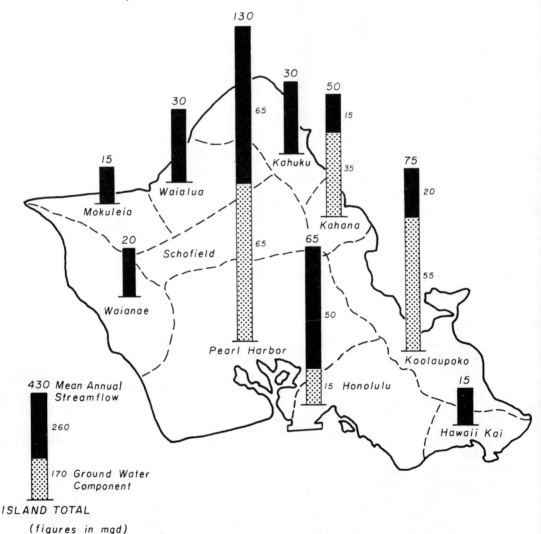

runoff is excellent, especially in the stream headwaters, although before reaching the ocean some streams may locally accumulate significant amounts of dissolved solids, nutrients, and coliform bacteria, primarily from sewage, industrial, and irrigation discharges. Also, because of their very flashy nature, many streams have high turbidity and suspended sediment concentrations during periods of heavy rainfall.

Perhaps the greatest potential threat to surface-water quality in many areas results from the close interrelationship between surface waters and groundwaters in many of Hawaii's drainage basins. Springs that issue from perched and dike-confined groundwater bodies represent natural discharge of excess storage from these high-level aquifers and provide a significant portion of the low-water flow of many Hawaiian streams. For example, Figure 8.11 shows the mean annual stream discharge from the various hydrologic areas along the Oahu coast and subdivides the source of discharge into surface-water and groundwater components. As can be seen, the groundwater component provides the most significant contribution to stream flow for several of the hydrologic regions, including most of the major stream basins on the windward coast. This is certain to become a source of major conflict in future years, not only on Oahu but also on the outer islands, because increasing groundwater development from the headwater areas of the stream basins will surely reduce downstream water supplies for irrigation as well as water for instream uses such as recreation, flora and fauna habitats, aesthetic enjoyment, and maintenance of chemical, biological, and physical water quality.

Flood, Erosion, and Siltation

Owing primarily to the very flashy nature of Hawaii's stream flow, flooding, together with the attendant problems of erosion and siltation, constitutes an additional serious water-resources problem in Hawaii. Despite the millions of dollars invested in flood-control works and related measures,

annual flood damage has been estimated to average over $1.8 million (State of Hawaii, Department of Land and Natural Resources 1980), and loss of land through erosion and siltation of inshore waters adds much more to this total each year.

In recent years, however, the emphasis gradually has been shifting from a purely flood-control approach to a more integrated floodplain management approach. The recent adoption of the federal Flood Disaster Protection Act of 1973 (Public Law 92-234) in Hawaii, which greatly restricts new construction in flood-prone areas, appears to be a positive step for better flood protection.

REFERENCES

Cox, D. C. "Water Development for Hawaiian Sugarcane Irrigation." *Hawaiian Sugar Planters' Report* 54 (1954): 175–197.

Ekern, P. C.; Lau, L. S.; Peterson, F. L.; Price, S.; and Pulfrey, R. 1971. "Hydrologic systems in Hawaii." *Proceedings of United States–Japan Bilateral Seminar in Hydrology.* Honolulu: n.p., 1971, pp. 186–201.

Hoffard, S. H. *Floods of December 1964–February 1965 in Hawaii.* U.S. Geological Survey Report R26. Honolulu: U.S. Geological Survey, 1965.

Peterson, F. L. "Water Development on Tropic Volcanic Islands—Type Example: Hawaii." *Ground Water* 10, no. 5 (1972): 18–23.

State of Hawaii, Department of Land and Natural Resources. *State Water Resources Development Plan.* Honolulu: State of Hawaii, 1980.

State of Hawaii, Division of Hydrography. *Bulletins* 1–13. Honolulu: State of Hawaii, 1935, 1938, 1939, 1940, 1942, 1946, 1947, 1960.

State of Hawaii, State Water Commission. *Hawaii's Water Resources, Directions for the Future.* Honolulu: State of Hawaii, 1979.

State of Hawaii, Water Resources Regional Study. *Hawaii Water Resources Plan.* Honolulu: State of Hawaii, 1979.

Takasaki, K. J. *Summary Appraisals of the Nation's Ground-water Resources Hawaii Region.* U.S. Geological Survey Professional Paper 813-M. Washington, D.C.: U.S. Geological Survey, 1978.

CHAPTER 9

SOILS
John Street

In several respects the soils of Hawaii are quite different from those of the continental United States. They are in many places very deep, very rich in iron and aluminum, virtually free of quartz sand, and extraordinarily permeable and resistant to erosion. These qualities reflect the conditions under which the soils developed— the year-round warmth of the tropics combined with abundant rain falling upon beds of dark, porous lava and deposits of volcanic ash.

Soils show the influence of the factors of soil formation: parent material, climate, topography, time, biota, and management. For the most part Hawaiian soils have developed on volcanic rocks, cinders, and ash of a basaltic or andesitic nature. Some coastal soils have formed on coral limestone and coral sands, while valley-floor and coastal-plain soils are commonly on alluvium. With the islands' immense diversity of climates—from desert to the wettest on earth and from perpetually warm to just short of eternal snow—there is a comparable multiplicity of soils. Terrain features are also varied, including such landforms as craters, cliffs, gently sloping volcanic domes, and alluvial plains. Plant cover ranges from simple lichens to tall, dense rain forest. Since it takes time for soils to develop from rock, volcanic ash, or beach sand and since soils differ from one stage of development to another, we find different soils on surfaces of divers ages.

The slopes of the active volcanoes of the island of Hawaii, with their lava flows of various and known ages, furnish the soil scientist with a natural laboratory for the study of soil formation—a laboratory with the further advantages of a great range of temperatures as one goes from sea level to over 13,000 ft (3,900 m) and of rainfall as one follows the contour from the perhumid windward flank of Mauna Loa to its desert leeward slope. Indeed Hawaii has been a major center for the study of tropical soils. Management of the island soils changed markedly over the past two centuries as Polynesian subsistence agriculture gave way to cattle ranches and they in turn in many areas were displaced by plantations of sugar and pineapple, now retreating before the monstrous growth of suburbia.

GEOGRAPHY OF SOIL USE

Less than one-twelfth of the land area of the Hawaiian Islands is under cultivation, a fraction about half that for the forty-eight coterminous states. Vast expanses of the flanks of Kilauea and Mauna Loa on the Big Island are covered with lava flows so recent that little or no soil has formed upon them. But even here one must distinguish between the rough jumble of clinkers that covers an aa flow and the smooth, ropy, massive surface of a pahoehoe flow. In the Puna district south of Hilo, an area of abundant rainfall, aa flows only a few decades old have been leveled by bulldozers and planted to papayas, while pahoehoe of greater age is not amenable to tree culture. In South Kona at about 1,000 ft (300 m) altitude, thousands of acres of macadamia orchards have been established upon the thin, stony soils that have developed on somewhat older flows. It is instructive to follow these flows down to the sea from the humid uplands to the semiarid coast. The vegetation becomes sparser and the soil thinner until there is virtually barren, fresh-looking lava near the shore. Moisture, working together with the plants it nurtures, is required to convert rock into soil.

Much of the interior of the island of Hawaii and the leeward coastal lands north of Kona are too dry to support agriculture without irrigation, even where the soils are adequate. Unfortunately, such water is not available and the stony desert and semi-desert soils in general support only poor pasture. On the other islands, too, aridity—primarily a phenomenon of leeward coasts—limits the use of otherwise satisfactory soils. Fortunately, water resources have been developed to permit the light supplementary irrigation of great fields of pineapple on the semiarid lands of Lanai and West Molokai and the copious irrigation of sugarcane on the dry lowlands of Maui, Oahu, and Kauai.

Steep slopes that can support but a thin soil and are prone to severe soil erosion if disturbed characterize the mountains that occupy much of west Maui, east Molokai, Oahu, and Kauai. For the most part these heavily dissected uplands are managed as protected watershed.

Temperature and sunlight also are related to the patterns of use of Hawaiian soils. Mountain areas that are very cloudy and wet, such as the windward flanks of Mauna Kea, Mauna Loa, and Haleakala at an altitude of about 3,000 ft (900 m), are unsuited for agriculture even though

their slopes may be moderate and their soils reasonably deep and stone free. Extensive virgin forests remain in such areas. Cool uplands with moderate slopes and precipitation and fairly deep soils support temperate-latitude vegetable cultivation and cattle range in the vicinities of Kula, Maui, and Kamuela, Hawaii. In these locales geologically recent volcanic ash has developed into dark, humus-rich, friable, porous soils with a high nutrient content.

In general, soil properties, save for depth and stoniness, are of less importance in determining the agricultural use of the land in Hawaii than are climate, slope, and the availability of water—the other significant physical constraints on the location of agriculture.

NATURE OF HAWAIIAN SOILS*

Zonal Soils

First to be considered are *zonal soils,* which bear a strong imprint from the climate in which they have developed. In the lands of moderate slope with rainfall in the 20 in. to 40 in. (50 cm to 100 cm) range and altitude of less than 2,000 ft (600 m), the most common soils, except on the geologically young island of Hawaii, are of the group *low humic latosols.* Again with the exception of Hawaii, these are the principal soils on which sugarcane and pineapple are raised. The soils are deep, with well-aggregated, friable topsoils that remain very firm when wet (this physical strength permits the oft-observed Hawaiian custom of parking automobiles on lawns—

*In this description the terminology will follow the *Soil Survey, Territory of Hawaii* . . . (Cline, M. G., and others. Washington, D.C.: U.S. Soil Conservation Service, Soil Survey Series 1939, no. 25, 1955) rather than the new *7th Approximation* (Soil Survey Staff. *Soil Classification: A Comprehensive System, 7th Approximation.* Washington, D.C.: U.S. Soil Conservation Service, 1960). The terms in the former are easier to remember, facilitate the recognition of similarities between soils, and lend themselves well to the explanation of soil genesis.

a practice that would have disastrous consequences on weaker mainland soils). Quartz sand is virtually absent from the soil since Hawaiian volcanic rocks contain no quartz crystals to be liberated upon chemical breakdown of the rock (chemical weathering). This is good for Hawaii's agriculture, as sandy soils tend to be dry and infertile—in the continental tropics, where the rocks are rich in quartz, the soils are poor.

When looking at road cuts (for example, in the vicinity of Wahiawa), the red soil appears to extend to depths of many tens of feet. However, since soil by definition must be the scene of organic activity, the material below a depth of 6 or 7 ft (2 to 2.4 m) is regarded simply as rotten rock. With warmth and moisture, which promote chemical weathering, the porous, permeable lava has, to a depth of many yards, undergone a complete transformation of its constituent minerals. In the process certain elements were carried away in solution, with the most soluble taking precedence. Bases such as sodium, calcium, magnesium, and potassium were the first to go, followed by silica. Due to this selective removal, the low humic latosols contain lesser proportions of silica and bases than the rocks from which they were derived and display relative enrichment by the less soluble elements: iron, aluminum, titanium, and manganese. The latter, which competes with iron for uptake by plant roots, may cause an iron deficiency in pineapple that is corrected by application of a ferrous sulphate spray.

In their natural state the low humic latosols range from neutral to mildly acid, but repeated fertilization with ammonium sulphate has made some of them quite acid. Texturally they are largely composed of clay, and the clay-sized particles are predominantly kaolinite, a clay mineral that has only a modest capacity to store water and nutrients. Organic matter content is fairly low—3 to 4 percent, as might be expected in a warm, fairly dry environment.

Humic latosols occur in climatically wetter areas than do the low humic latosols and often upslope of them. They contain less silica and alumina and more of the oxides of iron and titanium. The texture is still clay, but the proportion of kaolinite in the clay has decreased while that of the oxides of iron and titanium has risen. Humic latosols are characterized by good granular structure and a high capacity to store moisture and nutrients, thanks at least in part to their organic matter content of 8 to 10 percent. As is usual, with increasing rainfall comes higher acidity.

Humic ferruginous latosols characteristically occur upslope of low humic latosols on the geologically old surfaces of Kauai and of the Waianae Range of Oahu. At a depth of a few inches they have a dense horizon of high specific gravity containing very high proportions of the oxides of iron and titanium. These soils have poor structure, high erodibility, low capacity to store nutrients and water, and low permeability, not to mention a very high capacity for the fixation of phosphate fertilizer. They are regarded by a number of soil scientists as the ultimate soil—the end product of soil development in Hawaii. Underneath these old soils occurs a residuum so high in alumina and low in silica that it could be mined as an ore of aluminum.

Hydrol humic latosols have developed in areas of very heavy rainfall, primarily on volcanic ash on the windward slopes of Hawaii and east Maui. Very high organic matter content and phenomenal capacity to store water characterize them. When they are dried they shrink drastically and cannot be rehydrated to their former state. A weak structure ill adapts them to use of heavy machinery.

Red Desert soils, located on geologically young materials in dry places such as Kawaihae and Koko Head, have undergone very little weathering or leaching. They exhibit white calcium carbonate deposits and tend to be stony.

With increasing moisture the red Desert soils blend into *reddish Brown soils* favored with a friable, humus-rich topsoil of high native fertility that supports very nutritious pasture. They are similar to the soils of the southern Great Plains on the U.S. mainland.

Progressing further upslope along a continuum of increasing moisture on the southeast flank of Haleakala or above Kawaihae on Hawaii, reddish Brown soils merge into *reddish Prairie soils.* High in bases, with dark, humus-rich topsoil, the reddish Prairie soils contain no lime deposits and have lost some silica through weathering and leaching. *Latosolic Brown forest soils,* in a still moister environment, have lost even more silica and bases and tend to be slightly acid. Both types of soils are friable and have a high capacity for storing moisture and nutrients.

Intrazonal Soils

The *intrazonal soils* of Hawaii are those whose character has been strongly conditioned by impeded drainage or a high groundwater table. They may be considered under two categories: *mineral soils* and *organic soils.* All of the mineral soils are *plastic clays* that are easily converted into a structureless, impermeable paste when wet. They have a high content of exchangeable magnesium (that is, magnesium that may be extracted from the soil by plant roots) and the higher the magnesium, the more plastic the soils. These soils occur naturally on coastal plains, valley floors, and adjacent basal slopes at low altitudes in areas of low to moderate rainfall. The plains of southern and western Oahu and western Kauai encompass the largest expanses of plastic-clay soils. Water drainage from higher slopes over and through lava with a characteristic high magnesium content has enriched the lowland soils with magnesium. Man has also created plastic clays by flooding and cultivating fields for the culture of taro and rice. Except for flooded field culture the plastic clays tend to be less attractive for agriculture than the low humic latosols that commonly adjoin them. Hard when dry, sticky and soft when wet, they are difficult to work save when moist. They resist penetration of irrigation water, air, and plant roots, and their high magnesium content interferes with the uptake of potassium.

The propensity of the natural plastic clays to expand on wetting, shrink markedly on drying, and creep down slopes poses problems for construction. A notorious example of the costs of inadequate engineering precautions on a site with expanding clays is the Business Administration Building on the University of Hawaii Campus at Manoa, where cracks have had to be repaired and an entire wing dismantled.

Water-logged organic soils in the form of *peat bogs* exist on the cool, wet upper slopes of the mountains. The nearly level summit of Oahu's highest peak, Mount Kaala, is a bog, as are the highest parts of Molokai and Kauai. By far the largest bog, the Alakai Swamp, covers 15 sq mi (39 sq km) of the high interior of Kauai.

Azonal Soils

Soils that are very young with weakly developed topsoils are called *azonal soils.* They include the *alluvial soils* that have formed on stream-deposited sediments; the *regosols* that have developed on volcanic ash, cinders, and coral sand; and the shallow, stony *lithosols.* The alluvial soils occur in valley bottoms and coastal plains and, save for areas with excessively coarse sediments, are good for agriculture. Regosols are so sandy in texture that they retain little water or nutrients and hence are ill-suited for agriculture. Volcanic-ash and cinder regosols are extensive in the crater of Haleakala, Maui, and on the upper slopes of Mauna Kea and on the flanks of Kilauea, Hawaii. Soils developed on coral sands form a transverse belt in the isthmus region of Maui, are also fairly extensive in the western parts of Molokai and Kauai, and underlie the settlements of Kailua and Waimanalo on Oahu. With the advent of drip irrigation, cane cultivation is spreading on these soils on Maui.

The category of lithosols includes those areas that are stony either because they are covered by recent lava flows or are very steep. On moist steep slopes, such as those at the head of Manoa Valley on Oahu, soil forms very rapidly, but once it attains a depth of 2 ft (0.6 m) it becomes unstable, and heavy rains trigger landslides carrying the soil downslope into stream channels and toward the sea. It has been estimated that this process of soil formation and loss takes place at the remarkable rate of 1 foot (0.3 m) in 400 years in rain-drenched upper Manoa.

Figures 9.1, 9.2, and 9.3 illustrate the distribution of soil types on the principal Hawaiian Islands.

ECOLOGY OF SOIL MANAGEMENT

Archaeological evidence from Makaha Valley on Oahu and Halawa Valley on Molokai—layers of water-deposited topsoil mixed with charcoal and ashes—strongly suggests that long before the arrival of Captain Cook, Hawaiians cleared and burned forest on the slopes to prepare for planting gardens, thus inadvertently causing soil erosion. No doubt the Polynesian introduction of pigs to the islands also led to soil degradation. But it is also clear that damage from over a millennium of Polynesian land use was minuscule as compared with the havoc wreaked in the past two centuries.

Effects of Grazing Animals

Europeans who arrived in Hawaii in the last quarter of the eighteenth century introduced domesticated grazing animals: cattle, horses, sheep, and goats. The islands—essentially free of diseases and predators, with a flora that had evolved in the absence of large herbivores—afforded an idyllic environment for the rapid proliferation of the exotic beasts. Within a few decades hundreds of thousands of the hoofed creatures roamed wild, browsing and trampling vegetation largely lacking in the usual defenses of toxins, spines, and

offensive taste and smell. Not even the soils were adapted to resist the assault of the interlopers; earthworms had not colonized the remote Hawaiian Archipelago, and they were not present to restore the porosity, permeability, drainage, and aeration of soils compacted by the hooves. Bared of a protective mantle of plants and resistant to the infiltration of rain, rich topsoil was entrained by the water that coursed down the slopes during storms. Before long sterile subsoil was exposed creating red scars—some scars have resisted recolonization by plants to this day. Destruction of forest also precipitated landslides in soils no longer anchored to the slopes by the thick, strong roots of trees—a form of devastation garishly illustrated in the windward valleys of Oahu where removal of the land's epidermis has revealed great blotches of pink, rotten rock. The splotches of red in Waimea Canyon of Kauai (vaunted in the tourist blurbs) are the creation of the feral (wild) goats that roam the cliffs. On west Molokai, a sheep-raising venture by a Hawaiian *alii* led to formation of a badland landscape of deep, red gullies.

Erosion caused by grazing also led to the siltation of the Hawaiian fish ponds on the south shore of Molokai and to the transformation of the coastal waters between the reefs and the coral sand beaches into a vile, muddy mess.

Desolate Kahoolawe, stripped of its topsoil, with its hardened subsoil baking in the sun, is in its present sorry state as a consequence of its exploitation as a sheep ranch and of browsing by feral goats, contrary to common belief that it is a result of practice bombing by the Navy.

Gradually a realization dawned upon the landowners and rulers of Hawaii that indiscriminate grazing was ruining the land; feral animals were hunted and sharply reduced in numbers, and ranchers cut their herds to more nearly fit the carrying capacity of the range. However, as recently as 1960, cattle were still grazing on severely eroded lands on the Tongg ranch in the

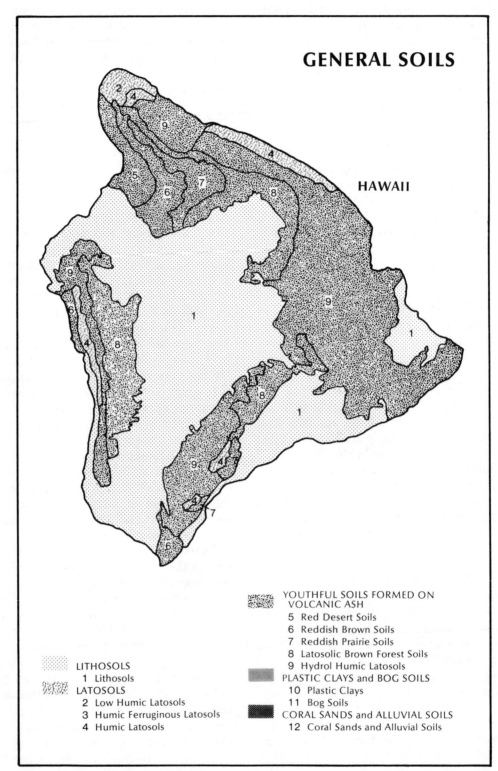

FIGURE 9.1.

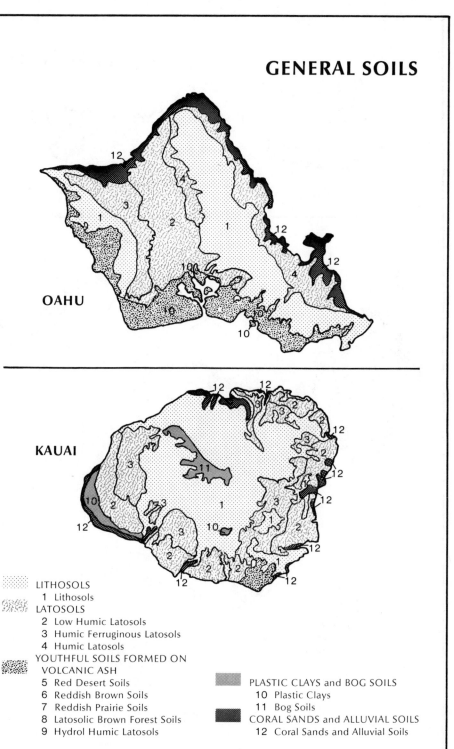

GENERAL SOILS

OAHU

KAUAI

LITHOSOLS
  1 Lithosols
LATOSOLS
  2 Low Humic Latosols
  3 Humic Ferruginous Latosols
  4 Humic Latosols
YOUTHFUL SOILS FORMED ON
VOLCANIC ASH
  5 Red Desert Soils
  6 Reddish Brown Soils
  7 Reddish Prairie Soils
  8 Latosolic Brown Forest Soils
  9 Hydrol Humic Latosols

PLASTIC CLAYS and BOG SOILS
  10 Plastic Clays
  11 Bog Soils
CORAL SANDS and ALLUVIAL SOILS
  12 Coral Sands and Alluvial Soils

FIGURE 9.2.

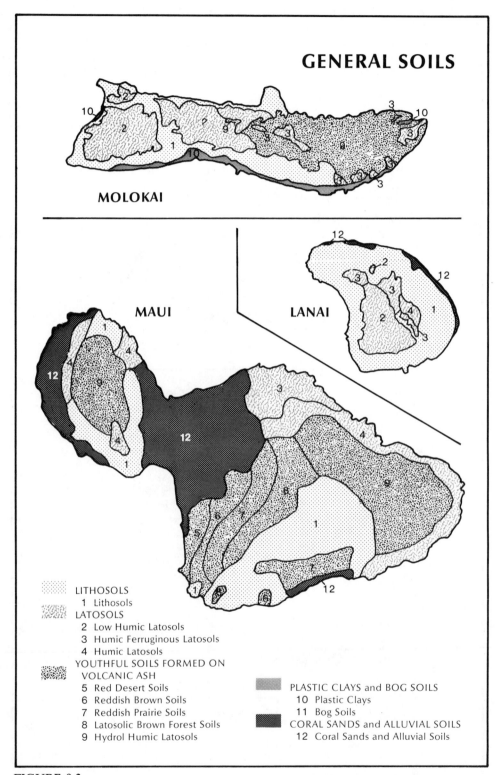

FIGURE 9.3.

Waianae Range of Oahu and on Molokai Ranch in west Molokai. And even today, in some localities, ranges are overgrazed and feral animals continue to desecrate the land. This is notably true on lands owned by the state of Hawaii. Hunters' lobbies have prevailed upon the state to maintain destructive herds of feral sheep on Mauna Kea and feral goats on the Na Pali coast of Kauai.

Influence of destructive grazing upon water resources became a concern of the sugar industry as it was developing irrigation works toward the end of the nineteenth century. The planters realized that a forest cover most effectively promoted the infiltration of rain water that nourished springs and groundwater. Therefore they supported control of feral stock, setting-up of forest reserves, and afforestation of denuded lands. In the early 1900s the Hawaiian Sugar Planters' Association built a station (now the Lyon Arboretum) in upper Manoa Valley, Oahu, for the purpose of introducing and testing tree species to be used in rewooding Hawaii's mountains. Consequently, Oahu is now much more forested than it was at the turn of the century.

Agriculture and Soil

Commercial agriculture, notably the cultivation of sugar and pineapple, has profoundly affected Hawaii's soils. Bare soil, such as that freshly turned by the plow, is very vulnerable to erosion, especially if the slope is steep and the rainfall intense. Many of the plantation fields are on slopes as steep as 10 percent, where high-intensity rain occurs frequently. Therefore the sugarcane and pineapple fields are at considerable risk of erosion at those times when the plant canopy does not fully shelter the soil. Fortunately, because cane generally is harvested only once every two years and pineapple is replanted only every four years, the erosion hazard is much less than if the fields were sown to annual crops such as corn or cotton.

In the pineapple industry, as with sugar, World War II stimulated mechanization. Many fields farmed by men and draft animals on steep slopes in the Koolau and Waianae Mountains of Oahu were abandoned, and herbicides displaced light cultivation for weed control. To improve the efficiency of the workers who pick pineapple, the fields were rearranged. Plantings along the curving contours of the land gave way to neat rectilinear patterns with straight rows across the general slope. As a consequence the rows run straight up and down the flanks of the shallow valleys that are oriented at ninety degrees to the general slope, and local erosion is severe. About one-tenth of the area of the pineapple fields is occupied by field roads of compacted earth, which shed water like a duck's back when it rains, thereby contributing to the erosion hazard.

Impact of Construction

Not only does the construction industry divert land from farming, it commonly wreaks such havoc upon the soils that they never can be restored to productivity. On sloping land, the effort to preserve the topsoil is rare; terraces are cut with bulldozers and when the buildings are ready for occupancy, the proud new owner can test his landscaping skills on a mixture of subsoil and rock. Downstream effects of construction on Oahu include the muddying of surfing beaches and the suffocation of the coral in south Kaneohe Bay by silt.

CHAPTER 10

VEGETATION

Lyndon Wester

The present-day vegetation of Hawaii is rich in species and most unusual in composition. The remarkable environmental diversity of the islands, coupled with their remote location, has resulted in a native flora in which 97 percent of the species are endemic, that is, found nowhere else in the world. These species evolved without the pressure to adapt to the ecological disturbances associated with human occupance.

After the Polynesians colonized the islands and more particularly after European settlement, there was wholesale replacement of native vegetation communities, and at least 273 species (15 percent of the flora) have been exterminated; 78 percent of those species that remain are considered to be endangered (Fosberg and Herbst 1975). (See Figure 10.1.) In their place a remarkable array of plants has been introduced to Hawaii by outsiders. At least 4,000 exotic species are cultivated in Hawaii, and an additional 600 species have become naturalized or maintain themselves as weeds or ruderals around human habitation.

Any consideration of the present-day vegetation of Hawaii must take into account not only the natural plant communities, many of which exist only as relicts in remote areas of difficult access, but also those created by humans. Many of these new associations of species are made up largely, or even entirely, of introduced plants. Almost all of the species most commonly associated with the Hawaiian Islands, such as the plumeria, the ornamental hibiscus, the coconut, and the taro (from which poi is made), were brought by settlers. An appreciation of Hawaii's unique native plants and an understanding of their precarious ecological status is most important in preserving the few remaining natural areas and in preventing any further extinctions or population depletion.

ORIGIN OF THE INDIGENOUS HAWAIIAN FLORA

In comparison with other regions, the Hawaiian flora is moderately rich in native species per unit of land area but poor in genera (Table 10.1). The 1,630 known native higher plants are believed to have evolved from as few as 407 different ancestral species that colonized the islands from elsewhere (Mueller-Dombois 1981). As they evolved with very little genetic exchange from the outside, they followed quite independent paths of development. Only 66 species native to Hawaii are found naturally in other parts of the world, and these are mostly "drift species" whose natural habitat is the coastal strand. They typically have seeds that float, and by this means they can migrate from one continental coast to another and become established on remote islands.

A consideration of the colonization of Hawaii by plants must take into account

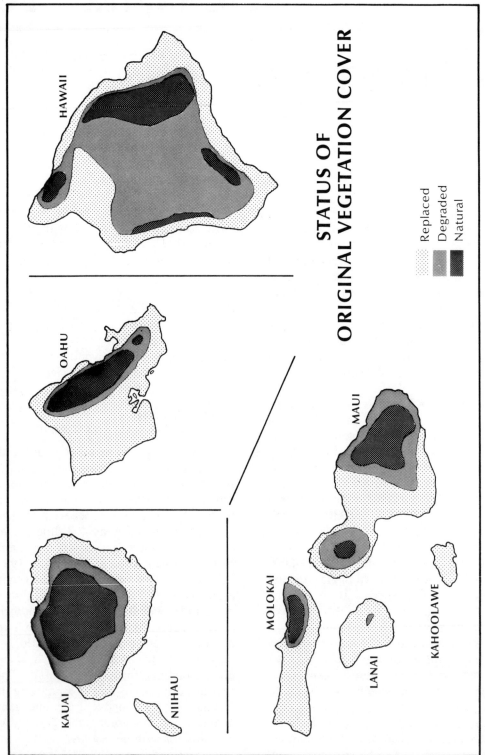

**STATUS OF
ORIGINAL VEGETATION COVER**

Replaced
Degraded
Natural

HAWAII

OAHU

KAUAI

NIIHAU

MOLOKAI

MAUI

LANAI

KAHOOLAWE

FIGURE 10.1.

Table 10.1   Native Genera and Species of Vascular Plants in Various Regions

Region	Area 1000 km^2	Genera No.	Genera % Endemic	Species No.	Species % Endemic	Species per Genera	Species per 1000 km^2
Hawaii	16.6	204	16.4	1,562	97.5	7.7	9.41
Alaska	1,479	355	0	1,366	5.9	3.8	0.92
Barro Colorado Islands	0.016	652	0	1,261	?	1.9	7,881.25
British Isles	308	545	0	1,443	1.2	2.6	4.69
Cape Peninsula, South Africa	0.47	533	0.2	2,256	7.0	4.2	4,800.00
Carolinas	217	819	0.1	2,995	0.8	3.6	13.01
Eastern United States	3,238	849	0.7	4,425	13.5	0.5	1.37
Galapagos Islands	7.9	250	2.8	701	25.0	2.8	88.73
Guatemala	109	1,799	?	7,818	?	4.3	71.71
Japan	377	1,098	1.5	4,022	34.1	3.6	10.67
New Zealand	268	393	9.9	1,996	81.1	5.0	7.45
Sonoran Desert	310	746	2.7	2,441	26.6	3.2	7.87
Texas	715	1,075	0.7	4,196	9.0	3.9	5.58

Source: Raven and Axelrod 1978; Hawaii data based on St. John 1973 and Fosberg 1948.

not only the means of dispersal available to propagules, but also the possible sources of immigrants and the character of the habitats available (Table 10.2). The transfer of seeds by flotation in seawater can satisfactorily explain the presence of only a small proportion of the flora. Furthermore, dispersal of plants by wind currents is probably only possible if the propagules are very tiny. The dust-sized reproductive spores of ferns are readily carried in this way, and so it is not surprising that Hawaii is rich in fern species. The seeds of most flowering plants, however, are much too large to be carried far by the wind, but it is possible that the three native orchid species and the very common ohia lehua (*Metrosideros collina*) migrated to Hawaii on air currents (Carlquist 1974).

The majority of native Hawaiian plants were brought by birds. Many upland plant species from wet habitats have small, fleshy berries that can be swallowed whole by medium-sized birds and carried in their intestines. In addition, some plant seeds have hooks, barbs, or a sticky coating that enables them to become attached to feathers. Still other plants have small seeds that,

Table 10.2 Origin and Mode of Dispersal of Ancestral Hawaiian Plants

		Place of origin of ancestral species by percent					Percent of species arrival by each mode of dispersal
	Mode of dispersal	Indo-Pacific	Australia	America	Boreal	Pantropic	
Ocean	Air flotation	3.0	2.2				1.7
	Frequent occurrence, seeds adapted to immersion	13.0	3.4	13.8		36.2	13.8
	Rare event caused by chance rafting	5.5	9.1	8.5		5.1	6.6
Birds	attachment by barbs, bristles, awns, etc.	49.0	45.5	40.4	7.1	17.2	41.0
	transport in digestive tract	11.5	11.4	5.3	14.3	3.5	9.2
	attachment with mud on feet	12.5	23.9	16.0	42.9	10.3	16.0
	attachment with viscid substances	6.5	4.5	16.0	35.7	27.6	11.6
	Percent of species from each region	43.3	19.3	20.6	3.1	12.7	

Source: Carlquist 1974, 56-58.

when mixed with mud, may be carried on birds' feet or other parts of the exterior.

Prevailing wind and ocean currents in Hawaii come from the northeast or east, and cold-front storms in the winter months may bring air from the north and northwest. However, plant immigrants from North America or northeastern Asia would find few suitable habitats in Hawaii. The closest ancestors of most Hawaiian plants grow in tropical Asia, Australia, or the islands of the western Pacific. In these regions there are many habitats similar to those found in Hawaii, but limited means to transport the seeds northwards. For these reasons it is not surprising that the Hawaiian flora appears to be derived from a small number of original colonists. It is possible that southerly air streams associated with Kona storms or the occasional hurricanes that reached the islands may have assisted airborne, waterborne, or birdborne migrations. Most dispersal was probably the result of water birds on meridional migrations or land birds that were blown out to sea and disoriented by storms, but able to fly great distances under comparatively calm atmospheric conditions to reach Hawaii by chance.

Considering that there were only 407 original higher-plant immigrants and that the islands are at least 5.6 million years old, it would appear that a successful establishment of a new species occurred only once in 14,000 years. Clearly, the arrival of a new plant species in Hawaii before human occupance was an extremely rare event.

COMPETITION BETWEEN INDIGENOUS AND ALIEN PLANTS

Not only was the indigenous Hawaiian flora derived from just a few species, but the number of individual immigrants was probably very low; most likely in many instances only a single seed or propagule arrived, and so the original pool of genetic diversity may have been very small. This has several important implications. The characteristics of the present-day endemic flora must have developed in situations quite different from those on continental land masses, and many of the highly successful species that evolved in the main centers of evolutionary innovation on continents failed to reach Hawaii. Those species that did arrive were distinguished principally by their dispersal ability rather than their proven success in direct interspecific competition. As a result, whole groups of plants and animals that have important ecological roles in continental ecosystems are absent, and other plants have evolved in Hawaii as substitutes to carry on similar functions. Considering the short time available and the limited genetic reservoir, they probably have not adapted as efficiently as their continental equivalents.

The failure of large herbivores to reach the islands had particularly important repercussions on the course of plant evolution, because the endemic island plants, having no need to protect themselves against grazing animals, had few thorns, bristles, or tissue toxins. When goats, sheep, and cattle were introduced they inflicted great damage on the vulnerable native vegetation, causing many plants to be replaced by exotic species that had long association with grazing animals.

Human habitation usually results in increased fire frequency, clearing, and many changes in soil properties—deterioration of structure by compaction, nutrient impoverishment by cropping, and enrichment by purposeful application of fertilizers or accidental concentration of waste. Many plants have adapted to these conditions and have evolved a close association with man. A few were brought to Hawaii by the Polynesians (Table 10.3), but a flood of new arrivals has occurred in the last 200 years. The results are summarized in Table 10.4. It appears that almost half the introductions (42.5 percent) are accidental. They might have been brought as impurities in batches of seeds of valuable species (since it is not possible to keep commercial seeds completely pure), carried in clothing of travelers or in the intestines of imported animals, or attached to objects such as cars or farm

Table 10.3 Plants Introduced to Hawaii by the Polynesians

Latin Name	Common Name	Food	Medicine	Wood	Dye	Ornament	Container-Wrappers	Fiber	Oil	Thatch	Poison	Soap	Weed
Aleurites moluccana	kukui, candlenut		x		x	x			x				
Alocasia macrorrhiza	ape, apii	x											
Artocarpus altilis	ulu, breadfruit	x		x			x						
Broussonetia papyrifera	wauke, paper mulberry						x						
Calophyllum inophyllum	kamani		x	x									
Cocus nucifera	niu, coconut	x		x				x	x	x			
Colocasia esculenta	taro	x	x										
Cordia subcordata	kou			x									
Cordyline terminalis	ti						x			x			
Curcuma domestica	olena, turmeric		x		x								
Digitaria setigera													x
Dioscorea alata	uhi, yam	x											
D. pentaphylla	piia, five leafed yam	x											
Eugenia malaccensis	ohia-ai, mountain apple	x											
Gardenia taitensis	tiare, gardenia					x							
Indigofera suffruiticosa	inikoa, indigo												x
Ipomoea batatas	uala, sweet potato	x											
Lagenaria siceraria	ipu, bottle gourd	x				x	x						
Ludwigia octivalvis	kamole, primrose willow												x
Merremia aegyptia	koali-kua-hulu												x
Morinda citrifolia	noni	x	x		x								
Musa spp.	maia, banana	x											
Nasturtium sarmentosum	paihi, nasturtium		x		x								
Oxalis corniculata	ihi, wood sorrel												x
Piper methysticum	awa		x										
Saccharum officinarum	ko, sugarcane	x						x					
Schizostachyum glaucifolium	ohe, bamboo				x								
Tacca leontopetaloides	pia, arrowroot	x	x										
Tephrosia purpurea	ahuhu										x		
Thespesia populnea	milo	x	x	x									
Urena lobata	aramina												x
Zingiber zerumbet	awapuhi kua hiwi, ginger					x						x	

Source: After St. John, 1973.

Table 10.4 Mode of Introduction of Naturalized Plants

	number	percent
Accidental	236	42.5
Ornamental	199	35.8
Crop (food, timber pasture)	121	21.8

equipment that had been in contact with the soil. Unfortunately, we have little reliable information about which of these factors might be of greatest importance, and the planning of more effective quarantine procedures is impeded.

It is extremely difficult to predict which introduced plants might have the capacity to naturalize and spread in Hawaii's (or any) environment so as to become pests in farmland or gardens or to threaten native plant communities. Many invasive exotic species are self- or wind-pollinated, grow and mature rapidly, produce large numbers of seeds, and have well-developed means of seed dispersal. Importation of new plants needs to be closely regulated, and those with the above characteristics should be strictly excluded.

VEGETATION PATTERNS

The first descriptions of the vegetation of Hawaii come from the records made by the earliest European explorers, but these depict an environment altered from its natural state by 1,200 years of Polynesian settlement; therefore any reconstruction of the original plant cover is speculative. It is known that before the arrival of humans the highly adaptable ohia lehua was the dominant species in many different ecological sites. The likely distribution of the main physiognomic vegetation types is illustrated in Figure 10.2.

Natural Vegetation Communities

Rain Forest. Closed canopy forests up to 50 ft (16 m) tall once covered areas of high annual precipitation. These splendid forests occurred from sea level up to 6,000 ft (1,900 m) but today have been almost completely replaced below 2,000 ft (650 m). Where the community persists the dominant tree is frequently the ohia lehua, but there is a great variety of other trees including the olapa (*Cheirodendron trigynum*) and many others. The community often has an understory of ferns, including the large tree ferns or hapuu (*Cibotium*

spp.) and vines such as the ieie (*Freycinetia arborea*). A dense mat of ferns, lichens, mosses, or fungi covers most available surfaces.

Dry Forest. Tree communities adapted to periodic drought occur in a variety of different temperature regimes and therefore display considerable floristic and structural diversity. The community tends to be more open than the rain forest with a well-developed understory of shrubs, vines, or herbs, which show adaptations to drought. The trees are not necessarily smaller than those of the rain forest; in fact, the magnificent koa trees (*Acacia koa*) with long, straight boles—prized by Hawaiians for the construction of canoes—grew in association with the ohia lehua in drier habitats at elevations above 6,000 ft (1,900 m). In contrast, communities at lower elevations on dry ridges consisted of short, low-branching trees. Important species included alahee (*Canthium odoratum*), akia (*Wikstroemia* spp.), halapepe (*Pleomele aurea*), and many others. Understory species included the ilima (*Sida fallax*); vines or creepers like the maile (*Alyxia olivaeformis*), huehue (*Cocculus ferrandianus*), or ulei (*Osteomeles anthyllidifolia*); and even some drought-tolerant ferns.

Unfortunately, most of the dry forest was altered by Polynesian habitation and more recently replaced by irrigated agriculture, pasture land, or urban development. Consequently, only small relicts of this once widespread community are left, and they are probably a poor representation of its former diversity.

Arid Scrub. The driest lowland habitats, on the leeward sides of the islands, supported a community of stunted trees or shrubs. This could be thought of as the driest phase of the "dry forest," but the low structure and shrub growth form of the dominants would not allow the community to be accurately characterized as a true forest. Here one would expect to find the more drought-resistant species such as the deciduous wiliwili (*Erythrina sandwicensis*) and ohe (*Reynoldsia sandwicen-*

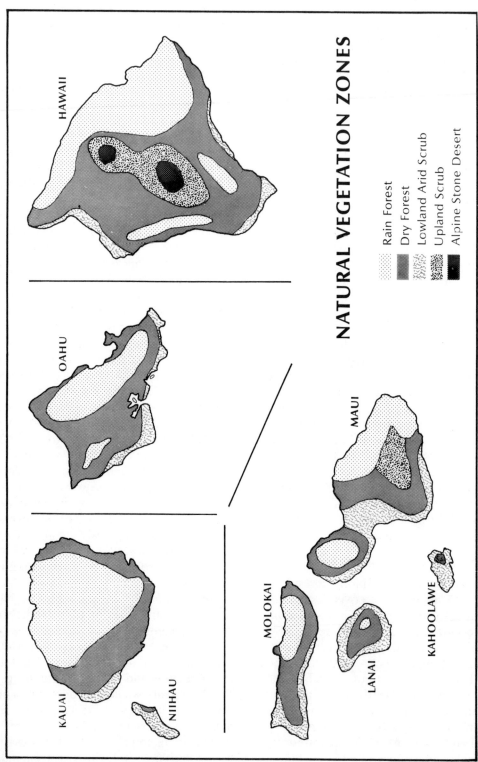

NATURAL VEGETATION ZONES

Rain Forest
Dry Forest
Lowland Arid Scrub
Upland Scrub
Alpine Stone Desert

HAWAII
OAHU
KAUAI
NIIHAU
MOLOKAI
MAUI
LANAI
KAHOOLAWE

FIGURE 10.2.

FIGURE 10.3.   A silversword (*Argyroxiphium sandwicense*) in bloom at the summit of Haleakala, east Maui.

sis) as well as other species with small, waxy leaves able to conserve moisture, such as lama (*Diospyros ferrea*), the sandalwoods ili-ahi (*Santalum* spp.), or aalii (*Dodonaea eriocarpa*).

Upland Scrub. Above 5,000 to 6,000 ft (1,700 to 1,900 m) the influence of the trade winds is slight, and these cold, dry uplands, which exist only on Maui and the Big Island, support a community of shrubs and low trees diminishing in height and density with elevation. In favored habitats open forests of koa and mamane (*Sophora chrysophylla*) may be found, whereas elsewhere species such as naio (*Myoporum sandwicensis*), pukiawe (*Styphelia tameiameiae*), aalii, and ohelo (*Vaccinium calycinium*) occur. It is also in this region that the most unusual, very rare Hawaiian silversword or ahinahina (*Argyroxiphium sandwicense*) is found.

Alpine Stone Desert. The peaks of Mauna Kea and Mauna Loa above 10,000 ft (3,200 m) are composed of recent lavas and cinders. Under the cold, dry conditions, these are mostly unvegetated, except for the occasional growth of mosses, lichens, or extremely drought- and cold-resistant annual herbs.

Strand Vegetation. The Hawaiian strand vegetation is the most cosmopolitan native plant community. Many species such as naupaka kahakai (*Scaevola taccada*), beach morning glory (*Ipomoea pes-caprae*), and the hau tree (*Hibiscus tiliaceus*) are found on beaches throughout the tropics. However, some of the most common and conspicuous species seen along the seashore today have been introduced, for example, the niu or coconut (*Cocos nucifera*), kamani haole *(Terminalia catappa*), milo (*Thespesia populnea*), and the tree heliotrope (*Messerschmidia argentea*). Even the mangrove (*Rhizophora mangle*) and its common salt-marsh associate, the pickle weed or akulikuli kai (*Batis maritima*), which are recognized for their ability to disperse over great stretches of ocean, failed to colonize Hawaii until they were introduced by Europeans.

Human-created Plant Communities

Extensive areas of the Hawaiian Islands have vegetation that is essentially a human artifact. Below an elevation of 2,000 ft (650 m) few native plants can be found, and the natural vegetation has been replaced even at much higher elevations in drier habitats. Plant species from Asia, tropical America, Africa, Australia, and elsewhere brought in as crop, ornamental, pasture, or reforestation species or simply introduced to the islands by accident, have colonized disturbed habitats. The communities show considerable floristic and structural diversity and, at least over a period of several decades, seem to be stable and able to reproduce themselves.

Guava Forest. At elevations below 1,500 ft (450 m) that receive 40 to 60 in. (102 to 152 cm) of rain per year a community can be found that is dominated by guavas (*Psidium guajava, P. cattleianum*) in association with other exotic trees such as

Christmas berry (*Schinus terebinthifolius*), kukui (*Aleurites moluccana*), and some native species such as koa and hau. The understory is composed of many exotic shrubs such as ti (*Cordyline terminalis*), coffee (*Coffea arabica*), and ginger (*Hedychium* spp.) or herbs such as honohono (*Commelina diffusa*); the canopy is often festooned with vines, among which various species of lilikoi or passion flower (*Passiflora* spp.) are common. Ferns are also abundant, especially the uluhe (*Dicranopteris linearis*) and sword fern (*Nephrolepis exaltata*). In this zone also are extensive areas of planted trees including eucalyptus (*Eucalyptus robusta, E. saligna*), silk oak (*Grevillea robusta*), ironwood (*Casuarina equisetifolia*), bamboo (*Bambusa vulgaris*), and many others. Many of the latter species grow vigorously and persist where they were planted, but do not spread.

Exotic Shrubland. In drier sites receiving between 20 and 40 in. (50.8 to 101.6 cm) of annual precipitation and subject to seasonal drought, the plant cover is low, more open, and dominated by many branching shrubs. Probably the most common species is the summer deciduous koa haole (*Leucaena latisiliqua*), along with lantana (*Lantana camara*), klu (*Acacia farnesiana*), and others. Where the shrubs do not form dense thickets so as to shade the ground, herbs such as the grass Natal red top (*Rhynchelytrum repens*), ilima (*Sida falax*), hialoa (*Waltheria americana*), and others may occur.

Kiawe Scrub. In the driest leeward sites at low elevation a community dominated by kiawe (*Prosopis pallida*) occurs. Where the long roots of this species can tap the groundwater table, majestic spreading trees can grow and survive in areas which are a climatic desert. Species that must depend on rainfall are few, but the native pili grass (*Heteropogon contortus*) and the exotic finger grass (*Pennisetum setaceum*) are conspicuous in the landscape.

Urban Vegetation

Urbanization generally destroys existing vegetation and replaces it with houses, streets, and tall buildings. Hence, the vegetation found in cities is usually introduced to provide an attractive setting for city dwellers. A study of street trees in Honolulu by Wesley Teraoka (1978) forms the basis for this brief discussion of urban vegetation in Hawaii (the city of Honolulu is deemed to be representative of other urban places in the state).

A number of early European visitors to Honolulu described it as dry, hot, dusty, and treeless. The introduction of domestic grazing animals by Cook and Vancouver, in 1778 and 1793, apparently had been responsible for much of the destruction of the city's flora. It was clear to many that something had to be done to make Honolulu a more attractive, livable place.

Many early residents planted gardens, but they were distinctly hampered in their attempts to beautify the city by the roaming pigs that uprooted plants and by the lack of a city water supply. It was not until 1851 that Nuuanu Stream became the source of Honolulu's water and a system of pipes brought water to local residents. Thereafter plantings of ornamental trees and shrubs became more common and successful.

Initially these plantings were by individuals but after 1900 the government took an active role in beautifying the city. While individuals continued to improve their house lots with plantings, the city government concentrated on street-tree plantings, that is, planting trees along the sides or in the median strips of the city's thoroughfares. In the most recent survey it was found that eighty species are included in the street-tree plantings of Honolulu. Thus, there is great diversity in the urban vegetation of Honolulu.

The highest-ranking species of the eighty accounts for only 9 percent of the total; the top ten species for 50 percent of the total. These are:

1. *Tabebuia pentaphylla* (Pink tecoma)
2. *Cordia sebestena* (Haole kou, foreign kou)
3. *Filicum decipiens* (Fern tree)

FIGURE 10.4.   This huge Chinese banyan spreads by means of aerial roots on the grounds of Iolani Palace, Honolulu.

4. *Cocos nucifera* (Coconut)
5. *Cassia fistula* X *Cassia javanica* (Rainbow shower)
6. *Bauhinia* spp. (Orchid tree)
7. *Chrysophyllum oliviforme* (Satin leaf, caimitillo)
8. *Delonix regia* (Royal poinciana)
9. *Koelreuteria formosana* (Golden-rain tree)
10. *Ilex paraguariensis* (Paraguay tea, yerba mate)

IMPORTANT COLLECTIONS OF PLANTS

A number of botanical gardens and arboretums exhibit important native and introduced plant species. On Oahu the Lyon Arboretum, a branch of the University of Hawaii; Foster Botanic Gardens; Wahiawa Botanical Garden; and the campus of the university itself have important collections.

The Olu Pua Botanical Gardens on Kauai and the Kula Botanical Gardens on Maui are likewise worth visiting.

PLANTS OF IMPORTANCE IN TRADITIONAL HAWAIIAN CULTURE

Sugarcane

Although sugarcane is most often thought of as a plantation crop introduced by white settlers in the early part of the nineteenth century, it was growing in the islands before they were visited by Cook in 1778. Early Polynesian settlers introduced it into the Hawaiian Islands—they planted it in gardens around home sites and used it as a food source, a sweetener, and a dessert.

The fiber of the stalk was made into a braid for hats, and the leaves were used for house thatching, although they were less favored than the more commonly used pili. Hawaiians recognized and had names for at least forty different forms of sugarcane and knew enough about the characteristics of the plant to have some proverbs and stories associated with the growth of sugar. They called one form *manu lele* ("flying bird") because "it was used to bring a wife's love back to her husband" (Neal 1965, 79).

In addition to its use as food the Hawaiians made a sort of short spear or dart out of the cane stalk, and a popular gambling game was played with contestants throwing the stalks. Mature sugarcane grows silvery flowers or tassels, and an ancient Hawaiian proverb or saying is "The sugarcane is growing white." According to Neal (1965) this is meant to be a tactful and friendly way of indicating that one is growing old.

Coconut

Ubiquitous in the Pacific tropics, the coconut has been used both for food and building materials. In Hawaii the coconut was less treasured as a food source but more utilized for other purposes (Krause 1974). Drums were made from the swollen base of the trunk, which also served as a calabash or food container.

The most important product was made from the fibers of the husk. They were the source of sennit (*aha*), made by twisting or braiding the individual fibers. The cordage made from *aha* was used for lashings in the canoes, and it generally served in place of nails in all sorts of building processes. The Hawaiian sennit was justly famous for its strength and durability; thick ropes were used for anchor cables (Krause 1974).

The shells of the nuts served as drinking glasses, as they sometimes do today when exotic tropical drinks are served to tourists. The drinking containers (*apu*) were used only for *awa*, a mildly narcotic drink (water was drunk out of gourds). The coconut shell was also used to make a number of musical instruments: a knee drum and a type of rattle.

Although the use of coconut as a food was less important in the Hawaiian Islands than it was in other Polynesian islands, it did serve in some desserts, usually in the form of a mixture of the raw grated flesh combined with taro. Today a popular sweet served at luaus is *haupia,* a coconut product. However, *haupia* and *pieleulu,* made with the Polynesian arrowroot and breadfruit, may have originated after the discovery of Hawaii in 1778 (Krause 1974, 12).

In addition to serving as an ornamental, the coconut today has a number of uses, some of them strikingly similar to uses by the ancient Hawaiians. According to Neal (1965, 119),

> The nuts have many uses, their shells for buttons, buckles, containers, lamp stands, charcoal for gas masks and automobile fuel; the fresh white pulp for food, flavoring, and feed for fowl and livestock; the wood (porcupine wood) for cabinets. The husks are made into cordage, mats, brushes, coarse textiles, and stuffing for upholstery. The leaves are plaited into screens to protect young cultivated plants on windy beaches; the young fresh leaves for hats and baskets. The midribs of the leaflets are used for mounting hibiscus flowers for bouquets.

Kukui

A large tree common throughout the Hawaiian Islands, the kukui, or candlenut tree, is the state tree of Hawaii. The leaves have a distinctive light green color, which stands out against the surrounding foliage. Frequently kukui trees form a line along streambeds or in low valleys.

The nut of the kukui was most valuable to the Hawaiians, chiefly for its oil, which could be burned in lamps made of stone. There was a time when the oil was exported commercially for use in varnishes and in some medicines. The nut itself was (and still is) used as a relish. It must be used sparingly, however, since the "rich uncooked nut is a drastic purge" (Neal 1965, 506).

The kukui has been the subject of a

number of Hawaiian legends and proverbs, because of the multiplicity of its uses. One legendary use of the nuts was by the Menehunes, the mythical little people of the islands, to make tops. According to other legends the oil of the kukui nut could be used to calm rough seas. A Hawaiian proverb, "The gum sticks to the candlenut tree," is a reference to a parasite, or to a child who clings unnecessarily to his mother (Neal 1965).

Koa

The tallest and most impressive of Hawaiian trees, the koa grows to heights of 50 ft (15 m) or more. Its wood is valuable today in the manufacture of furniture, novelties, and ukuleles. The ancient Hawaiians found its tall, straight trunks ideal for canoe hulls. Canoe building was practiced by skilled craftsmen, the *kahuna kalai waa,* who not only were excellent carpenters but also were adept at selecting and felling the ideal trees (Krause 1974). In addition to its use in canoes koa, now sometimes called Hawaiian mahogany, was used to make surfboards and calabashes.

Koas can be seen on mountain sides at elevations of 1,500 to 4,000 ft (450 to 1200 m). It has distinctive, small, crescent-shaped leaves and a light gray, smooth bark. A false koa, or koa haole, is a distinctly different species, a shrub widely distributed in the islands, particularly on lower mountain slopes and in dry lowlands. It is considered by some to be a weed.

On the island of Kauai the elepaio bird was the legendary god of canoe builders. If an elepaio, a shy forest bird, pecked at places on the fallen trunk of a koa, the tree was deemed to be unworthy of canoe making and accordingly rejected (Neal 1965). A less mythical explanation might be that the elepaio only pecked on trees that were rotted somewhat or whose wood was less hard for other reasons.

Ohia Lehua

The most common of native trees between elevations of 1,000 and 9,000 ft (300 to 2700 m), ohia trees are abundant and varied. The lehua blossoms are red and attractive; they are popular in leis and are the subject of a number of Hawaiian songs.

The commonest red form of the lehua blossom is the official flower of the island of Hawaii. The ohia wood is extremely hard and was useful to the ancient Hawaiians for making spears, idols, and mallets. Today the wood is used in interior furnishings, fuel, and furniture.

The red color of the lehua blossom has been associated in legend with the volcano goddess Pele, and according to one story Pele's sister, Hiiaka, possessed lehua groves in Kilauea, which the jealous Pele destroyed with a great flow of lava. Another Hawaiian goddess, Hina, was said to have assumed the form of an ohia lehua tree as she watched over a child at Waipio on the Big Island.

The tree itself varies from tall specimens to low shrubs, depending on the area of growth. The leaves are likewise varied in shape.

Sandalwood (Ili-ahi)

The ili-ahi, or Hawaiian sandalwood, was associated with one of the darkest periods of Hawaiian history. The aromatic tree was discovered growing in the islands, where it is native, by western traders who wanted it for trade with China. During the height of the sandalwood trade, roughly from 1810 to 1820, the harvesting of the trees was regulated by Kamehameha the Great, the islands' first monarch. Upon the king's death, however, the trade fell into the hands of the *alii,* who exploited both the trees and the commoners for maximum profit. Consequently, the forests were soon stripped, and the people were forced to work long hours harvesting the trees, at the expense of tending their crops. There was widespread hunger and even famine. The trade soon died out, ending the first really profitable industry in the islands.

Although sandalwood is still fairly common, large specimens are very rare in the islands. There have been efforts, dating from 1932, to plant seedlings and perhaps revive the trade.

Although it was the Chinese who first recognized the value of the wood, referring to the Hawaiian Islands as the sandalwood islands, the Hawaiians sometimes used the wood to treat tapa cloth, giving it a pleasant aroma. The sandalwood was either powdered or mixed with coconut oil for the purpose.

Hala

A native to Hawaii, as well as other Pacific islands, the screwpine or hala is abundant in the fiftieth state. It grows from sea level to about 2,000 ft (600 m).

The chief use made of the tree by native Hawaiians was of the leaves (*lau hala*). These were plaited into a number of materials such as mats, baskets, and clothing. In general, the same use is made of the leaves today, and there are a number of *lau hala* products on the market in tourist areas.

As the tree is common in residential areas it is not surprising to find *hala* used in place names: Hala Drive is a street in the Kamehameha Heights district of Honolulu.

The tree is distinctive in appearance due to its aerial roots, which give it the appearance of a "walking tree" (Neal 1965). When a mother has a number of devoted children, it is sometimes said of her that, "Her children are like the many rooted hala of the mountain side" (Neal 1965, 53).

Ti (Ki)

The ti plant, which is widespread in the Pacific from tropical Asia and Australia as far east as Hawaii, found numerous uses among the Hawaiians. Although not generally thought of as a food, the root of the ti plant was sometimes baked in an underground oven. It turned brown and was either eaten as a confection or, more rarely, as food when there was a famine. Even today ti leaves serve as wrappers for various foods and as plates.

Ti leaves were fed to horses and cattle and in that role served as important fodder. In the fishing method referred to as *hukilau,* a communal type of enterprise, ti leaves were often fastened to nets and dragged through the shallow coastal waters to attract fish. Ti leaves were widely used for house thatch, woven into garments (raincoats, sandals, and more recently hula skirts), and as sliding boards for children to slide down long grassy and muddy slopes.

One of the more interesting uses of the plant was in the manufacture of a liquor, *okolehau* (literally "iron bottom" after the method of distilling in iron pots). The drink was made from the distilled product of the fermented mash of the root.

There are a number of important ornamental uses of the plant. Hawaiians believed that a hedge of ti around a house site warded off evil spirits, and ti was used to make *kahilis* (emblems of royalty) according to one legend. Subsequently, *kahilis* were made from feathers. Hawaiian priests sometimes wore ti leis, as the plant was considered an emblem of divine power, or *mana* (Neal 1965, 204).

Wauke

The paper mulberry tree (wauke or sometimes *poaaha* in Hawaiian) was an early introduction into the Hawaiian Islands. It found wide use by the early Hawaiians, who used its bark extensively. The Hawaiian tapa (kapa) was used for clothing, paper, and bed clothes (Neal 1965, 302). The material made from wauke was washable, very warm, and long lasting. Hence it was more valuable than a similar product made from the bark of the mamaki.

One of the best-known Hawaiian legends concerns Hina and her son Maui. Hina was troubled that her tapa did not have a chance to dry, since the sun did not remain in the sky long enough. Maui, to help his mother, caught the first rays of the sun at sunrise and broke them off, thus slowing the sun in its path through the Hawaiian skies. Maui has long been associated with Haleakala, the "house of the sun."

FIGURE 10.5.   Taro in Hanalei Valley, Kauai.

Ulu (Breadfruit)

Some of the first Polynesian immigrants to Hawaii brought breadfruit trees with them. The tree had many uses: the wood for canoes, the bark for tapa, the sap for caulking the seams of canoes, and the fruit as an important food.

The popularity and value of ulu has made it the source of a number of myths, both in Tahiti and Hawaii. According to one legend Kamehameha did not make generous enough offerings to the volcano goddess Pele. She became angry and destroyed his ulu grove with a lava flow.

Uala (Sweet Potato)

The sweet potato plant arrived in Hawaii with early settlers from Tahiti and was an important food crop. On some islands it was even more valuable than taro. This was the case on the island of Niihau, for instance, where the considerable population ate the uala instead of taro.

The Hawaiian god of the sweet potato was Kane Puaa, literally "Pig Man," who used his piglike snout to cultivate the soil out of which the plant grew.

Taro (Kalo)

The most important food crop in ancient Hawaii and in other parts of Polynesia, taro was an introduction to the island by the first Polynesian settlers. Taro culture has been developed most extensively in Hawaii, and at one time there were close to 300 varieties in the islands.

The tubers of the plant, after boiling or baking and pounding, were made into poi, the most important food staple of commoners and royalty alike.

Poi is today an important food to many Hawaiians and part-Hawaiians. It also finds a place in tourist luaus, but apparently is thought of more highly as a novelty than for its taste. Rarely does a visitor to the islands claim to like poi; it is an acquired taste.

Other parts of the plant are also eaten: sprouts, stalks, and leaves. Taro is still grown commercially in the islands, although the acreage devoted to it is diminishing. Wet taro requires copious amounts of water, and in some regions taro farmers have been in competition for water supplies with urban developers. Hawaiian poi has been exported to the mainland United States and has been instrumental in treating various infant feeding problems, because poi is quite bland and is tolerated by infants who cannot tolerate other foods.

The Hawaiian commoner, *makaainana,* was traditionally a yeoman farmer who worked diligently in his taro patch. The islands' first king, Kamehameha the Great, could sometimes be found thigh-deep in a flooded taro field working a crop, presumably to demonstrate to his subjects the importance of the work.

REFERENCES

Carlquist, S. *Hawaii: a Natural History.* New York: American Museum of Natural History, 1970.

———. *Island Biology.* New York: Columbia University Press, 1974.

Fosberg, F. R. "Derivation of the Flora of the Hawaiian Islands." In *Insects of Hawaii,* vol. 1, edited by E. C. Zimmerman, pp. 107–109, 1948.

Fosberg, F. R., and Herbst, D. "Rare and Endangered Species of Hawaiian Vascular Plants." *Allertonia* 1 (1975): 1–72.

Krause, B. H. *Ethnobotany of the Hawaiians.* Honolulu: Harold L. Lyon Arboretum, 1974.

Mueller-Dombois, D.; Bridges, K. W.; and Carson, H. L. *Island Ecosystems.* Stroudsburg, Pa.: Hutchinson Ross, 1981.

Neal, M. C. *In Gardens of Hawaii.* Honolulu: Bishop Museum Press, 1965.

Raven, P. H., and Axelrod, D. I. *Origin and Relationships of the California Flora.* University of California Publications in Geography, 72: 1–134. Berkeley: University of California Press, 1978.

St. John, H. *List and Summary of the Flowering Plants of the Hawaiian Islands.* Memoir 1. Lawai, Hawaii: Pacific Tropical Botanical Garden, 1973.

Teraoka, W. "Street Trees of Honolulu." Master's thesis, University of Hawaii, 1978.

PART 3

HUMAN ACTIVITIES AND ECONOMIC GEOGRAPHY

CHAPTER 11

TOURISM

The economic geography of the state of Hawaii is dominated by tourism, the state's number-one industry. Tourism, or the visitor industry as it is sometimes called, brings in more revenues to the state government through taxes paid by tourists on their purchases and to individual hotel owners and shopkeepers in the islands than any of the other principal industries. Moreover, tourism provides a far greater number of employment opportunities for the residents of the state than does any other single economic activity. The attractions of Hawaii's mild climate, beaches, scenic resources, and friendly people have been recognized ever since Captain Cook reached the islands in 1778. The Sandwich Islands (as Cook named them for the Earl of Sandwich, an important political figure in the England of Cook's day and a staunch supporter of Cook's explorations) quickly became recognized by other explorers and traders in the Pacific as an ideal place to replenish supplies of food and water and make necessary repairs to their vessels. The crews of these early ships recognized the recreational attractions of the islands and their friendly people. The early visitors properly could not be called tourists, but their descriptions of the islands were instrumental in encouraging the visitor industry that was to follow.

HISTORY OF TOURISM

It is difficult to place a date on the start of tourism as an industry in the islands, but it is logical to trace the development of the visitor industry through the history of establishments specifically built to accommodate visitors. Surprisingly, the first hotel designed to house visitors was not on the beach at Waikiki or some similar coastal location but on the Big Island, in the Kilauea volcano district. The attraction, of course, was the volcano—its eruptive activities had been described by early missionary visitors to Hawaii. The Volcano House, built in 1866, was described in 1875 by Whitney (the account was reprinted in 1970, 82), "a commodious thatch house, standing on a grassy plat, under the lee of a hill which partially shelters it from the damp and chilly east wind that seeps over the crater. It is a comfortable one storey house, built expressly to accommodate tourists, having ample accommodations for all parties that have made the trip in the last ten years."

In 1867 the early industry was aided considerably by the inauguration of the first regularly scheduled steamship service from the U.S. mainland to Hawaii. Before then transportation to the islands had been uncertain at best and usually uncomfortable, since the vessels were designed primarily to carry cargo, and passenger accommodations were not good.

Just four years after construction of the Volcano House, visitors to the islands were apparently numerous enough to warrant the building of a second hotel. The Hawaiian Hotel in Honolulu opened early in 1872 and was mentioned by Charles Nordhoff in 1874 (the book was reprinted in 1974, 19), "From the steamer you proceed to a surprisingly excellent hotel, which was built at a cost of about $120,000, and is owned by the government."

It was not until 1894 that the virtues of Waikiki as a tourist destination were finally recognized, and the Seaside Annex was built. But even then other locations were favored, for just five years later, on August 5, 1899, the Haleiwa Hotel opened for business on the north shore of Oahu. Scott (1968, 759) referred to it as "one of the show places of the islands," and there were other reports of the delights of the hotel and the train ride from downtown Honolulu to the north shore of the island. The hotel continued to thrive until 1928, when it became a private club; during World War II it served as an officers' club.

As long as the rail line continued to operate, the Haleiwa Hotel, in one form or another, continued to thrive; the demise of the railroad after World War II spelled the end of the grand old hotel, and it was finally demolished in 1952.

Hotel development in the Waikiki district continued after the turn of the century with the building of the Moana Hotel in 1901 and the famous Royal Hawaiian in 1927. The Moana, the Royal Hawaiian, and the Halekulani, a gracious Waikiki hotel originally built as a private home, today are the only old low-rise hotels left in the Waikiki area.

In 1928 tourism development began in the Kona district of the Big Island with the opening of the Kona Inn.

Hotel development thereafter proceeded slowly, and many people who visited the

FIGURE 11.1.   SS *Oceanic Independence* makes weekly cruises among the islands, calling at ports on Hawaii, Maui, Kauai, and Oahu. It is a popular tourist attraction for both local residents and visitors.

islands prior to World War II remember when the beach at Waikiki had only the Moana, the Royal Hawaiian, and the unobtrusive Halekulani available for visitors. World War II, however, brought large numbers of military personnel to the islands, and although they certainly were not tourists, many remembered the islands with nostalgic delight. The fame of Hawaii as a tourist destination spread after the end of the war.

After its early beginnings the visitor industry grew slowly but steadily in terms of the numbers of tourists who came to Hawaii. In 1886 there were but 2,040 visitors, and in 1951 the annual count was only 52,000. Nevertheless, farsighted businessmen could see that the industry would flourish. The Hawaii Visitors Bureau was organized in 1903, and that organization today is still largely responsible for the

maintenance and growth of the visitor industry in the state.

Events and conditions both inside and outside of Hawaii have influenced the growth of tourism. In 1929 interisland air service was inaugurated, facilitating visits by Hawaii residents to other Hawaiian Islands. Transpacific air flights began in 1936, and the famous China clippers could carry wealthy passengers on a lengthy but comfortable flight to the islands. Sharp reductions in air fares in 1952 and 1963 gave a big boost to the industry, as did the inauguration of regular jet flights to Hawaii, which greatly shortened flying time. Interest in Hawaii increased in 1959, when the islands became the fiftieth state.

Two years after statehood 320,000 visitors came to Hawaii; in 1971 the visitor count reached 1,819,000 and in 1980 it was 3,934,504. The rise, while impressive,

FIGURE 11.2.   The beach at Waikiki on a January day, with Diamond Head and tourist hotels in the background.

FIGURE 11.3.   Where the beach is narrow or nonexistent, tourists seek the sun on lounges by the side of a swimming pool at one of Waikiki's large hotels.

has not been continuous. In 1979 DC-10 aircraft were ordered grounded after a tragic accident, and in the same year there was a strike of United Airlines employees. Both events resulted in the loss of business for the Hawaii visitor industry, and for the year 1979 there was a decrease of 9.2 percent in visitor arrivals.

The tremendous increase in the number of visitors in the decade of the 1970s was matched by hotel building on a previously unheard-of scale. At the end of 1980 there were 56,769 rooms available for tourists. Of this total, 42,575 units were in hotels and the remaining 14,194 in condominiums. Although most of the rooms were on Oahu, the neighbor islands (as the other major islands are referred to) had a total of 22,802 rooms, and the growth rate on Maui, Hawaii, Kauai, and Molokai had

exceeded that of Oahu. Maui was the island showing the largest growth in tourism with a gain of 1,580 rooms during 1980.

THE GEOGRAPHY OF TOURISM

From a geographic standpoint—and as a means of assisting the visitor industry in making its attractions more desirable to tourists—it is important to look both at where visitors come from and where they go while in the islands.

Of the 3,934,504 visitors to Hawaii in 1980, the great majority (2,348,591) came from the U.S. mainland, with more of them coming from the western states than from other regions of the country. The next-largest group of visitors came from Japan, with 570,000 arrivals in 1980. Canada provided 296,033 tourists, and the remainder

FIGURE 11.4.   A candy-shop window on Ka-lakaua Avenue in Waikiki advertises its wares in Japanese for the many visitors from Japan who vacation in the islands.

of the visitors in 1980 came from other countries in Asia and western Europe. There has been a steady increase in arrivals from European countries in the last few years, although the numbers are still small compared to the American and Japanese totals.

There are hotel developments for the accommodation of visitors on five of the eight main Hawaiian Islands: Oahu, Maui, Kauai, Hawaii, and Molokai. On Lanai, the number of rooms is limited to the twelve available at the Lanai Lodge. Since weather and climate are important factors in bringing tourists to the islands, most of the accommodations are located on the drier, leeward areas of the islands; there are some exceptions, particularly on the island of Hawaii.

Oahu

Most of the hotel and condominium rooms available for tourists are located on Oahu, particularly in the Waikiki Beach area. Waikiki has a marvelous climate and

a famous beach. Moreover, it is near the heart of Honolulu, with the attendant advantages of proximity to shopping centers, theaters, restaurants, and a number of cultural attractions. Most of Hawaii's people live and work in Honolulu, and the visitor who chooses to do so can see a part of the "real Hawaii" by leaving the Waikiki district and exploring other parts of the island. Nearby is Chinatown, for instance, and the downtown business district. Honolulu also has a number of historical sites worthy of a visit, including the state capitol, Kawaiahao Church, the Mission Houses Museum, and the Iolani Palace, Barracks, and old bandstand. The latter was built for the coronation of King Kalakaua in 1883.

The visitor to Oahu also can take advantage of hiking trails in the Koolau and Waianae mountains, fish for saltwater game fish, visit the *Arizona* Memorial, snorkel at Hanauma Bay and other sites, ride catamarans and canoes in the calm waters off Waikiki, and enjoy both board and body surfing at a host of beaches. On Oahu's north shore are surfing waves that attract world-class professional surfers from Hawaii, Australia, and the U.S. mainland. The Honolulu Zoo, Waikiki Aquarium, and Polynesian Cultural Center attract large numbers of visitors.

Waikiki is crowded, commercial, and in some cases tawdry. For visitors to Oahu who want to avoid the overcrowding of the Waikiki district, there are other hotels: one on the leeward side of the island at Makaha and the other at the northernmost point at Kuilima. Both hotels have golf courses—facilities not available at the Waikiki hotels, and both have attempted to attract tourists who wish to avoid the noise, bustle, and commercial atmosphere of Waikiki. However, neither hotel has been very successful; the vast majority of visitors to Oahu make a Waikiki hotel their destination. But most visitors to Oahu, particularly those who travel on planned tours, visit one or more other Hawaiian Islands before returning home.

FIGURE 11.5 (*above*). Visitors like to shop for souvenirs and Hawaiian clothing. Kalakaua Avenue, Waikiki's main street, provides a variety of things to buy. FIGURE 11.6 (*below*). For the visitor who wants to try deep-sea fishing, charter boats are available at Kewalo Basin, Honolulu.

FIGURE 11.7. Tour boats that take visitors on trips around Honolulu harbor and to the *Arizona* Memorial are an important component of the visitor industry.

FIGURE 11.8. A variety of attractions are available to the tourist at Waikiki Beach. Canoe rides are popular with many visitors; others want to learn to surf before leaving the islands.

Maui

Maui draws a great number of visitors interested in seeing another Hawaiian island, seeing more of rural Hawaii, and viewing volcanic scenery unavailable on Oahu. The shield volcano, Haleakala, with its great, eroded summit crater studded with cinder cones, is the big visitor attraction in the eastern part of the island. Most tourists content themselves with a drive to the summit and a look at the crater from a vantage point in the Haleakala National Park, but some spend one or more days hiking the rugged trails available.

The small community of Hana, reached only by a long drive along the Hana Highway—famous for its numerous curves, narrowness, and poor condition—is a prime tourist destination. Once there, visitors look for souvenirs at the Hasegawa General Store, an establishment designed to serve the needs of the local community with a large variety of both necessities and luxuries. Beyond Hana the highway continues on to the Seven Pools, a picturesque series of pools in a mountain stream, and to Kipahulu, the site of Charles Lindbergh's grave.

Most of the hotels on Maui are in the dry, leeward areas in the western portion of the island. The coastal strip between the town of Lahaina and the hotel development at Kaanapali provides accommodations for thousands of visitors. The attractions are fine beaches, golf, shopping, restaurants, night life, and Hawaiian history. Evidence of the latter can be found at Lahaina, a former capital of the Hawaiian kingdom that had its heyday in the boisterous days when whaling ships visited the islands. One of the attractions of the Lahaina waterfront is a visit to the *Carthaginian*, a restored whaler. Lahaina was also a mission station; restored houses and museums there depict missionary life.

The most recent and extensive hotel and condominium developments have taken place in the Kihei to Makena coastal area, on the lee side of the Haleakala volcano.

This, too, is a sunny area with good beaches and calm water. Snorkeling is popular at several locations, and golf and tennis are features at some of the larger, more sumptuous hotels. Maui's chief urban center is the Kahului-Wailuku conurbation, but there has been little development of tourist facilities in the area. In the West Maui mountain region, however, there is typical rainforest scenery and the famous Iao Needle in Iao Valley State Park.

Kauai

Many visitors to the islands rate Kauai as the most beautiful of the Hawaiian Islands. It has lush, green landscapes, spectacular cliffs, and beautiful beaches. Moreover, the island is less urbanized than Oahu or Maui, and the general atmosphere is quiet and pleasant. Some of the most spectacular geological landscapes are easily viewed by the visitor. There is Waimea Canyon in the western part of the island, which can be seen after a relatively short drive from any of the hotel locations. The Waimea River eroded a steep-walled, intricately carved canyon out of the single shield volcano that forms the island; the canyon is sometimes referred to as the Little Grand Canyon of the Pacific. Equally accessible is the Spouting Horn, a blowhole in the southeastern portion of the island that is a popular tourist attraction. One of the Hawaiian Islands' most beautiful amphitheater-headed valleys is Kalalau Valley on the Na Pali coast, which can be seen from a lookout point conveniently reached by automobile or can be entered after a long, strenuous hike on the Na Pali coast trail. The Na Pali coast, with its spectacular sea cliffs, can be seen only by those who hike the trail or by visitors who avail themselves of commercial helicopter flights that will take a passenger to one of a number of secluded beaches at the foot of the pali.

For the rugged tourist, there is the hiking trail in the Alakai Swamp, a very wet but beautiful region where a number of species of native birds can be viewed. A number of other hiking trails of varying degrees of difficulty are available, many originating from the Kokee State Park. Among the best known of the many fine beaches on the island is Lumahai Beach, where scenes for the movie *South Pacific* were filmed. The north shore of the island has the picturesque community of Hanalei, as well as some new developments at nearby Princeville. Hanalei Valley, where taro is still grown in a bucolic setting, is a popular place to visit.

The hotels mostly are located near Kapaa on the northeast coast and at Poipu Beach on the southeast shore. The Poipu Beach location has sunnier weather and has been the site of more extensive recent development. In addition to one of the finest body-surfing beaches in the islands and the nearby Spouting Horn, the Poipu Beach hotels offer proximity to the town of Koloa, a picturesque old community near the site of the first successful sugar plantation in the islands.

Hawaii

The Big Island provides great variety to the tourist. There are two separate visitor destination areas: Hilo and the Kona coast. Hilo's hotel district is on the eastern shore of the Waiakea Peninsula, which extends into Hilo Bay. The principal attraction is the Kilauea volcano and the Hawaii Volcanoes National Park, but they are about a forty-five-minute drive by automobile or tour bus. The Hilo area itself offers few delights to the tourist. There are no beaches very convenient to the hotels, and the climate is decidedly rainy. The picturesque Rainbow Falls can be visited and a short drive north on the wet Hamakua coast leads to Akaka Falls, a beautiful waterfall in an attractively developed state park. But the real attraction is the volcano, and the Hilo hotels are just a bit too far away to be a convenient stopping place for visitors whose interests are in Hawaii Volcanoes National Park.

Within the park itself is the Volcano House, a comfortable hotel featuring a

fireplace in the lobby with a fire that is said never to have burned out. However, the Volcano House (the successor to the original Volcano House built in 1866) has only thirty-five rooms. There are also cabins in the national park for visitors interested in more rustic accommodations. In addition to the Kilauea volcano, with its caldera and numerous craters, the park offers hiking trails, native vegetation, and a rugged trek to the summit of Mauna Loa. Many visitors drive through the national park on the way from Hilo to the Kona Airport, or vice versa, and some avail themselves of the opportunity to sample briefly some of the attractions. A longer, but more scenic, road from the park to Hilo is the Chain of Craters Road, with spectacular views of aa and pahoehoe lava flows, pit craters, and forests of native trees and ferns, and a view of the ocean with its rugged sea cliffs, arches, and stacks.

Hotels in Hilo can serve the tourist who wishes to see the Puna district, southeast of Hilo, as well as the waterfalls and the national park, but the combination of cloudy, rainy weather and the lack of attractive, convenient beaches has made most of the hotels unprofitable. Low occupancy rates have been the rule in the last few years, and some of the hotels have been sold for conversion to office buildings.

The Kona coast is different in many respects from the windward side of the Big Island. In the Kona district the climate features dry, sunny conditions for most of the year, but there is an area that gets its maximum rainfall in the summer months (see Chapter 6). There are some good beaches and some historic sites worth visiting. One of the best known of these is the City of Refuge at Honaunau, an authentically restored area of Hawaiian *heiaus* (temples), *kiis* (tikis), and other sacred sites. Another is Kealakekua Bay, the site of Captain Cook's landing on the island of Hawaii and of his death in 1779 during a fight with the natives of the island. North of the Kona district hotels, in the Kohala district, are the birthplace of Kamehameha the Great and the Mookini *heiau*, one of the most famous in the islands. The combination of dry, sunny weather, beaches, shopping, and history has been kinder to the Kona hotels than to those in Hilo. Occupancy rates are higher and there have been no recent closures. The area is served by Kona Airport, and many visitors to the Big Island fly from Honolulu to Kona, remain a few days in the Kona area, then drive to Hilo, visiting the Kilauea volcano on the way. They then fly out of Hilo for their return trip to Honolulu.

Molokai

Visitors to Molokai can enjoy the fine beaches at the western end of the island while staying at the relatively new Sheraton Molokai hotel. There are other places of interest to the visitor, including a look at the Kalaupapa Peninsula, site of the small town and medical facilities for leprosy patients. Most tourists are content to view the peninsula from a lookout point on the north shore of the island, but some actually visit the peninsula, either hiking the steep trail or arriving on a small plane. In either case permission from the health authorities must be obtained first, and the visitor must participate in a guided tour.

Other places of interest on Molokai are the numerous fish ponds on the south shore and beautiful Halawa Valley with its picturesque waterfall at the northeasternmost point of the island. Kaunakakai, the largest town on the island, has a few small hotels for those who prefer less-expensive accommodations, but the town itself has little to offer the tourist.

Lanai

Lanai really cannot be considered a tourist destination, but even this small island has daily scheduled flights from Honolulu and accommodations for a few visitors at the Lanai Lodge. The twelve rooms available for tourists serve the relatively few people interested in visiting the island and availing themselves of the opportunity to hike, fish, and hunt. There is a good beach

at Hulopoe Bay and an adequate small-boat and yacht harbor at nearby Manele Bay, but the Lanai Lodge is far from the ocean, located inland in Lanai City. Roads are rudimentary on the island, and travel by four-wheel-drive vehicle is necessary to reach some of the choicest sites for hunting, fishing, or hiking. A visit to Lanai is a different kind of vacation from the usual concept of Hawaiian tourism.

Activities

Visitors to any of the islands find a variety of things to do, aside from the traditional delights of the beaches and fine hotels. Cultural festivals of the various ethnic groups are held frequently, the celebration of the Chinese New Year with dragon dances and fireworks being a particularly popular diversion for residents and tourists alike. There are hula and ukulele contests at various times, and the music and dance are more authentically Hawaiian than the shows provided at the big hotels and night clubs.

Aloha Week is held each year in September and October, with special events designed to attract the tourists to the islands at a time of year when business is usually light. The Aloha Week parade and the Molokai-to-Oahu canoe race are the biggest events, but there is also the popular *hoolaulea*, a series of free entertainments held outdoors and largely provided by amateur dancers who are students at the many hula dance schools.

The islands have a large number of state and county parks, many in beachfront locations, some with cabins, campgrounds, hiking trails, and picnic facilities. Visits to historic sites, including *heiaus*, attract many tourists, and the more adventurous try their hands at sports such as hang gliding, wind surfing, scuba diving, sailing, and riding as passengers in sail planes.

There are a number of fine museums, most on Oahu, which visitors enjoy. The Bishop Museum, with its outstanding collection of Hawaiian artifacts and historical exhibits, is popular. There are also several

FIGURE 11.9. Aloha Week, a series of attractions designed to bring tourists to the islands, is advertised at the Royal Hawaiian Shopping Center in Waikiki.

military museums, including Army museums at Schofield Barracks and Fort De-russy, both on Oahu, and the U.S.S. *Bowfin*, a restored World War II submarine on the waterfront at Pearl Harbor.

TOURISM'S IMPACT

On April 1, 1980, the resident population of the state of Hawaii (excluding visitors and residents who were temporarily absent) was 964,691. If visitors to the islands were included, the resultant de facto population was 1,052,700. The difference of 88,009 was the number of tourists present, slightly over 8 percent of the de facto population. 1980 was not an atypical year for tourism. During the year there were 3,934,504 visitors who stayed overnight or longer, compared to 3,960,531 for the previous year.

Visitor arrivals decreased again in 1981, but the figures available for the first eight months of 1982 indicate a 2.4 percent increase in tourists over the comparable period of 1981. The impact of tourism can be assessed partially by noting the large increases in the number of visitors over the last fifteen years. The arrivals figures for 1970 and 1965 respectively were 1,746,970 and 686,828. It is clear that tourists are becoming an increasingly larger percentage of the state's de facto population.

A preliminary estimate of expenditures by visitors for the year 1980 is $3 billion. Expenditures for the years 1979 and 1978 were $2.6 billion and $2.2 billion respectively. In 1980 there were a total of 55,700 hotel rooms in the state, up from 51,782 in 1979, and hotel employment rose from

FIGURE 11.10.   Tour buses are an important component of Hawaii's visitor industry. They are available to take visitors to a variety of popular attractions.

23,735 in 1979 to 24,754 in 1980. No other single industry in the state employs more workers than the visitor industry. Of course, the total employment of Hawaii residents in the visitor industry encompasses much more than those who work in hotels. Others in the industry work in restaurants, shops, tour buses, and boats or are entertainers, greeters at the airport, travel agents, and so forth. Accurate data for these types of employment are not available, but the numbers undoubtedly are considerable.

The impact of tourism is much greater in some geographic regions than others. In Waikiki the majority of the people one sees on the streets and at the beach are tourists, while in central Oahu and in small towns on the neighbor islands tourists are rare. The only available information on tourist-to-resident ratios is for entire counties; these data indicate that the impact of tourism is approximately as great on the islands of Hawaii, Maui, and Kauai as it is on Oahu. However, on all the islands

there are many residents who never see a tourist and do not frequent hotels and restaurants where tourists congregate, and for whom the visible impact of the visitor industry is negligible.

Pros and Cons of Tourism

While most Hawaii residents agree that tourism is essential to the economic well-being of the islands, some are quick to point out the problems that the visitor industry brings. Some areas are overdeveloped and take on the appearance of "concrete jungles"—Waikiki is often cited as an example. Because the tourist is known to be able to afford the transportation to the islands, the hotel room and tour costs, and meals in restaurants in the tourist destination areas, prices for food, entertainment, clothing, souvenirs, and so on are generally higher than they would be otherwise if there were no tourism industry. For instance, Hawaii residents have long recognized that restaurant prices are higher

FIGURE 11.11.   Makers and sellers of leis have stands at the Honolulu International Airport. The flower industry is an important source of employment associated with tourism.

in Waikiki than elsewhere on the island of Oahu for what they assess as comparable meals. The Oahu resident, knowing this, usually chooses restaurants outside of Waikiki when dining out.

Some people argue that the additional fire, police, and other services required in tourist areas are not sufficiently paid for by tax revenues from the visitor industry. But the visitor to the islands pays the same 4 percent tax on purchases of food, clothing, hotel accommodations, tours, entertainment, and miscellaneous items as does the Hawaii resident, and the daily expenditure of the tourist is far greater than that of the local resident. In 1980 tax revenues from visitor spending amounted to $323 million, more than enough to pay for the added cost to the state of maintaining facilities and necessary services.

Another argument against tourism is that the industry changes the character of the islands; they are no longer scenic, quiet, and rural, but fast are becoming urbanized. While it cannot be denied that many areas are under increasing pressure to develop, it is by no means certain that the majority of island residents deplore this. Some see it as desirable, and even necessary for the Hawaiian economy.

The foremost point in favor of tourism is the employment opportunities the industry provides. In 1980 visitor expenditures generated 117,000 jobs. The direct employment in hotels has been noted, but there are also jobs in the construction industry, in transportation, and in entertainment fields that are clearly attributable to the presence of large numbers of visitors in the state. Tourism has done much to preserve some aspects of Hawaiian culture, such as music and dance. Most Hawaiian musicians would be hard pressed to make a living at their trade were it not for the tourists who want and can afford to be entertained.

THE FUTURE OF TOURISM IN HAWAII

The recent decline in the numbers of visitors arriving in the state has led many to question whether tourism can remain Hawaii's number-one industry and to argue that the state should attempt to diversify its economy. An assessment of tourism's future must include the factors in the islands and in the countries where visitors originate that encourage or discourage visits to Hawaii.

Conditions Outside Hawaii

The most important factor outside Hawaii influencing the state's tourist industry is the general condition of the economy. When the inflation rate is high and wage increases do not keep up, discretionary travel must be curtailed; tourist destinations suffer. Fluctuations in air fares—higher fares associated with increased costs of aviation fuel and lower ones resulting from increases in the number of airlines serving the islands and greater competition for the traveler's dollar—have a great effect on visitor arrivals in Hawaii.

Visits by Japanese tourists have shown a number of increases and dips depending on the state of the Japanese economy. Japan is particularly dependent on imported petroleum; its price can influence the nation's economy, and indirectly, the future of the tourist industry in Hawaii.

A cold winter in the United States, coupled with satellite television views of the annual Hula Bowl football game being played under bright blue skies at Aloha Stadium on Oahu, can increase the number of visitors dramatically in succeeding weeks.

The choice of Hawaii as the location of an important convention, such as the annual meeting of the American Legion or the American Bar Association, can mean a good year for Hawaiian tourism. If a competitor destination is selected, hotel occupancy rates in Hawaii will be lower.

Conditions in Hawaii

Tourists are attracted to the islands by climate, beaches, the sea, live volcanoes, Hawaiian culture, scenery, and the so-called Aloha Spirit. Residents of the state are most fortunate that they have these things, but they must insure that the quality of the environment is not degraded if visitors are to continue to spend their vacation money in the islands.

The climate presumably always will remain delightful and always tend to attract visitors. The Hawaiian tourist industry is not seasonal. In winter the islands' warm temperatures attract visitors who are anxious to escape the vicissitudes of winter at home. In summer it is frequently cooler in Hawaii than it is in many parts of the U.S. mainland or Japan. People can escape both heat and cold by a trip to Hawaii.

The Hawaiian Islands have a number of fine sandy beaches, but litter is a visible problem. While it may be argued that it is the tourists themselves who are spoiling the beaches, nevertheless if the beaches become unsightly, visitors will stop coming. Hawaii's residents also use the famed Waikiki Beach and must maintain it in an attractive condition. As swimming and water sports are such pleasant attractions, water quality must be maintained. In the past there have been occasions when the beaches have had to be closed temporarily because of water pollution.

Kilauea will continue to erupt, and visitors to Hawaii will continue to be attracted to the volcano district. There is little that is under the control of people living in the islands that can change the attraction of a live volcano of such benign accessibility.

An important attraction of the state is

its distinctive multi-ethnic culture. Tourists get to know a few words in the Hawaiian language, and they are treated to performances of Hawaiian music and dance. Hawaii has a distinct advantage in this regard over its principal mainland rival, Miami Beach. Hawaii is viewed as an exotic place with a foreign atmosphere, yet it is safely part of America. This seems to be an unbeatable combination for islands that hope to continue to attract visitors. The culture should be nurtured. The danger is that increasingly Hawaii is becoming just like other places, with the same traffic jams and fast-food restaurants as elsewhere. If the tourist industry is to thrive, the distinctiveness of Hawaii must be preserved.

Undeniably there is some spectacular mountain scenery in the state of Hawaii, and some of the state's landmarks—Diamond Head, for instance—are world famous. But one frequently hears that it is becoming difficult to see Diamond Head and the Koolau Range because of the number of high-rise buildings blocking the view. It seems to be true that developers are notoriously unconcerned about preserving scenic vistas. On Oahu the famous tuff cone, Punchbowl, is obscured by apartment buildings on its slopes. And, to a lesser extent, the same thing is happening on some of the other islands.

Finally, there is the Aloha Spirit. People in Hawaii are, for the most part, friendly and helpful to visitors. They are polite and gracious. They seem to welcome the visitor. But visitors are also the occasional victims of crime, and this has led to some bad publicity. The most important of Hawaii's attributes and one distinctly under local control is the spirit of Aloha. It must be preserved if the visitor industry is to flourish.

Problems

Tourism is the state's principal industry, so the state government has an obvious interest in the industry's good health. Some recent problems have to be dealt with. One is the tendency to build time-sharing condominium apartments as tourist accommodations. These have invoked the ire of some local residents who find that their neighbors change very frequently, have noisy parties, and usually do not care for their apartments as well as do permanent residents. Condominiums also have the undesirable effect of reducing hotel occupancy rates, so that employment in hotels is reduced.

The most important current problem is to counter the unfortunate publicity the islands have received because of crimes against tourists. There is crime in paradise, just as there is elsewhere; it must be brought under control in Hawaii, not just for the sake of the visitor industry but for the benefit of all Hawaii's residents.

REFERENCES

Bank of Hawaii. *Hawaii 81: Annual Economic Review.* Honolulu: Bank of Hawaii, 1981.

Nordhoff, C. *Northern California, Oregon and the Sandwich Islands.* Berkeley, Calif.: Ten Speed Press, 1974. (Centennial printing of 1874 edition).

Scott, E. B. *The Saga of the Sandwich Islands.* Lake Tahoe, Nev.: Sierra-Tahoe Publishing Co., 1968.

State of Hawaii, Department of Planning and Economic Development. *Data Book.* Honolulu: State of Hawaii, Department of Planning and Economic Development, 1981.

Whitney, H. M. *The Hawaiian Guide Book.* Rutland, Vt.: Charles E. Tuttle Co., 1970. (Facsimile reproduction of 1875 edition).

CHAPTER 12

MILITARY BASES

The history of Hawaii as the site for U.S. military installations predates the kingdom's annexation by the United States. In 1887 the kingdom of Hawaii and the United States renewed a treaty of commercial reciprocity, an event crucial to the further development of the sugar industry in the islands. The United States wanted a coaling station for its naval vessels in the Pacific and demanded from the island kingdom future rights to Pearl Harbor as the price to be paid for reciprocity. Hawaii agreed and the land and waters of Pearl Harbor were ceded to the United States. Interestingly, Pearl Harbor was not used for its intended purpose until after the annexation of the islands in 1898.

STRATEGIC LOCATION

U.S. military commanders value Hawaii's location in the central Pacific. No other advantages exist to stationing military units in the islands, since all of the needs of a modern military establishment have to be shipped in. The islands are without crucial natural resources such as oil, and at the time of the cession of Pearl Harbor to the United States for use as a coaling station they were without coal. It is undeniably more expensive to maintain a sizable military establishment in Hawaii than it would be to have the same forces stationed on the U.S. mainland. But the location of naval, air, and ground forces in the islands puts those forces closer to

potential trouble spots in the western Pacific.

U.S. naval units used Pearl Harbor for the first time in the Spanish-American War. Hawaii has been an important base for all conflicts since the islands became a part of the United States, with the exception of World War I, which had little effect in the Pacific. Nearly half a million service personnel were in the islands during the peak mobilization periods in World War II. Hawaii was also an important military way station for units on the way to Korea and Vietnam, during conflicts in those countries.

MILITARY LAND USE

All of the armed forces—Army, Navy, Air Force, Marine Corps, and Coast Guard—have units in Hawaii. In the state as a whole, 5.9 percent of the land is owned or leased by the armed forces. The Army is by far the biggest user of the military lands, with 71 percent of military acreage under its control. The Navy has 25 percent of the military lands; this includes Marine Corps bases, which are under the control of the Secretary of the Navy.

Although for the state as a whole military land use is not excessive, it is for the island of Oahu. Twenty-six percent of Oahu's land is owned or leased by the federal government for military purposes. Since Oahu is but the third largest of the Hawaiian Islands and contains 79 percent of the population,

FIGURE 12.1.   The main gate of Hickam Air Force Base, adjacent to the Honolulu International Airport.

competition for land is keen. Some view the military presence as detrimental to the welfare of the state, but most of Hawaii's residents recognize that the military is an important component of the economy and that military activities in the islands are beneficial.

Military Headquarters

The importance of Hawaii to the U.S. defense establishment is emphasized by the presence in the islands of important Pacific commands. The headquarters for the Commander in Chief Pacific, who commands all military units in the Pacific and Indian Oceans, is located at Camp H. M. Smith in the Honolulu suburb of Aiea. The Commander, Fleet Marine Force Pacific, is also headquartered at Camp Smith; all Marine Corps units in Hawaii, the western Pacific, and aboard navy ships are under his command. Commander, Fleet Marine Force Pacific, is subordinate to Commander in Chief Pacific (CINCPAC).

Another of CINCPAC's subordinate commanders is the Commander in Chief of the Pacific Fleet, with headquarters at Makalapa, a Honolulu neighborhood just outside the gates to the U.S. Naval Base at Pearl Harbor. The fleet has units at San Diego and Long Beach, California, as well as at Pearl Harbor and at various bases in the western Pacific. Units of the fleet are sometimes cruising in the Indian Ocean. In addition to surface ships—aircraft carriers, cruisers, frigates, and the like—the Pacific Fleet has a powerful submarine force, whose commander also has headquarters at Pearl Harbor.

Hickam Air Force Base is the headquarters for the Commander, Pacific Air Forces, whose units include fighter and attack squadrons as well as logistic aircraft of the Military Airlift Command. The largest planes in the world, C5A's of the Military Airlift Command, are regular visitors to Hickam Air Force Base. They provide cargo and personnel transportation for units in Hawaii, as well as using Hawaii as a refueling station on their way to the western Pacific.

Important Army units in Hawaii include the 25th Infantry Division at Schofield Barracks in central Oahu. Headquarters'

FIGURE 12.2.   The main gate at Schofield Barracks in central Oahu.

staffs for a number of Army activities are stationed at Fort Shafter in the Kalihi district of Honolulu.

Important Military Land Holdings and Bases

Aside from the 26 percent of Oahu's land under military control, the largest military base in the islands is the Pohakuloa Training Area on the Big Island. Four percent of that island is devoted to providing land and facilities for training and maneuvers for the 25th Infantry Division and Marine Corps troops stationed on Oahu. Pohakuloa is in the saddle area between the Mauna Loa and Mauna Kea volcanoes; its isolation and extensive acreage provide ideal conditions for training troops in ground tactics under conditions simulating actual combat.

On Oahu the largest single land holding and use by the military is the Army's Schofield Barracks and the associated Kahuku-Kawailoa Training Area. The latter is a large parcel of leased land that extends north from Schofield Barracks almost to the north shore of the island and provides thousands of acres for military exercises and maneuvers.

Other sizable holdings of the Army include Fort Shafter, Tripler Army Medical Center, Fort Derussy, a recreational facility at Pokai Bay on the leeward coast of Oahu, and the Kilauea Military Camp in the Hawaii Volcanoes National Park.

Tripler Army Medical Center is one of the best staffed and equipped military hospitals in the United States. It provides medical and surgical services for military personnel, their dependents, and retirees. In addition, it serves as the Public Health Service hospital for the islands and serves a number of patients from the Trust Territory of the Pacific.

Fort Derussy occupies expensive real estate in Waikiki and includes the Hale Koa, a hotel up to the standard of commercial hotels in the area. The Hale Koa was built with nonappropriated funds (profits from Army, Navy, and Air Force exchanges) and is for the use of military personnel and their dependents. The beach at Fort Derussy is open to the public as are all beaches in the state.

Kilauea Military Camp is a unique facility in the volcano area. There are cabins and dormitory-type housing for military personnel and their dependents from all the services. It contains the usual post exchange activities, including a cafeteria and retail store. In addition, tours of the volcano's attractions are provided at nominal cost. It, too, is financed by nonappropriated funds from the profits of military exchanges in the islands.

Navy and Marine Corps bases include extensive facilities at Pearl Harbor: a naval station, a supply depot, the Pearl Harbor Naval Shipyard, and the Pacific Fleet Submarine Base. Elsewhere on Oahu are the Barbers Point Naval Air Station, in the Ewa district; the Kaneohe Bay Marine Corps Air Station; and extensive ammunition storage areas, principally in Lualualei Valley in the leeward district of Oahu.

The Air Force conducts most of its activities and virtually all of its operational flights from Hickam Air Force Base, located contiguous to the Honolulu International Airport and sharing some of its runways.

Wheeler Air Force Base, in central Oahu adjacent to Schofield Barracks, is a World War II airfield now used for a number of small, miscellaneous Air Force units and activities, as well as flight operations by Army helicopter units.

Other Air Force land holdings are Dillingham Field near Mokuleia on the north shore of Oahu and Bellows Air Force Station on the windward coast, both inactive for ordinary operational use. Bellows has a number of recreational facilities for Air Force personnel, and Dillingham Field is extensively used by the local civilian glider flyers. It is used occasionally for military exercises, but for the most part it can be considered to be a small civilian air field.

The U.S. Coast Guard has a base on Sand Island in Honolulu harbor and operates aircraft from the Naval Air Station at Barbers Point.

All of the military services have housing for their personnel, but service families also live in the local communities. Foremost among the military housing areas is Aliamanu Crater, a tuff cone in which 2,600 housing units have been built. Other housing areas are located on the military bases and at Iroquois Point near the western shore of Pearl Harbor.

The islands of Maui, Kauai, Molokai, and Lanai have no installations of any consequence. Kahoolawe, however, is completely under military control and is used for live bombing and firing exercises. Other live firing areas are in the Kahuku-Kawailoa Training Area and in Makua Valley, a beautiful amphitheater-headed valley on the leeward side of Oahu.

ECONOMIC, SOCIAL, AND CULTURAL IMPACTS

The number of military personnel and their dependents in the islands varies somewhat from year to year, but is always a sizable percentage of the overall population of the state. With approximately 110,000 military personnel and dependents, the military component of the state's population is almost 13 percent of the total. The impact of this military population on the economy and social fabric of the state is accordingly great.

Economic Impacts

Expenditures by the federal government to maintain military establishments in Hawaii are the second largest source of income in the state. There are about 20,000 civilian jobs at military bases, making the federal government one of the biggest employers in the islands. The Pearl Harbor Naval Shipyard is a particularly important provider of jobs for skilled trades people, while the headquarters activities utilize a great many clerical workers as well as middle-management-level civilians.

In addition to the direct employment provided by the military bases, the economy of the state benefits by the presence of service personnel who spend a portion of their incomes locally. This spending can be particularly important in communities near the larger bases, such as Wahiawa near Schofield Barracks.

Periodically there are threats to reduce personnel allowances at military bases or to move units to the mainland. These threats to the Hawaiian economy are treated seriously by the state and the Hawaiian congressional delegation.

Social Impacts

Service personnel are generally young males and many are single. They form a large segment of the young adult population of the state. Some military personnel mingle freely and amicably with local youths; some soldiers, sailors, and airmen, however, rarely leave the military bases, choosing instead to obtain all they require in food, shelter, and recreation from military sources.

There have been instances of less than friendly relations between military personnel and their contemporaries in the local communities, but, in general, the problems are not serious.

Some complaints have been aired that the military has usurped too much prime recreational land and that many desirable beaches are restricted to use by servicemen and servicewomen. In most cases, however, local unit commanders have been able to arrange for sharing of facilities. For example, the air field at Dillingham Field is regularly used for recreational purposes by local glider pilots. On Ford Island, in the middle of Pearl Harbor, there is a World War II landing strip no longer of use for modern high-performance military air operations. Local pilots use it to practice touch-and-go landings; aircraft landings and takeoffs take place in proximity to work at some of the offices used by the Navy on the island.

In communities where military-civilian relationships are liable to be sensitive there are regular meetings among prominent military and civilian personnel to insure that problems are solved before they become serious. In one instance Marine Corps enlisted men from the Kaneohe Bay Marine Corps Air Station were instrumental in improving facilities in a nearby state park. Local residents treated them to a luau (a traditional Hawaiian feast) as a reward for their efforts.

There have been occasional complaints that military housing is in competition with housing built and rented to service families by local developers. Most Hawaiians, however, feel that provision of housing to servicemen and servicewomen on the military bases eases the strain on the housing market in the nearby communities and tends to keep housing costs down. Since Hawaii has the most expensive housing costs in the nation, in many cases exceeding the national average by more than 100 percent, taking the service personnel out of the local housing market is both necessary and beneficial.

Helicopter flights provided by Army aircraft and crews are a regular part of the MEDEVAC service that transports people in need of emergency medical services to hospitals.

Activist groups question the use of Kahoolawe and Makua Valley as bombing targets, and others have complained of the alleged storage of nuclear weapons at some of the Navy ammunition depots. Despite the conflicts between the military, environmentalists, and peace activists, the tolerant attitude that Hawaiians have toward different racial, ethnic, and cultural groups makes the Hawaiian Islands a good place to maintain military establishments.

Cultural Impact

Although military personnel have no distinctive culture in the sense of separate language, religion, art forms, or music, the military forces in Hawaii nevertheless have a distinct cultural impact on the state.

On Armed Forces Day military bases are open to the public and a number of special events take place. The Navy periodically opens ships for public visiting, and foreign navy ships invariably are proudly displayed to the Hawaiian public. An annual naval exercise, with ships from

FIGURE 12.3.   Navy ships, one U.S. and one Australian, side by side on the Honolulu waterfront. The vessels were open to visitors after participating in a Pacific-wide naval exercise.

FIGURE 12.4.   USS *Bowfin,* a restored World War II submarine with an impressive war record, is moored at Pearl Harbor and is visited by both tourists and local residents.

the United States, Australia, New Zealand, Canada, and Japan, usually concludes with an "open house" on several of the ships.

Military museums are found at several of the installations: the submarine base at Pearl Harbor, Schofield Barracks, and Fort Derussy. The *Arizona* Memorial, only recently transferred officially from the Navy to the National Park Service, has been an important visitor attraction for many years; it is popular with tourists and local residents alike. The memorial sits atop the sunken battleship U.S.S. *Arizona*, a victim of the Japanese attack on the U.S. Fleet at Pearl Harbor on December 7, 1941.

A World War II fleet submarine, U.S.S. *Bowfin*, was the oldest ship in the "mothball fleet" at Middle Loch, Pearl Harbor. Because the vessel had a proud combat record and a number of Navy personnel, both active and retired, were interested in establishing a new type of museum, money

was raised to refurbish the ship. It now is open to visitors.

Finally, in Hawaii parades usually have one or more military bands or marching units taking part. The Marine Corps Drum and Bugle Corps and the Army's 25th Division Band are particularly sought after, but the Navy and Air Force also provide music on the occasion of parades and other public events.

REFERENCES

Bank of Hawaii. *Hawaii 80: Annual Economic Review*. Honolulu: Bank of Hawaii, 1980.

Department of Geography, University of Hawaii. *Atlas of Hawaii*. Honolulu: University Press of Hawaii, 1973.

State of Hawaii, Department of Planning and Economic Development. *Data Book*. Honolulu: State of Hawaii, Department of Planning and Economic Development, 1980.

CHAPTER 13

AGRICULTURE: PLANTATIONS AND DIVERSIFIED FARMING

Hawaii is one of the few states that grow sugarcane, and the sugar industry has been important in the islands since its beginnings in the early part of the nineteenth century. Pineapple has been an important crop since the end of that century, and other crops and livestock are also grown.

The history of Hawaii was dominated by the all-important sugar plantations for almost one hundred years, and sugarcane still is grown on thousands of acres of land. Pineapple, also a plantation crop, still is the basis for a large industry, but faces competition and problems that have caused recent declines in production. Papayas, macadamia nuts, coffee, cattle, and several other crops contribute to Hawaii's agricultural income.

HISTORICAL BACKGROUND OF SUGAR PLANTATIONS

Captain Cook found sugarcane growing in the islands when he arrived in Hawaii in 1778; the plant had been brought to the Sandwich Islands from the Polynesian homelands of the original settlers. Hawaiians recognized the food value of the cane and used it as a sweetener. The plants were found at house sites, where they frequently formed windbreaks in addition to being used as an occasional tasty treat. No attempt was made to mill the cane and produce crystalline sugar, however.

The first recorded attempt at sugar production from cane in the islands took place in March 1819 when Don Francisco de Paula Marin, an avid horticulturist, reported that he had extracted juice from the cane. He and others were unsuccessful at producing crystalline sugar, but in 1825 sugar was finally crystallized.

Ten years later, Ladd and Company founded the first successful milling enterprise at Koloa, on the island of Kauai. In 1837, when the first commercial crop was harvested, 2.1 tn (1.9 t) of raw sugar were marketed. The industry grew rapidly. By 1838 twenty mills were in operation in the islands, eighteen animal powered and two water powered.

Three problems had to be solved: land, water, and labor. Land was acquired by lease from the *alii* and in some cases by grant or lease from the king. Initially the *alii* also provided the labor, by simply assigning the work to the *makaainana* who occupied the land in a classical feudal arrangement. The problem of water to irrigate the notoriously thirsty sugarcane plants was eventually solved by a number of large irrigation projects that brought water from the wet windward sides of the islands to the sunny leeward regions.

The labor problem continued, however. Hawaiians did not take to plantation life, preferring instead to work on their individual small farms or to seek employment in Honolulu, particularly in the rapidly growing port area. Moreover, the Hawaiian population was decreasing at an alarming rate as newly introduced diseases of European origin took their toll of native people who had no natural immunity. Sugar planters realized that they needed additional sources of cheap farm labor.

Various immigrant groups worked on the plantations, as the Hawaiian government permitted the planters to bring in foreign labor under contract. Among the immigrants were Pacific Islanders, Scandinavians, Poles, Russians, Germans, Chinese, Japanese, Portuguese, Filipinos, and Koreans. Some of the initial immigrant-labor groups did not remain long on the plantations, but the arrival of the Chinese in 1852 heralded an influx of Asians who worked efficiently and for relatively long contract periods. In 1868 the first Japanese immigrants arrived, followed in 1878 by Portuguese. Filipino immigration began in 1910, and Filipinos are currently the most numerous of the ethnic groups to be found on the plantations. Intermarriage and the migration of each immigrant group from plantations to cities resulted in the mix of cultures and peoples that characterizes Hawaii today.

Eyewitness Accounts of the Industry

Two years before the arrival of the first Japanese workers to Hawaii the islands were visited by Mark Twain, who provided some valuable descriptions of the sugar industry. In 1866 he wrote, "This country is the king of the sugar world, as far as astonishing productivity is concerned" (Twain 1975, 257). The "astonishing productivity" referred to was as much as 13,000 lb/acre (5,900 kg/ha) on "unmanured soil" and averaged 6,000 lb/acre (2,700 kg/ha) on the island of Maui. One hundred years later productivity on the Hawaiian plantations reached 11.12 tn/acre (10.08 t/ha), but at the time that Twain was so impressed with Hawaiian sugar yields, in Louisiana yields were but 2,500 lb/acre (1,135 kg/ha).

At the time of Mark Twain's visit there were twenty-nine small plantations in Hawaii, and the total annual yield was 27 million lb (12,258,000 kg). The average pay for a sugar worker was $100 per year, which, according to Twain, was about the same as the cost to feed and clothe a slave. Since the sugar planters did not have to incur the initial purchase price of a slave, estimated to be between $500 and $1,000, the economics of labor on the plantations was quite favorable.

Sugar was fetching a good price on the American market, more than twice the price of Louisiana cane. This favorable price differential was partially offset by a sugar duty on Hawaiian sugar of three cents per pound.

Then, as now, there were some distinct advantages to growing cane in Hawaii. The cane crop never fails, it can be cut whenever ripe, and the mills can be operated year round. Twain's observations were that sugar matured in eighteen to twenty months on Maui's low ground, but took twenty-two to thirty-six months to ripen on the Ulupala Kua plantation at 2,000 to 3,500 ft (610 to 1,067 m) elevation. In the hot, dry, sunny environs of Lahaina cane was ready to be cut in nine to ten months, and the average ripening time for the islands of Oahu, Hawaii, and Kauai was one year.

Sugar plantations were changing the appearance of the land.

> Being painted snow white, the mill building and the tall chimney stand out in strong contrast with the surrounding bright green

cane fields. A long elevated flume in front, and a laboring overshot wheel of large diameter; at one side a broad inclosure peopled with coolies spreading "trash" to dry; half a dozen Kanakas feeding cane to the whirling cylinders of the mill and a noisy procession of their countrymen driving cartloads of the material to their vicinity and dumping it— these things give the place a business-like aspect which is novel in the slumbering Sandwich Islands. (Twain 1975, 265)

The Kanakas referred to by Twain earned an average of $6 to $8 per month and were serving on written contracts. Their pay was somewhat lower than the average of $100 per year for other plantation laborers.

Twain was keenly observant and witnessed what he saw as the eventual demise of the Hawaiian race. "The sugar product is rapidly augmenting every year, and day by day the Kanaka race is passing away" (Twain 1975, 270). What Twain did not foresee was that improved health and living conditions and the intermarriage of Hawaiians with other racial groups would save the Hawaiians from extinction. Today, approximately 20 percent of Hawaii's population is part-Hawaiian.

Hawaiian labor was augmented by what Twain called coolie labor. The Chinese immigrants, according to Twain, were former pirates, cripples, and lunatics. At least one of their characteristics made them good workers when carefully supervised since "their former trade of cutting throats has made them uncommonly handy at cutting cane" (Twain 1975, 271).

Charles Nordhoff (1974, 56–64) had some other observations about Hawaii's sugar industry in 1874. He described the great yields, as did Twain, particularly on the island of Maui, but in the intervening eight years profits had diminished and bankruptcies had occurred. Among the numerous problems were variability in climates, procedures, and cane types, as well as difficulties in economically shipping the sugar to the mainland United States. Honolulu was the only good port, while Kahului, Hanalei, Nawiliwili and one or two

Oahu plantations had "tolerable" landings. There was a need to ship directly from island plantations to the United States rather than transshipping the milled sugar via Honolulu.

By 1874 the agency system was well established, and the agents' fees, debts, high interest rates, and distant markets were becoming problems. Many of the plantations were owned by "absentees," and this too was a problem. In addition to the high costs of building and maintaining irrigation systems, there was a need for taro fields, pastures, and sources of wood nearby. Nordhoff concluded that cooperation among the various growers was needed to alleviate these difficulties.

Reciprocity Treaty

Many of Hawaii's problems were solved by the Reciprocity Treaty of 1876. Hawaiian sugar had enjoyed a favorable market in the United States during the years of the Civil War, when the southern states were not selling sugar to the north. After the war, however, Hawaiian sugar had to compete with American-grown cane, and the three cents per pound duty was troublesome.

The Reciprocity Treaty contained only two articles. The first listed the Hawaiian products that could enter the United States duty free. The most important of these was "Muscavado, brown or other unrefined sugar, meaning hereby the grades of sugar heretofore commonly imported from the Hawaiian Islands, and now known in the markets of San Francisco and Portland as 'Sandwich Island Sugar'." An associated set of products, "Sirups of sugar-cane, melado and molasses," was also covered by the treaty, as well as arrowroot, castor oil, bananas, nuts, vegetables, hides and skins, rice, pulu, seeds, plants, shrubs or trees, and tallow (Whitney 1970, 130).

Article 2 enumerated the American products that could enter Hawaii duty free. This list was long, containing both agricultural and manufactured goods. Since the Hawaiian market was small and of no great consequence to American producers, while Hawaii's economic life depended on sales of sugar to the United States, the treaty was criticized by some as one-sided. Nevertheless the United States obtained great political gains by the treaty. Thereafter Hawaii would become an economic dependent of the United States and eventually would become part of the nation.

Industry Changes and Improvements

After 1876 sugar was without rival in the economy of the islands. The contract-labor system provided the workers needed for the expanding industry and at the same time changed the cultural geography of the islands. According to Nordhoff, the system was to be praised, as it provided for regular hours of employment, decent food and pay, churches, and medical care. Sugar workers did not always agree, and there were a number of attempts to organize to gain better pay and working conditions. These eventually succeeded, but not without a good deal of labor strife. In 1946 the sugar workers, now represented by the International Longshoremen's and Warehousemen's Union, struck for two and a half months. They won better pay and shorter hours, but lost some of the benefits provided by the plantation owners under the old system of paternalism.

While labor was organizing, so too was management. The cooperation among growers first recommended by Nordhoff was achieved with the formation of the Planter's Labor and Supply Company in 1882, which later became the Hawaiian Sugar Planters' Association in 1895. In 1906 the California and Hawaiian Sugar Refining Corporation (C and H) was founded, and thereafter all Hawaiian-grown cane was marketed by C and H.

During its history the Hawaiian sugar industry has been marked by increasing mechanization, higher yields (both per worker and per acre), and higher wages for the workers. In 1853 steam replaced animal- or water-power on a Hawaiian plantation at the old Ladd and Company mill

at Koloa, Kauai, and thereafter other improvements followed in planting, harvesting, milling, and transportation. Yields were improved by the introduction of new strains of cane, specially bred for Hawaii's climate and soils. These improvements in all phases of the sugar industry of the islands were achieved largely through work by the Hawaiian Sugar Planters' Association, which maintains strong research facilities and efforts. Generally increasing yields and sufficiently high prices have thus far been able to keep up with high labor costs; the industry, while by no means the economic power it was in the past, is important to the economy of Hawaii.

SUGAR IN HAWAII TODAY: LAND USE

Sugar is grown commercially on the islands of Hawaii, Maui, Oahu, and Kauai (1980 production is shown in Figure 13.1). In 1979 the sugar industry accounted for 259,906 acres (105,262 ha) in the state. Of this, 218,773 acres (88,603 ha) were devoted to growing of cane: 91,683 acres (31,132 ha) on Hawaii; 47,719 acres (19,326 ha) on Maui; 45,812 acres (18,554 ha) on Kauai; and 33,559 acres (13,591 ha) on Oahu. In addition to the cultivated land, sugar companies used 41,133 acres (16,659 ha) for roads, reservoirs, mill sites, and irrigation systems.

Climate on Sugar Lands

Figure 13.1 shows that on the islands of Hawaii and Kauai some cultivated acreage is in the wet windward regions; additional acreage on those islands and the sugar fields on the islands of Maui and Oahu are in dryer leeward areas. "Average annual rainfall on some sugarcane land exceeds 200 inches, while on others it is as low as 15 inches" (Hawaiian Sugar Planters' Association 1980, 5). Consequently, irrigation is necessary on some acreage. About 55 percent of the sugar lands in the state are irrigated; these fields are higher producers, yielding 63 percent

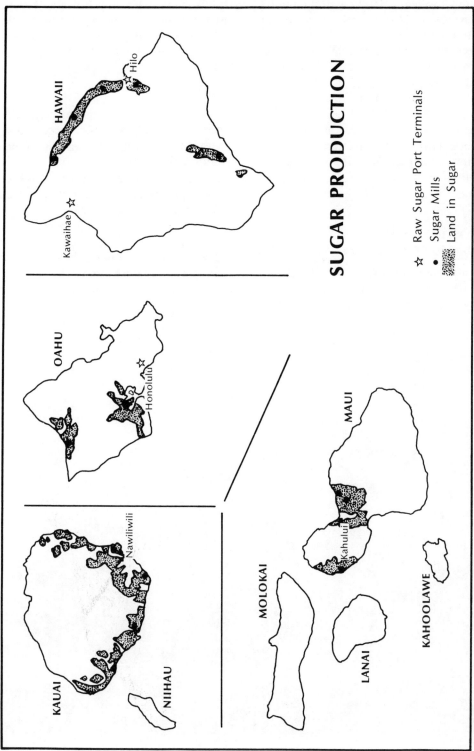

SUGAR PRODUCTION

☆ Raw Sugar Port Terminals
● Sugar Mills
▨ Land in Sugar

HAWAII

Hilo

Kawaihae

OAHU

Honolulu

KAUAI

Nawiliwili

NIIHAU

MOLOKAI

MAUI

Kahului

LANAI

KAHOOLAWE

FIGURE 13.1

of the sugar in the islands.

Although sugar requires tremendous quantities of water, the best yields are in the sunnier areas where there is a potential for increased photosynthesis. Well-irrigated fields in the hottest, sunniest regions produce the best yields.

The growing season in Hawaii is virtually year round; the average age of a sugarcane crop in the islands at harvest is two years. These two characteristics are a consequence of Hawaii's climate with its predominately winter rainfall.

OPERATIONAL METHODS IN THE SUGAR INDUSTRY

The operations required to produce sugar in the islands have been adapted to Hawaii's soils, climate, and economy. Plant-ing, harvesting, milling, transportation, refining, and marketing are all carried out to make best use of the resources of the state and the characteristics of the market, generally the western part of the United States.

Planting

Sugarcane is propagated vegetatively: short pieces of cane, or "seed," are cut from the harvested cane and subsequently planted. The planting is done completely mechanically, with machines dropping the seed cane in rows and covering the plantings with soil. Since sugarcane will grow from the stubble left after the cane is cut, it is not necessary to replant after each harvest—ratoon crops can be obtained from the original planting. Anywhere from two to four ratoons are usually harvested before the fields are prepared for replanting.

FIGURE 13.2.   Mechanized planting of sugarcane on the Waipio Peninsula, Oahu. The machine lays the seed cane into prepared furrows, then covers the cane with earth.

FIGURE 13.3. Harvesting sugarcane, Oahu. The grab crane is used to load the cut cane into trucks.

Harvesting

Harvesting, too, is a mechanized operation. First the acreage to be harvested is burned in order to destroy the leaves without harming the stalks, which contain the sugar. This avoids the necessity of bringing the useless cane leaves into the mill, where they would then have to be disposed of as waste. Burning is carefully controlled and is done in small patches, usually about 15 acres (6 ha).

Following the burning, while the field is still smoking, the mechanized harvesting operation begins. On most plantations two tractorlike machines are used: the pushrake and the lilikoi. The pushrake cuts the cane at ground level and pushes it into rows; grab cranes subsequently are used to load the cane onto trucks. The lilikoi has comblike rakers in front that scoop up the cane stalks left in the field by the pushrake and push them into bundles to be picked up by the crane.

Even with the operation of the pushrake and the lilikoi some stalks of cane are missed. These are cut by hand by the one employee not operating a machine, the "scavenger," who uses an old-fashioned cane knife to cut the remaining stalks, which are then added to the piles of cane.

A V-cutter is used on some of the plantations instead of the pushrake and lilikoi. The machine has a V-shaped blade with a vertical cutting wheel at the front. On some of the nonirrigated fields mechanical harvesters cut the cane into short lengths and clean it with forced air.

Irrigation

Sugar planters in Hawaii were primarily responsible for developing many of the island's water systems, and they still operate an extensive system of wells, tunnels,

FIGURE 13.4.   Although almost all sugarcane is cut mechanically in the islands, there is still some hand cutting done. Here, seed cane, which would be damaged too severely if mechanically harvested, is cut by hand.

ditches, flumes, irrigation troughs, pumps, and pipes for drip (trickle) irrigation.

Furrow irrigation, in which the water is brought to the field by flumes and portable irrigation troughs and then allowed to pour into the furrows, is still the principal irrigation method employed. But the drip system is now being used on about 30,000 acres (11,000 ha) or approximately 25 percent of the sugar lands. In the drip method, flexible hoses with small holes are laid in the fields. The water is thus brought more directly into contact with the individual plants, and the method is more efficient in its use of water. Moreover, the drip method can be automated, and therefore requires less labor for its operation.

Milling

Thirteen sugar mills grind the cane and extract the sugar. In the milling process, after the cane is washed and passed through rollers to squeeze out the juice, the bagasse (waste) from the milling process must be disposed of. Bagasse, after some processing, now is being used extensively as a fuel for mill operations. On some plantations all power required for milling is provided by burning bagasse, and in some cases excess electrical power is sold to the electric utility companies.

The cane juice is then clarified and centrifuged, the resultant products being molasses and crystalline sugar. The sugar crystals produced are "raw sugar," which must go through a refining process before becoming acceptable as a food item.

Transportation

Raw sugar is transported by truck to the sugar loading terminals at the ports, where it is loaded on board ships in bulk.

Specially designed sugar ships are operated by C and H to transport the bulk raw sugar from terminals in Hawaii to Crockett, California, the location of the large C and H refinery.

Refining and Sales

The refining process consists of melting the raw sugar, then purifying and recrystallizing it. C and H operates two refineries, the large one at Crockett, California, and a much smaller one at Aiea, Oahu. The Crockett refinery has a capacity to melt 960,000 tn (870,720 t) of raw sugar annually, while the Aiea refinery melts only 40,000 tn (36,280 t) per year, all of it for the local Hawaiian market. The output of the Crockett refinery is marketed as C and H sugar throughout the western continental United States; C and H is the refining and marketing arm of the Hawaiian sugar industry.

ORGANIZATION AND MANAGEMENT

The Hawaiian sugar industry is operated as an agricultural marketing association and cooperative under the Capper-Volstead Act. The stock of C and H is owned by fifteen sugar companies in the islands in substantially the same proportion as the amount of raw sugar each company provides to the C and H refineries and markets through C and H.

The Sugar Companies and Independent Growers

Table 13.1 shows, by island, the sugar companies, acreages, and production for the year 1979. Twelve of the sugar companies both grow and mill their sugar; two, Gay and Robinson and Mauna Kea Sugar Co., are growers only, using the milling facilities of other companies. Hilo Coast Processing Co., a processor only, provides milling services for Mauna Kea Sugar Co. and for 292 independent growers organized as the United Cane Planter Cooperative.

Olokele Sugar Co. mills its own cane as well as that produced by Gay and Robinson. The small acreage, 6,143 acres (2,488 ha) of the United Cane Planter Cooperative is either owned by individual growers or leased from larger sugar companies.

A fairly wide range of productivity is evident. The best yields, up to 14.09 tn/acre (31.56 t/ha), are generally in the hotter, sunnier leeward districts.

With the exception of the United Cane Planter Cooperative, all sugar companies in the islands are subsidiaries of one of the so-called Big Five companies: Castle and Cooke, Alexander and Baldwin, C. Brewer, Theo H. Davies, and AMFAC. The Big Five got their starts as agents or factors for sugar growers and have expanded both their agricultural and other business operations. Cooperative arrangements in milling, harvesting and marketing (through C and H) are facilitated by the consolidation of ownership in the hands of five companies.

Employment and Wages

Hawaiian sugar workers are unionized and are exceptionally well-paid agricultural employees. As of August 1, 1982, the lowest classification of worker received a minimum wage of $6.70 per hour. For the highest grade of worker the pay rate was $9.49 per hour. In 1981 the total payroll for sugar workers was $157,286,500. All employees are full time; there is no seasonal employment in the Hawaiian sugar industry.

While it is clear that sugar workers in the islands are well paid in comparison to other agricultural employees in the United States and overseas, the sugar industry in Hawaii does not provide employment for many. The industry is highly mechanized. Much of the mechanization has been developed by the work of the Experiment Station of the Hawaiian Sugar Planters' Association, which has also been instrumental in developing new and improved varieties of cane and devising better pest-control procedures.

Table 13.1
Hawaiian Sugar Companies with Acreage and Production for 1979 (Raw Value)

	Total Canefield Acreage		Acreage Harvested		Production	
	acres	hectares	acres	hectares	tons/ acre	metric tons/ hectare
HAWAII						
Hilo Coast Processing Co. (Processor only)					9.39[a]	21.03
Mauna Kea Sugar Co. (Grower only)	17,722	7,177	8,478	3,434		
United Cane Planter Coop. (Grower only) .... (292 member-growers)	6,143	2,488	3,567	1,445		
Davies Hamakua Sugar Co. ...	35,636	14,433	15,008	6,078	10.52	23.56
Ka'u Sugar Co., Inc.	16,037	6,495	5,367	2,174	11.32	25.36
Puna Sugar Co., Ltd.	16,145	2,648	6,944	2,812	8.16	18.27
TOTAL HAWAII	91,683	37,132	39,364	15,942	9.85	22.05
KAUAI						
Gay and Robinson (Grower only) ....[b]	2,667	1,080	1,259	510	14.09	31.56
Kekaha Sugar Co., Ltd.	8,066	3,267	4,039	1,636	12.10	27.09
The Lihue Plantation Co. ...	17,347	7,026	9,117	3,692	8.67	19.41
McBryde Sugar Co., Ltd.	12,905	5,227	6,486	2,627	8.80	19.78
Olokele Sugar Co., Ltd.	4,827	1,955	2,344	949	12.68	28.40
TOTAL KAUAI	45,812	18,554	23,245	9,414	10.00	22.40
MAUI						
Hawaiian Commercial & Sugar Co.	34,250	13,871	14,214	5,757	12.40	27.78
Pioneer Mill Co., Ltd.	8,776	3,554	4,402	1,783	11.53	25.83
Wailuku Sugar Co.	4,693	1,901	2,370	960	10.89	24.40
TOTAL MAUI	47,719	19,326	20,986	8,499	12.05	26.99
OAHU						
Oahu Sugar Co., Ltd.	18,271	7,400	9,480	3,839	11.30	25.31
Waialua Sugar Co., Ltd. ...	15,288	6,192	7,535	3,052	10.49	23.48
TOTAL OAHU	33,559	13,591	17,015	6,891	10.94	24.49
TOTAL--ALL ISLANDS	218,773	80,603	100,610	40,747	10.60	23.73

Source: Adapted from Hawaiian Sugar Planters' Association 1981.

[a]Includes production of Mauna Kea Sugar Co. & United Cane Planter Coop.
[b]Gay & Robinson sugarcane milled by Olokele Sugar Co., Ltd.

THE FUTURE OF SUGAR IN HAWAII

The population of the Hawaiian Islands is now nearly 1 million (964,624 according to the 1980 census), and land is becoming increasingly more valuable. The economy of the state has diversified. Agricultural industries are no longer the kingpins of the Hawaiian economy and there are many who wonder whether the land used by sugar plantations might not be better used for housing and other industries. There is enormous pressure to convert land to non-agricultural uses.

The success of the Hawaiian sugar industry to date has been due to generally increasing productivity that has kept pace with increasing wage rates. Until the end of 1974 the U.S. Sugar Act maintained a degree of stability in sugar prices by controlling the supply of raw sugar in the United States through a series of quotas for the various domestic and foreign producers. Since the demise of the Sugar Act, sugar prices have fluctuated as demand has risen and fallen compared to supply. The instability of sugar prices has created additional difficulties for the industry in Hawaii.

Sugar acreage has been maintained at around 220,000 acres (89,100 ha) for the period from 1908 to the present. Productivity measured by tons of sugar per acre increased from five or less in the years up to 1923 and has been generally increasing since. The peak year, 1966, produced an average for Hawaiian plantations of 11.2 tn/acre (10.09 t/ha). Production has decreased somewhat since then, causing industry leaders to wonder whether or not productivity can continue to keep up with rising expenses. It should be noted, however, that productivity per acre in Hawaii is close to being the highest in the world and far exceeds figures for plantations in the continental United States. In Florida 1979–1980 yields were but 3.46 tn/acre (3.14 t/ha); yields in Texas and Puerto Rico were even less with the former at 2.70 tn/acre (2.45 t/ha) and the latter 2.25 (2.04).

While Hawaiian cane sugar certainly ranks high compared to other competitive cane industries, sugar beets and sweeteners made from corn syrups must be considered. "During the past 17 years consumption of corn sweeteners has increased from about 13 pounds per capita to 38 pounds per capita. Per capita consumption of other caloric sweeteners—sugar, honey and other syrups—has declined slightly during the same period." (Hawaiian Sugar Planters' Association 1980, 19).

Yet another problem for sugar in the islands may be a shortage of water. Sugar is a prodigious user of water: it is said that it takes a ton of water to raise a pound of sugar. As water supplies grow more critical it may be tempting for government decision makers to give preference in the use of land to less-thirsty industries or uses. Much of the water use in the sugar industry is for irrigation, and much of this water returns to the groundwater reservoirs of the islands; nevertheless sugar competes for available water with industry and urban uses.

Finally, the sugar industry is no longer vital to the economy of the state. Tourism now is. Hence, public policies will undoubtedly support the growth of tourism in the islands, perhaps neglecting the sugar industry. The parent companies in the sugar industry are large and diversified and might use the land for more profitable residential or recreational purposes. Already in central Oahu much land has been taken out of sugar production as new housing communities have been built. This trend is likely to continue. If the population of the islands increases only moderately, the sugar industry will probably be maintained at close to its present level. But if population growth continues in the next decade at the level of the 1970s, less and less sugar acreage will be planted in Hawaii.

PINEAPPLE

Both fresh and canned Hawaiian-grown pineapple is an important product in supermarkets in Hawaii and on the U.S. mainland. Pineapple is so closely associated with Hawaii that there is the erroneous impression that the fruit is native to the islands, or was a very early introduction. In fact, pineapple is a relative newcomer.

Pineapple occupies far less agricultural land than does sugar and has considerably less impact on the economy of the state.

Historical Background

At the end of the nineteenth century sugar so dominated the Hawaiian economy that there was real fear that unless additional agricultural products were introduced, the economy of the islands would be in danger of collapse should something unforeseen happen to the sugar crop. Efforts were made to diversify the agricultural economy with rubber, coffee, and sisal; all attempts were unsuccessful. The pineapple industry finally succeeded.

Sugarcane was growing in Hawaii long before 1778, having been introduced by early Polynesian settlers, but pineapple was unknown to the islands before 1813. In that year Don Francisco de Paula Marin, the Spaniard who was responsible for so many horticultural introductions, reported that he had planted pineapple. The variety was apparently Wild Kona, a species found growing wild in the 1880s.

The California gold rush inspired the first attempt at commercial pineapple growing in Hawaii; 12,000 pineapples were shipped to California in 1849 and 1850, but the enterprise was not profitable.

In 1882 the partnership of Ackerman and Muller began a canning operation in the North Kona district of the Big Island. The firm of Theo H. Davies, then primarily an agent for sugar growers, tried unsuccessfully to market the fruit for them. The Wild Kona pineapple did not have the sweet flavor that consumers desired.

In the same year John Kidwell arrived in the islands; four years later he imported from Florida the first commercially successful variety of pineapple, the Smooth Cayenne. The fruits were planted near Waipahu, Oahu; a later crop was planted in Manoa Valley and a cannery built. But the enterprise failed.

Hawaii's successful pineapple industry has long been associated with James Dole, who came to the islands at the turn of the century, having recently graduated from Harvard University. Dole had family connections in Hawaii: Daniel Dole, an early missionary, was his grand uncle, and Sanford Dole, first president of the Hawaiian Republic, was distantly related. In 1901 the Hawaiian Pineapple Company was organized, and 75,000 pineapples were planted near Wahiawa, Oahu. In that year the company's payroll was $4,720. In 1903 the first pineapple pack consisted of 1,893 cases, and in that same year a cannery was built. The primitive canning operation required that broken slices of the fruit be inserted into holes in the tops of the cans, which were later soldered shut.

In the following year the cannery was enlarged as was the output. The pack of 8,810 cases in 1904 soared to 25,022 cases in 1905. The success of Dole's new industry created confidence in the agricultural enterprise by others; Oahu Railway and Land Company extended its narrow gauge line from Waipahu to Wahiawa, and the American Can Company established a plant in Hawaii.

The success of pineapple as a plantation crop led others to grow the fruit. By 1908 there were eight pineapple packers in the islands, and a campaign was begun to sell "Hawaiian Pineapple" in the United States.

Pineapple plants could be grown and harvested much more efficiently than they could be prepared for canning. The first real innovation in the Dole cannery was the invention in 1914 of the Ginaca machine. This device could size, peel, core, and cut the ends from the pineapple and could handle 100 fruits per minute. Ginaca's invention is still the heart of the cannery operation.

Pineapple research was begun in 1914, initially under the Hawaiian Sugar Planters' Association, which started a pineapple research branch. In 1923 a separate Pineapple Research Institute was founded, which was in operation until 1971, when Dole Pineapple withdrew from the institute and set up its own research facilities. In 1973 additional pineapple research was begun at the University of Hawaii.

Expansion of the industry was accelerated in 1922 with the purchase of the island of Lanai and additional acreage on Oahu by the Dole company. In that year 30,000 additional acres (12,000 ha) were acquired. Expenditures on Lanai totaled $4 million and included the building of Lanai City and a small harbor at Kaumalapau.

After World War II, 2,000 Filipinos were

brought to the islands on 3-year farm labor contracts, and at the height of the industry (1958) there were ten pineapple companies growing and canning fruit in the territory. Pineapple plantations were begun on the islands of Molokai and Kauai, and intensified production took place on Oahu and Lanai. In addition to seven Hawaiian pineapple companies, there were three big mainland fruit companies with plantations and canneries in Hawaii.

But changes in economic conditions forced the industry to retrench, and today only three companies still do business in Hawaii: Del Monte, Dole, and Maui Land and Pineapple Company. The Dole and Del Monte canneries are in the Iwilei district of Honolulu; the Maui cannery is in Wailuku. The Dole cannery is the largest fruit cannery in the world.

THE PINEAPPLE INDUSTRY TODAY

The Smooth Cayenne (*Ananas comosus*), a member of the Bromeliad family, is a collective fruit. It grows as high as 2 or 3 ft (0.6 or 0.9 m) and spreads to 3 or 4 ft (0.9 or 1.2 m). Flowering occurs at twelve to fourteen months. The fruits that develop are almost seedless, and they are ready for harvesting after about twenty months. The initial fruit weighs about 5 lb (2.27 kg); but second, or successive, crops—ratoons—weigh only about half that. The first fruiting produces one fruit per plant and the ratoon crops two, since the usual procedure is to leave two shoots after the first harvesting, and each shoot produces its own separate fruit.

Planting

A field that is to be replanted after one or more ratoon crops have been harvested is plowed, and the old plants are cut up and incorporated into the soil. Sometimes the old plants are burned, and the resultant debris is plowed into the prepared field.

Tractorlike machines fumigate the ground, apply fertilizer, and lay strips of black plastic. The latter, which has precut holes equally spaced on both sides, serves as a mulch. It conserves moisture, retards the growth of weeds, prevents evaporation of the fumigants, hastens growth by keeping the soil warm, and increases the action of certain beneficial bacteria.

Actual planting is done by hand and is decidedly hard, "stoop" labor. The crowns, slips, and shoots of the pineapple plant are used, and each is hand planted in the precut holes. A skilled planter can plant several thousand plants in a single day.

Growing Pineapple

The pineapple usually requires little or no irrigation when grown in typical Hawaiian locations, but it does require a good deal of care if maximum yields are to be obtained. Herbicides must be applied, as well as liquid fertilizer, hormones, insecticides, and iron sulphate. The latter is required despite the high iron content of Hawaiian soils, because the pineapple plant is incapable of absorbing the iron through its root structure.

All of these operations, plus occasional sprinkling with water when conditions are exceptionally dry, are carried out with the use of a mechanical boom sprayer.

In Hawaii pineapple is grown at elevations as high as 3,000 ft (914 m) and in locations where the annual precipitation is as little as 25 in. (63.5 cm). Hence pineapple does not compete with sugar for available land or water, although it is possible to grow the two crops on adjacent acreage. This is done in central Oahu, and occasionally land is shifted from one crop to another.

Harvesting

Picking pineapple is a labor-intensive operation, since it has not been possible to mechanize the harvesting process completely. Pickers walk behind a boom on which a conveyor belt runs. The hand-picked fruits are placed on the belt and conveyed to a bin suspended from a truck mechanism. As the truck drives slowly

FIGURE 13.5. A pineapple field in central Oahu, with the Waianae Range in the background. Note the plantings on the moderate foothill slopes.

through the field on previously prepared dirt roads, the pickers keep pace. If the fruit is destined for the cannery, the crowns are removed by the pickers, and a certain number of crowns are saved for use as planting material. If the fruit is to be marketed as fresh fruit, the crowns are left on. Despite the hot sun pineapple pickers must wear heavy clothing to protect them from the leaves of the plant, which are very sharp.

Land Use in the Pineapple Industry

At the beginning of 1983 there were about 40,000 acres (15,800 ha) planted in pineapple on three islands: Lanai, Maui, and Oahu. The most recent loss of acreage was due to the closing of a 3,300 acre (1,300 ha) plantation of the Del Monte Corporation on the island of Molokai, leav-

ing the island without pineapple for the first time in decades. Total acreage was down considerably from 1969, when 62,400 acres (25,272 ha) were in pineapple on four islands. Now there are 12,000 acres (4,860 ha) on Oahu, 12,000 acres on Maui and 16,000 acres (6,500 ha) on Lanai. The latter, all in one plantation of the Dole company, is said to be the largest pineapple plantation in the world.

Production and Sales

Pineapple production in 1979 was 681,000 tn (617,667 t), up slightly from the 675,000 tn (612,225 t) of the previous year, but far below 1969's production of 915,000 tn (829,905 t). The 1979 crop was valued at $190.2 million.

Hawaiian pineapple is in competition with foreign-grown and processed fruit. The pineapple that comes from outside of Hawaii has the advantage of much lower labor and production costs, particularly the canned product. The one advantage enjoyed by Hawaiian pineapple in its principal market, the mainland United States, is lower transportation costs for the fresh fruit. Consequently, the concentration in recent years has been on increasing the marketing of fresh fruit and decreasing the cannery output.

Employment

Most of Hawaii's pineapple is harvested during the summer months, and part-time labor is utilized for picking and cannery work. Full-time employees are unionized, and high wages (for agricultural workers) are the norm. The use of temporary laborers during the summer months, who are paid much lower wages, reduces the labor costs considerably. In 1979 there were 4,979 full-time-equivalent workers in the industry, with an average annual pay of $12,402 per employee. During the 1970s, as earnings per full-time-equivalent employee rose from $6,759, the number of full-time-equivalent employees dropped from 7,779 to the 1979 figure of 4,979. Were it possible to completely mechanize the planting and picking process, employment would drop even further.

The Future

Hawaiian-grown pineapple is in competition not only with the foreign-grown products but with other canned fruits as well. It is difficult to predict what the future of the Hawaiian pineapple industry will be, but it is clear that the trends in recent years are cause to be pessimistic. One large mainland company, Libby, McNeil and Libby, sold its Molokai acreage to Dole, which tried unsuccessfully to run the plantation at a profit. When Dole ceased operations, pineapple acreage was reduced drastically. Pineapple is grown on land eminently suitable for urban development, and much acreage has been lost in central Oahu to housing developments.

FIGURE 13.6. This pineapple is actually a water tower on the grounds of the Dole Pineapple cannery. Located in the Iwilei district of Honolulu, it is the largest fruit cannery in the world.

On the optimistic side is the increase in the fresh-fruit market for Hawaiian pineapple. The fruit can be shipped in refrigerated containers to the West Coast of the United States in five days, and air shipments take only hours. The fresh-fruit market is profitable and is increasing in volume.

Castle and Cooke, Inc., parent company of Dole Pineapple, also has pineapple plantations in other tropical areas, chiefly the Philippines, where production costs are much lower than in Hawaii. But the Dole cannery is the world's largest and naturally there is reluctance to discontinue its operation, in view of the large investment in it. Another large investment in pineapple is the island of Lanai, with its 16,000-acre (6,480-hectare) plantation, Lanai City community development, and the harbor at Kaumalapau, on the southwestern coast of the island, constructed especially for the shipment of pineapple to the Honolulu cannery.

Another factor in the competition for land use in the islands, particularly on Oahu, is a potential shortage of water. Pineapple is not the prodigious user of water that sugar is. If there is to be a competition for land between urban development and agriculture, from the standpoint of water usage it would be wiser to maintain pineapple plantations in preference to sugar acreage.

Pineapple will continue to be produced in the islands for some time, but it is difficult to see how production can be increased, and in fact the industry probably will get smaller.

DIVERSIFIED FARMING

All agricultural activities other than the growing and processing of sugar and pineapple are arbitrarily classified here as diversified farming. Among the more important crops grown in the islands are papayas, macadamia nuts, coffee, and fruits and vegetables for the local market. Diversified agriculture consists both of crops grown for export and those grown to feed the population of Hawaii.

Also included are raising cattle, for both beef and dairy purposes, and the production of poultry, eggs, and pigs. Not included is the growing of marijuana (*pakalolo*), an illegal activity for which few accurate statistics are available (it is possible that the most valuable crop in the islands is *pakalolo*, far surpassing sugar).

State Agricultural Policy

The islands are growing in population, and there is intense pressure to reclassify agricultural land and make it available for urban uses. The stated policy of the state government is to resist reclassification and thus preserve land for agricultural uses. The reason for this policy is to maintain the islands' current degree of self-sufficiency in food production. Hawaii does not produce nearly enough food crops or animal products to feed its population. Food imports from the U.S. mainland are necessary—taking additional land out of agricultural production would only make the lack of self-sufficiency worse.

Another reason for maintaining land in agriculture is to preserve an old, traditional life-style practiced by some part-Hawaiians: raising crops, particularly taro, on small plots of land and remaining in rural areas,

far from the hustle and bustle of the modern cities and towns.

Between 1970 and 1980 the overall number of farms decreased by 200 and the farm acreage by 330,000 acres (133,650 ha) (Table 13.2). The monetary value of both diversified crops and livestock increased considerably, but some of that increase can be attributed to inflation. Proportionally, the greatest loss of farmland was in Maui County, reflecting the urban boom on the island of Maui during the decade of the 1970s.

Crops

The overall loss of farm acreage between 1970 and 1980 was at the expense of the plantation crops, sugar and pineapple, rather than in diversified agriculture. Table 13.3 shows that the volume of crop marketings for all listed crops except taro and coffee was up between 1970 and 1980, with the drop in coffee production particularly drastic. Despite the drop in production of coffee and taro, the value of crop sales was up for both, as well as for the other crops listed. Particularly noteworthy is the increase in value of flowers and nursery products, which are rapidly becoming one of Hawaii's most successful agricultural exports.

Livestock

Some of the largest landholdings in the state are cattle ranches. Although the Bishop Estate, holder of the largest acreage, is not a ranch, the Parker Ranch ranks second. There are other large ranches on the islands of Hawaii and Maui, with somewhat smaller spreads on the other islands. The sole commercial activity on Niihau is the raising of cattle and sheep. Nevertheless the state is not nearly self-sufficient in beef and other meat products. More than 60 percent of the beef consumed in the state is imported.

The reasons for low productivity in the state's cattle industry are partially misfortunes of geography and partially inefficiencies in production. All cattle feed must be shipped into the state, at considerable

Table 13.2
Number of Farms, Farm Acreage, and Value of Crop and Livestock Sales, by
Geographical Areas: 1970, 1980

Geographic area and year	Number of farms	Farm acreage acres (x1,000)	Farm acreage hectares (x1,000)	Value of crop and livestock sales ($1,000) Diversified Crops	Value of crop and livestock sales ($1,000) Livestock
State total:					
1970	4,500	2,300	932	21,919	41,648
1980	4,300	1,970	798	90,625	81,249
Hawaii Co.:					
1970	2,500	1,340	543	11,265	13,294
1980	2,500	1,150	466	55,540	22,446
Maui Co.:					
1970	650	526	213	3,139	4,060
1980	500	420	170	12,016	10,073
Oahu:					
1970	930	152	62	5,820	22,380
1980	1,000	125	51	18,504	43,009
Kauai Co.:					
1970	420	282	114	1,695	1,914
1980	300	275	111	4,565	5,721

Source: Hawaii Agricultural Reporting Service, Statistics of Hawaiian
          Agriculture (annual).

expense. Most recent increases in both milk and beef prices have been attributed to rising feed and shipping costs. But the beef production cycle in Hawaii is unusual and not very efficient. Cattle are shipped on the hoof by barge from neighbor islands to Oahu, where they are fed with imported feed grains at a feedlot in the Ewa (southwestern) district of the island. The cattle lose considerable weight in the shipping process, being very susceptible to seasickness on the often rough channel crossings. After being fattened up at the feedlot, the steers are transported by truck for slaughter in Honolulu. The meat is then sold to restaurants or on the local market.

If the feedlot operations were located on the islands where there are the largest ranches, shipping costs could be reduced considerably since it is far cheaper to ship dressed, packaged meat than cattle on the hoof. Moreover the severe weight loss due to seasickness could be avoided.

Food Prices

Virtually all Hawaiian-grown produce or livestock products are as expensive or more expensive compared to products shipped to the islands from the mainland United States. Even fruits such as bananas, which grow in many residents' yards, cannot compete with imported products.

The generally small size of Hawaiian farms precludes economies of scale such

Table 13.3
Acreage in Crop, Volume of Crop Marketings, and Value of Crop Sales:
1970, 1980

	1970	1980
Acreage in crop (1,000 acres):		
Vegetables and melons (harvested acreage)	3.2	3.9
Fruits, excluding pineapples	3.3	5.2
Coffee	3.9	1.9
Macadamia nuts	8.7	13.4
Miscellaneous crops	3.6	4.9
Volume of crop marketings (1,000 lb.):		
Vegetables and melons	54,798	70,680
Fruits, excluding pineapples	36,241	67,800
Coffee, parchment	4,300	1,450
Macadamia nuts, in shell	13,216	33,390
Taro	8,555	6,400
Value of crop sales ($1,000):		
Vegetables and melons	6,889	18,501
Fruits (excluding pineapples)	3,488	12,983
Coffee (parchment)	1,449	2,175
Macadamia nuts (in shell)	2,868	24,174
Taro	736	1,280
Flowers and nursery products	4,225	27,441

Source: Hawaii Agricultural Reporting Service,   Statistics of Hawaiian
          Agriculture (annual).

as those recognized on farms in California, from which much of the food eaten in Hawaii comes. Added to that is the cost of fertilizer that must be shipped into the state.

Crops grown for export do better, however, largely because the farms are generally larger and the operations are controlled by some of the large Hawaiian corporations, which can employ mechanization to a larger degree than can the small farmer. Papayas are grown profitably for the Japanese market, and macadamia nuts are a well-known, popular Hawaiian export. The success of the flower and nursery-products industry

has already been noted; much of this production is for export to the mainland United States. The exception to the success of the export crops is coffee. Hawaii's justly famous Kona coffee is an excellent product that could be featured in fine restaurants on the mainland. Production has been down, as Table 13.3 indicates, chiefly because the coffee farms are small family-owned enterprises, and production costs are high.

Of the crops grown for local consumption, the one with no competition from outside the state is taro. Taro production is hard work, and there have been some difficulties in obtaining sufficient irrigation water for the crop, particularly in areas where urban uses of water compete with agriculture. But poi, the food made from the taro root, is still a popular item in the Hawaiian diet, and prices are high. The high prices have stimulated interest in growing the crop by many who now see it as an important commercial enterprise rather than merely food for the immediate family.

The Future?

Although the policy of the state to maintain small farms and farm acreage seems to have been generally successful, the ultimate goal of self-sufficiency in food production is farther off than it has ever been. Production of food for the local market has not kept pace with population increases, and much land devoted to diversified agriculture is used to grow export crops. There seems to be nothing in the future that might change the situation. The limited land available for agriculture in the state is slowly diminishing, while the population of the state is rising at a fairly rapid pace.

REFERENCES

Hawaiian Sugar Planters' Association. *Hawaiian Sugar Manual for 1981*. Honolulu: Hawaiian Sugar Planters' Association, 1981.

Neal, M. C. *In Gardens of Hawaii*. Honolulu: Bishop Museum Press, 1965.

Nordhoff, C. *Northern California, Oregon and the Sandwich Islands*. Berkeley, Calif.: Ten Speed Press, 1974. (Centennial printing of 1874 edition).

Philipp, P. F. *Diversified Agriculture of Hawaii*. Honolulu: University of Hawaii Press, 1953.

Roberts, J. O. *Pineapple in Hawaii Today*. Honolulu: The Pineapple Growers Association of Hawaii, 1977.

State of Hawaii, Department of Planning and Economic Development. *Data Book*. Honolulu: State of Hawaii, Department of Planning and Economic Development, 1980.

Twain, M. *Letters from Hawaii*. Honolulu: University Press of Hawaii, 1975.

White, H. A. *James D. Dole, Industrial Pioneer of the Pacific: Founder of Hawaii's Pineapple Industry*. New York: The Newcomen Society in North America, 1957.

Whitney, H. M. *The Hawaiian Guide Book*. Rutland, Vt.: Charles E. Tuttle Co., 1970. (Facsimile reproduction of 1875 edition).

CHAPTER 14

WATERFRONT INDUSTRIES

As one would expect for an island state, the waterfront is important to Hawaii. Virtually all the goods consumed in the state arrive by ship, and a number of other industries are associated with the ocean—for instance, commercial and recreational fishing and tour boat operations, an important component of the tourist industry. Emphasis will be given to commercial fishing and shipping.

COMMERCIAL FISHING

Commercial fishing is not an important industry in the state, measured by the number of people employed, the tonnage of fish caught, or the dollar value of the industry as a percentage of the gross state product. However, because fishing was important in the past to Hawaiians, there are those who hope the industry can be rejuvenated. In 1978 there were only 2,574 people employed in commercial fishing and but 277 motorized fishing boats. Sales totaled $12,118,649, a miniscule percentage of wholesale sales in the state.

The largest components of the industry are the aku (skipjack) and ahi (yellowfin) tuna fisheries. In 1978 aku accounted for 6,794,086 lb (3,084,515 kg) caught and sales of $4,358,429. Ahi sales, much smaller but still significant, were $2,471,847, and the catch totaled 2,010,648 lb (912,834 kg).

The Aku Fishery

Aku are fast-swimming, predatory tunas that inhabit the warm tropical oceans. In the Hawaiian fishery they are taken by pole and line from a sampan-type fishing vessel. The boats, numbering only about fifteen for the entire industry, are generally small, old, and limited in capability. Schools of aku are sighted by noting the presence of bird flocks, and the sampan captain maneuvers his boat into the school of feeding fish. Live baitfish are then thrown overboard to induce a feeding frenzy by the aku. The boats are equipped with water nozzles near the waterline that are operated to stir up the water and further stimulate the frenzied activity of the fish. Fishermen on the sampans catch the tuna with short bamboo poles and lines, to which are attached barbless hooks

Because live bait must be used, one serious problem is the bait fish. A species of small anchovy, the nehu, is used. Fishing sampans must first spend several hours catching nehu, which are kept alive in bait wells aboard the fishing vessel. However, mortality is high in the nehu before they are used as bait; for that reason, as well as lack of adequate refrigeration and living facilities aboard the sampans, the boats cannot remain out overnight. Consequently the catch is relatively small and the op-

FIGURE 14.1 The *Sea Queen* is an aku fishing boat of the Japanese sampan type. It is shown at its home port of Kewalo Basin, Honolulu.

eration is not efficient. The aku are sold fresh to supermarkets or other stores, or to a cannery that markets the catch as Coral Brand tuna. The cannery is a unit of Bumble Bee seafoods, a subsidiary of Castle and Cooke, Inc. The Bumble Bee cannery depends both on the catch of local fishermen and imported tuna to maintain operations at a profitable level. If the cannery depended on the catch of Hawaiian-based fishermen alone, it could not stay in business.

Earnings by fishermen are on a share basis and depend on the skill and good fortune of the fishing-boat captain. More fishing is done in the summer, when the weather is generally better and more aku are in Hawaiian waters. Consequently many fishermen can work at other jobs during certain times of the year. Earnings of com-

mercial fishermen vary considerably from year to year and from boat to boat, but it is safe to say that they are not large, and it has been difficult to attract local Hawaiian residents into the business.

Both the state of Hawaii and the federal government have programs of research and low-interest loans to assist the industry; these have achieved some limited success.

The Ahi Fishery

The ahi, which include yellowfin as well as other deep-swimming tunas and some billfish, have different habits and must be caught with different techniques. Since they inhabit deeper waters, the pole-and-line method cannot be used. Moreover, ahi are much larger, some weighing 200 lb (90.8 kg) or more; they could not be caught by a single fisherman with pole and line. Instead the long-line method is used. In this technique a long horizontal line, buoyed to remain on the surface, is strung out from the vessel. Attached to the long line are short vertical lines to which are affixed one or more baited hooks. After the line has been played out, a suitable time period is allowed to elapse before the line is retrieved. The catch is then removed from the lines and refrigerated.

The bait used need not be live, hence the ahi fishery does not have the same problems with bait as does the aku fishery. But the remaining problems are similar. Boats are old and in poor repair, and earnings in the industry are not high. The fish are marketed daily at a fish auction, and a single ahi, weighing more than 200 lb (90.8 kg), might bring in more than $1,000. High prices prevail during the Christmas–New Year season, when fresh ahi are highly sought after for sashimi, a dish highly prized at the New Year season by Hawaiian residents of Japanese origin. At other times the ahi bring in much less.

Ahi boats generally stay out for ten days or so before returning with their catch. The long liners must therefore be equipped with refrigeration and living quarters suitable for voyages of that length. As with the aku fishery, there are federal and state programs designed to help the industry, but results have not been encouraging.

SHIPPING

An island state needs efficient shipping services if an adequate standard of living is to be maintained. Components of an efficient shipping industry include port facilities and ships. In Hawaii both components of the industry work efficiently to provide residents of the state with the goods they require.

Ports

There are state-owned ports at Honolulu, Oahu; Hilo and Kawaihae, Hawaii; Kahului, Maui; and Port Allen and Nawiliwili, Kauai. These are deep-water ports with project depths of 35 ft (10.6 m). In addition there are a number of small barge harbors on the islands of Molokai and Lanai. Only the sparsely inhabited island of Niihau is without regular port facilities, but the needs of Niihau residents are provided for by landing craft of World War II vintage operated by the island's owner from Kauai. In general, the port facilities on each island are suitable for the needs and the stage of economic development of the island.

The port of Honolulu can handle the most modern of container ships and roll-on–roll-off vessels. Hilo and Kahului are equipped to offload roll-on–roll-off vessels, whil Nawiliwili can accommodate small, feeder container vessels and tugs and barges. Molokai and Lanai must be supplied by tug-and-barge operations, but the small populations of these islands do not require more sophisticated port facilities. In the case of Lanai the island's owner, Castle and Cooke, Inc., owns and operates the port and the tug-and-barge line, which imports food and manufactured goods and exports the island's pineapple crop.

The West Coast to Hawaii Trade Route

Most of the general cargo arriving in the islands comes from the United States by regularly scheduled vessels operated by three companies: Matson Navigation Co., United States Lines, and Hawaiian Marine Lines. Matson, which has about 80 percent of the trade, operates modern container vessels and roll-on–roll-off ships. Container ships of United States Lines call at Honolulu on less frequent schedules. Hawaiian Marine Lines provides an efficient tug-and-barge service from the mainland and has captured the majority of the trade from the Pacific Northwest. The regular container ships of both Matson and United States Lines call only at Honolulu, but Matson's roll-on–roll-off vessels call at Hilo and Kahului as well.

Exports from the state are generally limited to sugar and pineapple. Pineapple is shipped fresh or canned by container ship,

FIGURE 14.2.   Shipping at Kahului Harbor, Maui. *Above*, a tug and barge with cargo from Honolulu; *below*, a Japanese factory fishing vessel being assisted by a harbor tug prior to tying up at one of the piers.

but sugar must be shipped in bulk. The one notable inefficiency in the trade between Hawaii and the U.S. West Coast is the lack of back-haul cargo from the islands. Consequently, except for pineapple shipments, most container ships return to the mainland empty of cargo, and shipping costs are correspondingly higher than they would be if the vessels could be profitably employed on both legs of the journey. In the case of bulk shipments that situation does not prevail, as ships carrying raw sugar to the C and H refinery in California are frequently loaded with grain for the return voyage to the islands.

Petroleum Shipments

Crude oil arrives by tankers from Southeast Asia and the United States. Large crude-oil carriers discharge their cargoes at offshore moorings near Barbers Point, Oahu; from there the petroleum is piped to oil refineries at Campbell Industrial Park in the Ewa district of the island. Refined petroleum products arrive in smaller tankers in Honolulu harbor, and gasoline and other products are transshipped to the neighbor islands by barge.

Interisland Shipping

Cargo that cannot be shipped directly from the mainland to Oahu's neighboring islands is transshipped from Honolulu. Interisland shipments are made in a variety of ways.

The *Mauna Kea*, Matson's small self-contained vessel, carries containerized cargo from Honolulu to Nawiliwili, Kahului, and Hilo. It is Matson's primary link with the island of Kauai and serves as a secondary link with the islands of Maui and Hawaii, which can order merchandise directly from the mainland and receive it via one of the roll-on–roll-off vessels.

A regularly scheduled, regulated, common-carrier tug-and-barge service is provided by Young Brothers, Ltd. Weekly and biweekly schedules are maintained to all neighbor islands except Lanai and Niihau. Shipments to and from Molokai are largely dependent on this service, but contracted tug-and-barge services are used to ship pineapple and sand.

The island of Lanai is privately owned by Castle and Cooke, Inc., and has a port built by the owners to provide for shipments of pineapple from the island to Honolulu and for imports of food, fuel, and other essentials. Isleways, a subsidiary of the island's owners, provides the service.

The island of Niihau is operated as a cattle and sheep ranch. Cattle shipments are made via landing craft operated by the

owners, Niihau Ranch. The landing craft also provide essential imports to the island. Port facilities are not necessary, since there are three suitable landing sites, one of which should be usable no matter what the wind and surf conditions.

Conclusions

Both overseas and interisland shipping are efficient and adequate for the state's needs, as are port facilities. As the state grows in population, however, additional or improved ports may be needed. In the last few years improvements to the port of Kahului were made, and another port on Oahu is contemplated. It would be located in the Ewa district of the island, near the site of the island's oil refineries and heavy industries.

REFERENCES

Ahsan, A. E.; Ball, J. L.; and Davidson, J. R. *Costs and Earnings of Tuna Vessels in Hawaii.* Honolulu: University of Hawaii Sea Grant Program, 1972.

Campbell, A. *A Voyage Round the World from 1806 to 1812.* Honolulu: University of Hawaii Press, 1967. (Facsimile reproduction of the third American edition of 1822).

Comotini, S. *An Economic Analysis of the State of the Hawaiian Skipjack Tuna Fishery.* Honolulu: University of Hawaii Sea Grant Program, 1977.

Morgan, J. "Honolulu Harbor: Heart of Hawaiian Commerce." *Sea Grant Newsletter* 8, no. 7 (July 1978):1.

State of Hawaii, Department of Planning and Economic Development. *Hawaii Tuna Fishery Development Plan.* Honolulu: Department of Planning and Economic Development, 1977.

CHAPTER 15

URBANIZATION: SIX PROPOSITIONS

Willard T. Chow

THE BEST OR WORST OF HAWAII?

Hawaii has long been noted for its ethnic diversity, dramatic natural landscapes, wide climatic variations, spectacular beaches and surf, rare and endangered biota, centralized form of government, royal heritage, and Aloha Spirit. Rarely have its towns and cities received much acclaim, notoriety, or scrutiny. Urban problems commonly have been defined by mainland standards and treated with mainland remedies prescribed by mainland consultants. The implicit assumption is that the way in which cities evolved in the islands is neither unique nor deserving of special attention. This chapter will challenge some of the prevailing assumptions about the context in which the islands have urbanized.*

*The author is grateful to Clarence Tom of the Department of General Planning, City and County of Honolulu, and to Tom Dinell of the Urban and Regional Planning Department, University of Hawaii at Manoa, for their comments on an earlier draft of this chapter. The author, of course, assumes all responsibility for any errors that may have been made. The views expressed in this chapter do not represent those of the City and County administration in which the author serves.

Hawaii's Towns

Although much has been written about rural Hawaii, relatively little has been said about its towns and cities. Ironically, Hawaii's towns have long served a variety of functions: the prime destination areas for most of its visitors, the ladder of socio-economic mobility for most of its residents, and the locus of decision making for most of its institutions. The towns of nineteenth-century Hawaii provided opportunities for missionaries to proselytize, investors to turn a profit, visitors to rest and relax, workers to find employment, students to learn, and administrators to manage. The rural hamlets, villages, camps, ranches, farmsteads, and plantations of that period were far from being as exciting, dynamic, or tolerant as the towns, even though they may have been more comfortable, picturesque, healthy, and affordable places in which to live. Many ethnic groups were recruited to work in rural Hawaii, but few found the situation to be to their advantage. Most of these immigrants resettled in Honolulu, even though they were often jammed into urban tenements, forced to labor for long hours at low wages, and thrust into a cauldron of racial and cultural tension.

The cosmopolitan city that emerged by 1920 did not win national design awards, but it filled most immigrant groups with a sense of hope and provided them with opportunities that were not available in rural areas.

Metropolitan Honolulu has since become an important node in a transnational system of cities. Towns like Hilo and Lahaina are also integral parts of that system. Connected to other metropolitan centers by modern telecommunications and air transport service, the bustling cities and towns of Hawaii are no longer remote. They have grown in population as old functions have expanded and new functions have emerged to take advantage of markets and improvements in transpacific communication and transportation networks.

The "awakening" of Honolulu during the 1960s and many of the outer-island towns during the 1970s has not been gentle. The cities and towns of "paradise" now resemble other American cities with similar functions and suffer from similar economic, social, environmental, and governmental problems. Population growth in Hawaii, compared to other states, has accelerated since the 1950s; most of this growth continues to be concentrated on Oahu or metropolitan Honolulu. Water shortages, siltation, and traffic congestion suggest that the carrying capacity of Oahu soon may be exceeded. Oahu's population density in 1980 was 1,387 per sq mi (535 per sq km), while that of Kauai was only 75 per sq mi (29 per sq km) and the Big Island's was even lower, at 24 per sq mi (9 per sq km).

Many people see Hawaii's growth as healthy, the high cost of living as necessary, and new construction as indicative of progress. Others insist that further urbanization will destroy the uniqueness of Hawaii by undermining the social and ecological fabric on which many of Hawaii's life-styles depend. They assert that urban Honolulu is seldom perceived by visitors as the most attractive feature of the islands.

Challenges to Planning

Pioneering efforts by the state of Hawaii to manage urban growth through statewide zoning started in 1961 and by means of the recently adopted State Plan were inspired by grave concerns about uncontrolled urban development, particularly in Honolulu.

Maintaining the integrity of local networks in the face of metropolitan expansion requires much more than disjointed, parcel-by-parcel decision making. Managing growth involves coordinating island-wide services and facilities such as water, sewer, drainage, transport, schools, and parks. City planning must be more than just zoning: it must attempt to resolve inherent conflicts between cosmopolitan and metropolitan networks and needs. Unfortunately, despite the state's planning efforts, little progress has been made during the past two decades in this direction. Strict land-use regulations and elaborate review procedures that were begun in order to combat urban problems have in turn created other problems— such regulations have not necessarily resulted in livable cities and viable neighborhoods.

It is possible, while advocating "highest and best use" principles, lofty standards, and bold solutions, to lose sight of the functions of old streets, neighborhoods, and rural communities and the need to preserve their integrity. Many modern planners favor building places whose physical form is impressive and modern. Although the weathered quarters, substandard structures, and neglected streets of old Hawaii look neither impressive nor modern, they have provided disadvantaged residents with entrepreneurial opportunities that no longer are open to them in the sprawling suburbs and technocratic towers of metropolitan Hawaii.

Six propositions are set forth to challenge some long-standing beliefs about the context in which cities in Hawaii evolved and the way by which their future can be better planned.

COLONIAL TOWNS

Proposition One: *Whaling did not urbanize the islands. Urbanization did not really begin to accelerate until the twentieth century.*

The whaling industry, to be discussed in Chapter 16, had a profound impact on the morals, health, and economy of the Hawaiian kingdom, and particularly on the town of Lahaina. Nevertheless whaling did not "urbanize the islands," as Gavan Daws contends (Armstrong 1973, 90). In fact, few towns were founded by transient whalers, blossomed under their auspices, or bore the imprint of their ideals. It was the foreign missionaries and merchants who shaped the small but lively towns of nineteenth-century Hawaii. They brought with them conflicting, but definite, ideals about how the islands ought to be settled, civilized, and transformed.

Ohana

The high population densities of ancient Hawaii were made possible, according to Handy and Pukui (1972, 1–6), by intensive inland cultivation and the careful allocation of offshore fishing rights. The ancient Hawaiians did not live in villages or towns but instead were organized into *ohana,* dispersed rural communities of people tied by ancestry, birth, or sentiment to a particular region, homeland, or *aina.* Coastal and inland households of an *ohana* were obliged to exchange food, utilitarian items, and services. Although a century and a half of Christianity, ranches, plantations, commercial rice cultivation, fishing, and urbanization have taken their toll, *ohana* as a spirit and institution remains a cohesive force in the country districts, where many urban Hawaiians still have their roots (Handy and Pukui 1972, 15–16).

Towns—with their emphasis on individualism, specialized skills, cash economy, formal education, and impersonal relationships—were not in keeping with the traditional Hawaiian life-style in which the community, subsistence activities, gifts, oral communication, and social obligations were much more important. Many of the native Hawaiians were nonetheless drawn to the port towns, where they often were employed as laborers, servants, or sailors.

Origin of Port Towns

The arrival of Captain Cook in 1778 ushered in the China fur trade in which Hawaii functioned as a supply station and wintering area. In 1804 King Kamehameha built stone storehouses for royal goods near the sheltered port of Kou (now Honolulu), which had previously supported a fishing village, and exacted fees from visiting vessels for its use. Thereafter the booming sandalwood trade kept the kingdom's major ports at Honolulu and Lahaina busy, the royal treasuries full, and the waterfront bustling with transient sailors. One of the earliest western structures in Hawaii was a fort overlooking Honolulu's harbor. Originally built by the Russians in 1816 at the foot of Fort Street, the fort was finished by Kamehameha near what is now Aloha Tower.

The earliest towns of Hawaii were foreign enclaves transplanted into a semifeudal society. When the first Congregationalist missionaries arrived from New England in 1820, Honolulu was composed mainly of grass houses, half a dozen stone or wooden buildings, a few small stores, and several thousand inhabitants. It nonetheless had nearly everything to sell that could have been found in the crossroad store at Brookfield or Cornwall or on the waterfront at Boston.

There were chandleries, trading posts, grogshops, where white men dispensed sea stores, pea jackets, cooking pots and rum. . . . The grogshops flourished like the green bay tree. They offered not only drinks but gambling, fiddling, singing, hornpipes, wrestling and often downright brawls. Here jack-tars, glad to get their feet on firm earth, could hear the news of the world (six months old) and find robust and ribald comradeship. But more immediately than any of these wares or pleasures, the crew of incoming vessels wanted women. If the Islands were the paradise of the Pacific, it was because there every Adam had his Eve (Loomis 1951, 40).

Oahu was less populated than Maui until 1835 and overshadowed by the Big Island in terms of population until 1872. However, it had the most secure harbor in the Sandwich Islands and the only good harbor within 2,000 mi (3,200 km) of the Pacific whaling grounds, so the town of Honolulu functioned initially as a mercantile, recreation, and supply center for foreign ships (not as a central place or administrative center). Although Liholiho (Kamehameha II) moved the royal court to Honolulu in 1820, the towns of Hilo, Kailua, Lahaina, and Hana, each with around 2,000 inhabitants (Schmitt 1977, 30), were nearly as large as the capital city. The construction of wharves and rigging docks at Honolulu harbor by Kamehameha III and the establishment during the 1820s of the first Christian church on the site of what is now Kawaiahao Church in Honolulu paved the way for the city's growth as a mercantile and missionary headquarters. Merchants' and missionaries' houses initially clustered between Fort Street and Kawaiahao Church within walking distance of the bustling harbor.

The Missionary Influence

Missionary stations were established in Honolulu, Lahaina, Kailua, Hana, and Hilo during the early 1820s to convert and educate the chiefs and natives. Towns were an integral part of the missionary life-style. The New England missionaries were so effective that by 1853 Hawaii was no longer regarded by the American Board of Commissioners for Foreign Missions as a foreign mission. The missionaries were then encouraged by the king to become citizens of Hawaii and were given lands, houses, and livestock that the missions had acquired (Kuykendall and Day 1976, 77). The imprint of New England ideals was evident. Charles Nordhoff made the following observation in the 1860s: "The white frame houses with green blinds, the picket-fences whitewashed until they shine, the stone walls, the small barns, the scanty pastures, the little white frame churches scattered about, the narrow 'front yards,' the frequent schoolhouses, usually with but little shade: all are New England, genuine and unadulterated" (Judd 1961, 58). The missions, anxious to impose their own sense of physical and moral order, contributed much to the townlike character of Kailua, Waimea, Lahaina, and Honolulu (Creighton 1978, 37).

The rising demand by whaling ships for locally grown food drew an increasing number of natives into the port towns. By 1831 nearly 40 percent of the native Hawaiians had learned to read and write (Judd 1961, 53). Many of those who were educated in missionary schools settled in the port towns to which they brought their livestock and produce for sale. By mid-century between one-fourth and one-third of all native Hawaiians were permanent or semipermanent urban residents according to Gavan Daws (Armstrong 1973, 90). Unfortunately, many could not find work or were not prepared to cope with city life, where they were not supported by the *ohana*. About 2,000, or one-fifth, of the young native men enlisted as sailors from 1845 to 1857 (Kuykendall and Day 1976, 91), a factor contributing to the decline of the native birthrates.

Early Honolulu

Honolulu, finally declared a city and the capital of the kingdom by Kamehameha III in 1850, supported a population of 11,445 in 1853, including most of the foreigners in the kingdom. Early Honolulu was a vibrant but relatively small frontier town. Its population of 14,000 in 1860 was only one-fourth that of San Francisco. Yet Lewis Mumford (1961, 9–10) reminds us that cities are much more than concentrations of people:

> even before the city is a place of fixed residence, it begins as a meeting place to which people periodically return: the magnet comes before the container, and this ability

to attract non-residents to it for intercourse and spiritual stimulus no less than trade remains one of the essential criteria of the city, a witness to its inherent dynamism, as opposed to the more fixed and indrawn form of the village, hostile to the outsider.

Early Hawaiian towns attracted both natives and foreigners, but retained few of them as permanent residents before 1876, when the treaty of commercial reciprocity was negotiated. Reciprocity permitted duty-free trade between the United States and Hawaii and gave sugar from the islands the advantage over imports from other foreign countries.

Although Honolulu was called a city, during the 1800s it still retained small-town characteristics. Its status as a port town and missionary station had not yet been superseded by other urban functions.

PLANTATION CAMPS AND COMPANY TOWNS

Proposition Two: *The cane fields were not a racial melting pot; the plantations took advantage of racial differences to combat strikes.*

Tadd Fisher, a sociologist, contended that the early plantation camps and company towns were a racial "melting pot," responsible in large measure for the establishment of harmonious race relations in the islands (Fisher 1973, 9–11). As Chinese, Japanese, Portuguese, Koreans, Puerto Ricans, and Filipinos were all residents of those early camps at one time or another and presumably suffered the same long hours and lack of comforts, it might be assumed—since they suffered equally and had the same problems—that residence in one of the camps naturally would lead to increased understanding and reduced racial bias. Fisher's contention has the ring of truth, and many Hawaiian residents tend to accept it uncritically.

Development of Plantations

The development of rural Hawaii into ranches and sugar plantations during the nineteenth century admittedly was stimulated by expanded demands for meat by the whalers and gold seekers and for sugar after reciprocity. Not until land, labor, and capital all became available, however, did development accelerate.

In the Great Mahele of 1848, Kamehameha III divided the land into "crown lands" and "*kuleana* lands" for the common people. The act finally allowed land to be held and transferred under fee-simple title and subsequently gave foreigners the same rights as natives to hold, buy, and sell land. The Great Mahele helped to pave the way for both the creation of large rural estates and resettlement in cities. One of the chief motives of the Great Mahele, according to Handy and Pukui (1972, 16–17), was to keep the Hawaiians on their land, even though country Hawaiians in the middle of the nineteenth century had little understanding of what private ownership meant. Paradoxically, the act did not have this effect. Many Hawaiians continued to seek opportunities in towns, selling or giving their parcels of land to foreigners or allowing the land to revert to public ownership. Given the prospect of a larger market and the security of private land ownership, foreign investors plowed their capital into irrigation systems, sugar mills, and land acquisition during the 1860s and 1870s. The critical remaining problem was labor.

The native Hawaiians, afflicted by epidemics and sinking birthrates, declined in number from an estimated 250,000 at the arrival of Captain Cook to 57,000 in 1872. Disease, not urbanization, was responsible for the losses. As early as 1852 Chinese laborers were recruited to build the irrigation ditches, work the cane fields, and operate the mills, but by the 1860s many of them had returned to China. Others had left the plantations to cultivate vegetables, raise poultry, or grow rice, or had settled in the town of Honolulu to work as entrepreneurs or domestic servants. An additional 55,000 Chinese immigrants were brought to the islands between 1877 and

1890 to meet the needs of the sugar plantations. The Bureau of Immigration also recruited Japanese, Portuguese from the Madeira Islands, Germans, and Scandinavians. Prior to 1886 the Chinese were the most numerous immigrant group in the islands, and many Hawaiian residents feared that Chinese were becoming too influential economically in the towns and on the plantations. About 180,000 Japanese were recruited from 1886 to 1908 in order to dilute the influence of the Chinese, who still outnumbered the Japanese in the census of 1890.

The Chinese, however, had a positive impact on both rural and urban Hawaii. Most of the irrigation systems of Hawaii were built by Chinese coolies. Many married native women, raised part-Hawaiian children, and settled in rural villages and outer-island towns as farmers and fishermen. The main reasons why so many Chinese left the plantation camps were the paucity of women on the plantations and the onerous (by contemporary standards) working and living conditions they had to endure (Lind 1967, 74).

Conditions did not improve in this buyers' market until the turn of the century, after Japanese plantation workers began to press and strike for better working conditions. The Japanese chose to remain on the plantations and felt that their future lay in settling down (Kuykendall and Day 1976, 279). Efforts to import Filipino workers began in 1910 in response to strikes by Japanese plantation laborers. The Filipinos have constituted the largest ethnic group employed by the plantations since 1922, succeeding the Japanese, who dominated during the previous three decades, and the Chinese, who prevailed until the mid-1880s (Lind 1967, 75).

Modern Plantations

Hawaii's sugar workers now earn more than any other agricultural workers in the world, but these gains were won by bitter strikes and collective bargaining. The contract-labor system was terminated with annexation, but the plantation camp with its company housing, company store, and company-controlled social facilities changed little until after the Second World War (Meller and Horowitz 1971, 31).

Urbanization in Hawaii from 1880 until World War II was driven more by push than pull factors. Caucasians, Caucasian-Hawaiians, and Chinese were the only groups to concentrate in Honolulu during this period. The Hawaiians tended to remain in rural villages, farms, and ranches. Relatively few of the Japanese and Asian-Hawaiians remained on the plantations. Most of them eventually resettled in the larger port and mill towns like Hilo, Lahaina, Lihue-Nawiliwili, and Wailuku-Kahului, where outer-island public schools were situated in 1920, or escaped to operate their own farms in places like Kona. The Filipinos were the only group to stay on the plantations and to benefit from the long struggle for improved working, housing, and educational conditions after World War II.

Agriculture, which accounted for 34 percent of the civilian jobs in the state in 1940, provided only 3 percent in 1975 (Schmitt 1977, 122–125). Tourism succeeded sugar as Hawaii's second largest source of income (behind military expenditures) by 1960. The changing economic structure of the islands after World War II was clearly reflected by shifts in patterns of urbanization.

The portion of Hawaii's population residing in small places with less than 10,000 residents declined from 1940 to 1960. But during the last two decades, while the portion residing in towns of 2,500 people continued to diminish, Hilo, Lahaina, and Wailuku, all of which had declined in population during the 1950s, rebounded with the boom in tourism. Waipahu, Wahiawa, Aiea, Pearl City, Kailua, and Kaneohe continue to grow as burgeoning metropolitan suburbs. Much of the urban fringe and many of the outlying visitor destination areas have been transformed dramatically since statehood, as highways and airports were built or expanded to meet their needs.

With the growth of the cities has come increasing ethnic and racial diversity. In the urban neighborhoods Japanese, Chinese, Caucasians, and Filipinos live side by side, whereas in the original plantation camps they had been segregated. But integration came slowly; Honolulu first developed into a number of ethnic neighborhoods.

FROM COSMOPOLITAN
TO MIDDLE-CLASS HONOLULU

Proposition Three: *The purpose of zoning and urban renewal was not to implement community policies; it was rather to protect commercial and residential property owners from changes caused by increasing urbanization.*

The state of Hawaii adopted a unique strategy in 1961 to manage urban growth through effective statewide land-use classification—in effect a form of zoning; therefore one might think that the purpose of individual zoning decisions was to implement a plan. Since a plan implies that long-term policies are to be implemented, zoning of individual properties and areas of the state or of a city presumably should be the case-by-case actions required to support the plan's desired objectives. In actuality, zoning preceded the 1978 State Plan by seventeen years, and even those zoning decisions made subsequent to 1978 have not, in many cases, supported the objectives of the State Plan.

The City and County of Honolulu, organized in 1907, passed its first subdivision regulations in 1911 and its first zoning ordinance in 1922. The influx of Japanese and Filipino immigrants and mainland servicemen and their dependents raised the demand for housing in the city. Zoning was imposed, apparently to protect property owners in middle-class neighborhoods and the central business district (CBD) from the intrusion of noxious or incompatible activities. Manufacturing, commodity wholesaling, automobile repair

shops, and working-class dwellings were expanding and could no longer be confined by deed or lease restrictions to the inner ring around the CBD. Blight was threatening property values in middle-class commercial and residential districts.

Origins of Honolulu's
Ethnic Neighborhoods

The practice of residential congregation into ethnic communities and segregation into racial enclaves had already begun by 1884, when the city's population was only about 20,000. Chinatown had become a densely settled residential quarter, vulnerable to both disease and fire, by the 1880s. Its small shophouses functioned as wholesale importers, retail stores, residences, banks, post offices, and social centers for Chinese from the same village or of the same clan. On the other hand, the two- and three-story frame mercantile houses and residences of upper-class Honolulu were not designed for multiple use.

The growth of Honolulu during the first two decades of the twentieth century was prompted by the migration of plantation workers. The Portuguese congregated on the slopes of Punchbowl, the Chinese gravitated to Chinatown, and Japanese concentrated in fishing communities like Palama or farming villages like Pauoa. Some of the former plantation laborers also settled in small farming camps at the edge of the city, which in 1930 included Waialae Nui, Wailupe, Palolo, Kalihi-Uka, and upper Manoa (Lind 1967, 62–63). Still others settled on the poorly drained flatlands of Kakaako, McCully, Moiliili, and Waikiki to the east. There they raised taro, ducks, pigs, rice, vegetables, bananas, and flowers for local markets; clustered into fishing communities; or worked at nearby warehouses, repair shops, and other industrial sites.

The Europeans and Americans preferred to reside in the cooler areas of Nuuanu, Makiki, and Manoa, where Victorian mansions still remain, or along the beach from

Waikiki to Kahala, to which major streets were extended.

Nineteenth-century Honolulu was a pedestrian city whose narrow streets and alleys were oriented toward the waterfront. Government offices, warehouses, churches, banks, stores, and taverns all clustered near the port. The first hotel was built at Richards and Hotel Streets in the heart of downtown Honolulu shortly after the first steamships arrived in 1870. The first mule-drawn street railway was not established until 1888: travel prior to mass transit was by foot, horse, carriage, or bicycle. After streetcars were electrified in 1903, the well-to-do could commute from outlying neighborhoods.

At the time of annexation in 1898, Honolulu had a well-defined central business district. The CBD was bordered by the inner ring of districts composed of industrial, commercial, and working-class residential uses. The specialized outer ring consisted of upper-class residential neighborhoods, connected to the CBD by streetcars, and scattered ethnic villages or camps oriented to farming and fishing. Of the 39,000 residents in Honolulu in 1900, 23 percent were Chinese, 21 percent were native Hawaiian, 16 percent were Japanese, 12 percent were Portuguese, and 11 percent were part-Hawaiian. Only 18 percent were Caucasian (other than Portuguese). Ethnic working-class people were housed in mixed-use districts, while middle-class people were housed in single-purpose residential quarters.

Expansion of the City

The emergence of industrial quarters in Iwilei, on the western side of Nuuanu Stream, began slowly with expansion of sugarcane cultivation, which raised the demand for irrigation, harvesting, and milling equipment. The opening of the railroad and pineapple canneries after the turn of the century also increased the demand for machine shops, metal works, and warehouses. Iwilei attracted industrial activities because it was near the harbor, adjacent

to working-class residential districts, and serviced by rail lines that ran along the waterfront. The city of Honolulu accounted for less than 12 percent of the manufacturing in Hawaii (by value added) in 1899, but more than 28 percent in 1919.

Residential subdivisions opened in Kapahulu and Kaimuki, which was at the end of the trolley line in 1905, and on the slopes above Makiki to meet the demands of middle-class Oriental, Portuguese, and part-Hawaiian families prior to World War I. Upper Manoa, part of Maunalani Heights, Pacific Heights, St. Louis Heights, Wilhemina Rise, and the slopes of Diamond Head were developed by the 1920s to house the rapidly expanding middle-class Caucasian population of the city at a time when trolleys were still the principal mode of transportation. The poorly-drained marshes between Waikiki and Kakaako were occupied by stable immigrant farming, fishing, and laboring communities, which continued to support their own ethnic language schools, religious institutions, and customs until World War II. The Chinese who moved out of Chinatown into middle-class neighborhoods were gradually replaced first by Hawaiians, and then by Japanese and Filipino plantation workers. The Japanese population of the area adjacent to Chinatown, which was much less than the Chinese population there in 1900, has exceeded its Chinese population since 1920 (Glick 1936, 27). Situated between stable ghettos like Japanese Palama and Chinese Chinatown, transitional slums such as Hell's Half Acre, the red-light district near the Iwilei railroad terminus, had also emerged (Lind 1967, 54).

The large swampy area behind Waikiki was not reclaimed until the 1920s, when the Ala Wai Canal was dug. Only two of the city's five hotels were in Waikiki in 1917; the others were located in downtown Honolulu. Honolulu of the 1920s and 1930s, according to Judd (1961, 151), still had the "sleepy and gentle tempo of a charming small town." The western edge of the city was committed to naval, military, industrial, or agricultural uses. Although the old trail down the Nuuanu Pali was improved and paved for two lanes of automobile traffic during the 1920s, the present tunnel was not constructed until the late 1950s. Suburban expansion began after World War II. Pearl City, Kailua, and Kaneohe, the first, second, and fourth largest towns in the state in 1980, had fewer than 2,000 residents each in 1940. Honolulu, like most American cities of comparable size before World War II, was still a compact, CBD-oriented, low-rise city heavily dependent on mass transit. In the words of Lewis Mumford (1975, 89), "One might define Honolulu as a great park, partly disfigured by a careless weedy undergrowth of buildings."

Changing Patterns

The English Standard public schools, limited to children proficient in the English language, began in 1924. They were established largely in response to demands by middle-class parents, who could not afford private schools, to prevent their children from learning Pidgin English in public schools. While these special schools helped to raise the caliber of public education in Honolulu, they also helped to maintain patterns of racial and socioeconomic segregation until the 1950s, when the schools were terminated. Although the English Standard schools were meant for Caucasian children, who made up 77 percent of their enrollment in 1924, only 29 percent of the students were Caucasian in 1947 (Hormann 1950, 38–39). The middle class burgeoned with the arrival in Honolulu of military officers, proprietors of small businesses, and federal officials and their families from the mainland and the economic success of first- and second-generation Chinese and Japanese immigrants.

Supported by bountiful water resources and small farms, the populations of both rural Oahu and urban Honolulu more than tripled between 1900 and 1940, while the population of the outer islands increased by only 75 percent. In 1900 62 percent of

the people in the territory were on the outer islands and only 26 percent were in the city of Honolulu. By 1940 only 39 percent were on the outer islands and 42 percent were in Honolulu, where jobs in sugar processing, pineapple canneries, military and naval installations, and reclamation and construction activities expanded.

The United States acquired the right to use Pearl Harbor in 1887 in exchange for extending reciprocity but did not dredge the channel at its entrance or build roads, locks, and docks for a naval base until the end of World War I. Plans were developed by the Army for a series of forts to guard Honolulu harbor and Pearl Harbor, a centrally located garrison post, gun emplacements and observation posts along the coast, and a network of roads to reach all parts of the islands (Kuykendall and Day 1976, 215). Schofield Barracks in central Oahu was first occupied in 1901 and became the largest garrison post in the country. Luke (on Ford Island in Pearl Harbor), Wheeler, and Hickam air fields were established after World War I. The expansion of naval and military installations on the west side of town generated unprecedented civilian employment opportunities in west Honolulu and central Oahu, eventually brought millions of service personnel and their dependents to the island, created work for local contractors and suppliers, and diversified the economy of the territory. Defense spending was the islands' primary source of income from World War II until 1971, when tourism took the lead.

As in so many other American cities whose ethnic neighborhoods clustered at the edge of the central business district, disadvantaged ethnic groups in Honolulu were accommodated in urban villages, shophouses, and mixed-use districts. Not until the Second World War, after many of these communities were rezoned or cleared to make way for industrial and highway expansion, did Honolulu have a housing problem. Slum clearance, urban renewal, and public redevelopment only became fashionable after the wartime housing shortage and downtown decline. Fortunately, not all the immigrants to Honolulu after 1940 really needed low-cost housing in these districts. The new middle-class mainland families could afford to reside at the fringe and did not need help from special inner-city ethnic institutions. Most of the Filipinos and South Pacific islanders who came to Oahu after the war were able to work and reside in the small plantation towns and farming communities outside of the city, where their modest needs were generally met.

The vast majority of disadvantaged immigrants to urban Honolulu nonetheless have had difficulty finding affordable housing in single-purpose residential areas. Middle-class aspirations and rapidly increasing urban densities prompted city officials to impose higher subdivision and building standards in order to prevent the spread of slums. Blight in the eyes of planners was defined by traffic congestion, poor access to interior blocks, inadequate parking, poor sanitation, and aging and deteriorating buildings (Central Business District Consultants, 1961, 14). Connectivity and form, not functional viability, were the principal criteria. By such standards, blight in mixed-use, ethnic districts had always existed. Not until the Housing Act of 1949 and the later decline of CBD property values, however, did public officials really care.

The urban poor, who had usually worked and resided in what are now substandard structures on nonconforming properties, were priced out of the private housing markets even before the war, when few new houses were constructed and the demand for homes soared. Although many new walk-up apartments and single-family dwellings were built between the two wars, most were of much better quality and thus too expensive for the poor, many of whom lived in walk-up tenements along Kukui, Queen Emma, and School streets and along Hall Street, which no longer exists. Downtown Honolulu, built to serve the retail needs of middle-class residents, was victimized by the postwar growth of Ala Moana Shopping Center and the automobile—not by its adjacent working-class communities.

METROPOLITAN HONOLULU

Proposition Four: *High-rise redevelopment does not necessarily prevent urban sprawl; both can occur at the same time.*

When population pressures create the need for additional housing, urban development is needed. The choice might be to build high-rise apartments in a relatively confined central location, or planners might choose to extend the city's boundaries horizontally by permitting construction of single-family homes with individual yards. Logically, it would seem that selecting the high-rise plan would preclude urban sprawl, and expansion of the city horizontally would obviate the need for high rises. Honolulu's development seems to refute this logic.

The phenomenal growth of metropolitan Honolulu since World War II was made possible by both rapid suburban and high-rise expansion. The physical character of Honolulu has been dramatically transformed since statehood in 1959 in order to accommodate the connective and spatial needs of a rapidly suburbanizing region. Honolulu, whose international airport ranks eleventh in the country in terms of air traffic, became part of two vast urban systems, connecting the metropolitan centers of North America with those of Asia and Australia–New Zealand. Suburban development was encouraged by the construction of federally financed "interstate" highways, the rapid subdivision of agricultural land, the extension of sewer and water services, and the influx of capital from large mainland institutions.

Growth rates for suburban and rural Honolulu (the rest of Oahu) have been much higher than those for urban Honolulu since 1950. Urban or central Honolulu, which held half the state's resident population in 1950, contained only 39 percent in 1978. Urban fringe (suburban and rural Oahu) communities accounted for 41 percent of the state's population in 1978, compared to only 21 percent in 1950.

Community opposition to proposals to redevelop older single-family residential neighborhoods into townhouses, duplexes, and low-density apartments has usually been intense, even where the existing structures were neglected. Most residents continue to be attached to their neighborhoods, even those people who can afford new luxury apartments or larger houses in the suburbs and those whose children no longer reside with them.

Like most Americans, most of Hawaii's families would prefer to reside near people with similar values and interests and in dwellings where they have some privacy. Most would also like to enjoy the sunshine, flowers, fruit trees, and backyard barbeques that make living in Hawaii especially attractive. The importance of semiprivate, outdoor space is rooted in the island lifestyle. Small lanais or gardens were usually provided in older mixed-use districts. Unfortunately, such space was not required for new apartments. Of all the land resubdivided on Oahu from 1946 to 1962, only 0.2 percent was converted into two-family dwellings, and 3 percent was redeveloped into multi-family dwellings. The lion's share was resubdivided into single-family housing (on smaller lots) (Vargha 1962, 23).

Instead of upzoning many areas moderately, city and county officials upzoned those areas on which developmental pressures focused (such as Makiki, McCully, Moiliili, Waikiki, Salt Lake, and Pearl Ridge) into medium-rise and high-rise apartments during the 1960s and early 1970s.

The number of new building permits annually authorized for private multi-family units on Oahu consistently exceeded the number authorized for single-family units from 1965 to 1978 (Bank of Hawaii 1980, 25). The previous pattern in which single-family units dominated from 1946 to 1957 was thus reversed. The numbers of new single-family units authorized for both windward and central Oahu have been higher than they have for central Honolulu (tax key areas 1–2) since 1973. The shortage of single-family houses, duplexes, and townhouses in central Honolulu has driven up prices in the past decade (Bank of Hawaii 1980, 11). Only 45 percent of Oahu's housing units were owner occupied in 1979, which was well below the national average of 59 percent in 1977 (State of Hawaii, Department of Planning and Economic Development 1980).

The "highest and best use" of land was based on its zoning potential, not on its environmental carrying capacity. The relationship between high-density zoning and the availability of water, sewer, drainage, parks, mass transit, and other public services was sometimes ignored. Concrete towers were erected to maximize the profitability of the parcel. They were not expected to enhance the environmental quality of the surrounding neighborhood, nor were they obliged to meet the needs of families with young children. The strident mix of old single-family dwellings and towering new apartment buildings that characterizes so much of urban Honolulu was not anticipated. It should have been expected and could have been avoided.

New housing in central Honolulu was usually built in the form of high-rise apartments that often offered magnificent views of the city (and other high-rise buildings), air conditioning, and other aesthetic amenities. Such features are better suited for temporary vacation stays by visitors than for long-term occupancy by island families. According to Thomas Creighton (1978, 78),

By the early 1960s, the city was losing its moderately low, reasonably uncrowded look and starting on the road to metropolitan densities. . . . High-rise apartments began to appear in unlikely, scattered places, since the city's zoning map had ignored visual considerations. Valuable sight lines and view planes were lost as tall, often bulky, generally unrelated structures were built—up the sides of Punchbowl, into Nuuanu Valley, back of Waikiki, on the close-in slopes of lower Makiki Heights, at the base of Diamond Head, in Kahala, and of course as part of the burgeoning Hawaii Kai environs.

The rise of residential condominiums is, at least in part, attributable to the strong desire for home ownership in the face of sky-rocketing prices for single-family housing. Condominiums are supposed to raise the density of residential developments, provide shared common areas, lower the cost of each unit, and thus reduce the price to prospective buyers, who would otherwise not be able to afford a home. Condominiums give owner occupants a tax advantage and an opportunity to share in the appreciation of the property, neither of which would be open to renters. Moreover, they are much more attractive to lenders than cooperatives, whose notes are difficult to sell on the secondary mortgage market.

The construction of new condominiums could have relieved Honolulu's housing crunch if they had been built as townhouses, located in mixed-used areas, and designed as garden apartments. Rarely, however, were new condominiums in central Honolulu so designed. "In Honolulu the trend was toward mainland big city modernism—without the benefit of the creative talents that megalopolitan architecture needs in order to have form and visual organization. . . . In the way it used its central city land, Honolulu, which could have had its own colorful tropical character, matured as carelessly and as drearily as any other American metropolis" (Creighton 1978, 80). Too much of central Honolulu has been rezoned to high-rise apartments that cannot be easily served by firefighting equipment. Too little land has been used for walk-up apartments that are less expensive to build. Over 70 percent of the condominiums on Oahu in 1978 were part of high-rise structures, in contrast with 28 percent on the neighbor islands (State of Hawaii, Department of Planning and Economic Development 1979, 351). Townhouses were only about 17 percent of Oahu's condominiums. Unfortunately,

most of them were built on the fringe, not in town. Townhouses, duplexes, and cluster developments, most of which are well designed and carefully planned, have become more the exception than the rule in central Honolulu.

The City and County of Honolulu does have provisions for "customized zoning" in the form of planned developments, special design districts, and historic, scenic, or cultural districts, but they have not been used to provide a wider range of housing or commercial opportunities, with the possible exception of the Chinatown Historic District. According to Geoffrey Fairfax (n.d., 13–15),

> If stronger architectural expression is needed anywhere in Honolulu today it is most certainly in the area of high-rise buildings. Here particularly, with the indulgent tropical climate and limitless variety of materials, diversity prevails. In hotel and apartment high-rise structures balconies feebly assist in establishing a design direction, but in all high-rise structures, including office buildings, a convincing statement is rarely made. . . . Small board and batten houses, well-mellowed with age and toil, bow to the large containers of increased densities and move quietly from the scene. Creeping into Honolulu's architectural fabric are meaningless globs of concrete block apartments that disregard the value of the land—showing little concern for those who must dwell within and no concern for the countless others who are forced to view their exteriors.

Although city planning in Honolulu dates back to 1915, when the City Planning Commission was established at the urging of Lewis Mumford, public zoning, subdivision, and infrastructural decisions did not necessarily follow long-range city plans, nor were they evaluated in a comprehensive manner. The city fathers of Honolulu, as in most cities, failed to heed the advice of Charles Mulford Robinson (1906, 6) to "let all improvements be a development, not a remaking, of the old." Not until 1969 did the Hawaii Supreme Court rule that rezoning decisions had to conform to long-term comprehensive General Plan objectives, as provided in the Honolulu City Charter. Updating the 1964 General Plan, according to the court, had to be based on comprehensive studies of changing conditions and trends (Marshall, Kaplan, Gans, Kahn, and Yamamoto 1975, 34–35). A new Oahu General Plan was finally adopted in 1977, long after the foundations of spot zoning and high-rise sprawl in Honolulu had already been laid.

THE COST OF SPRAWL

Proposition Five: *Urban sprawl not only raises the cost of public services and eliminates scenic opportunities but also raises the cost of food and undermines rural life-styles.*

Urbanization can occur either by converting more nonurban land to urban use or by using existing urban lands more intensively. The urban fringe can be developed in a contiguous manner or in a leap-frog process; the latter is labeled suburban sprawl. Existing urban lands can be redeveloped to encourage high-rise housing on relatively few properties or lower-density housing on a larger number of contiguous parcels. It is clear that high-rise sprawl, which characterizes so much of metropolitan Honolulu, was just one of several possible development alternatives. High-rise sprawl can be extremely profitable for those who own urban lands that are rezoned for high-rise structures or large chunks of rural land that are rezoned into single-family housing. Low-density redevelopment within or at the edge of existing urban areas also raises land values, but it spreads the "unearned increment" out among more landowners.

The rural life-style, now being threatened by private landbanking in anticipation of further suburban and outlying resort development, actually throve on Oahu prior to statehood. Oahu had more acres in vegetable and taro production than any of the other counties and more land in fruit

orchards than all of the other counties combined in 1951 (Philipp 1953, 168). Family farming on Oahu was bolstered by the increasing demand for food to feed the city's growing resident, visitor, and military populations after World War II. About 46 percent of the family-sized fruit and vegetable farms in Hawaii were on Oahu in 1948 (Philipp 1953, 179). The spread of urbanization on Oahu closely followed major highway improvements and the expiration of agricultural leases. Private efforts to convert agricultural land into residential land were facilitated by the extension of drainage, water, and sewer systems. "The loss of rich, fertile and valuable agriculture lands" resulting from urban sprawl was a matter of grave concern to city planners, as indicated in the City and County's 1959 General Plan (Honolulu, Planning Department 1959, 10–11). Efforts by the Bernice P. Bishop Estate to develop 6,300 acres (2,520 ha) of agricultural land in central Oahu, Heeia, East Honolulu, and Koko Head and by Kaneohe Ranch (Castle Estate) to develop 8,000 acres (3,200 ha) of land in Kailua and Kaneohe were already well underway by the late 1950s in response to federal antitrust activities. Yet little was done by the city and county to maintain the viability of small farming on rural Oahu.

Of the 14,000 acres (5,600 ha) of agricultural land on Oahu redesignated by the State Land Use Commission to urban use from 1962 to 1975, over one-third were in central Oahu (Lowry and McElroy 1976, 21). Statewide zoning, which was established in 1961 as part of Hawaii's pioneering land use law, failed to protect prime agricultural lands and reverse the prevailing patterns of scattered suburban development that raised the cost of providing public infrastructure and services for fringe communities. It nonetheless lengthened the process and expense of housing development. The impact on housing prices was especially acute on Oahu, where the supply of land for new housing was already constrained by insularity, terrain, increasingly stringent subdivision regulations, and highly concentrated patterns of rural land ownership. Land-use control as implemented by the State Land Use Commission proved to be a cumbersome instrument for guiding and managing growth (Lowry and McElroy 1976, 27).

According to the City and County of Honolulu Planning Department (Honolulu Planning Department 1971, 3), 10,000 to 12,000 acres (4,000 to 4,800 ha) of land on which residential use was permitted were vacant during 1968–69. A more recent study (Honolulu Department of General Planning 1980, 5) contends that there is already enough residentially zoned land to meet Oahu's housing needs until the year 2000. Apparently, a great deal of land has been locked into development agreements or held for resale, rather than for immediate development into new housing.

The impact of soaring housing prices on Oahu has been especially burdensome on the disadvantaged country people who lease land or rent homes in what is now left of rural Oahu. The demand for country living has escalated as Honolulu's affluent population, who can afford to keep horses, own a weekend home, or invest in a tax shelter, has expanded. What will happen to country residents whose life-style is rooted in small commercial farming, subsistence agriculture, horticulture, and fishing? Keeping "da country country" has become a rallying point for many of those on the Waianae and windward coasts of Oahu who have nowhere else on the island to turn. The profitability of landbanking, and eventual development into resort or suburban communities, continues to reduce the availability of land on Oahu suitable for crops and livestock. The development of East Honolulu, Kaneohe, and Kailua during the late 1940s; Halawa, Aiea, and Pearl City during the 1950s; and Mililani-Waipio and Hawaii Kai during the late 1960s not only eliminated a great deal of agricultural land, it also uprooted rural residents who fished and raised livestock,

nursery products, fruits, vegetables, taro, or flowers for local market and subsistence consumption.

Although many of these crops can be grown in prime agricultural areas on the neighbor islands, such as Kula on Maui or Kona and Puna on the Big Island, the extra cost of interisland shipping is ultimately borne by local consumers. The cost of food prepared at home in Honolulu has thus risen faster since 1967 than any other item on the consumer price index (State of Hawaii, Department of Planning and Economic Development 1979, 226). The irony is that Oahu, with only about 10 percent of the land in the state, has more potentially productive agricultural land (classified in 1968 as "very good" or "good") than any of the other islands (State of Hawaii, Department of Planning and Economic Development 1979, 336). The number of acres in farms is nonetheless much lower on Oahu than it is on any of the other islands. Much of the state's prime agricultural land is located in rapidly suburbanizing central Oahu.

Unfortunately, the so-called "quiet revolution" in land-use controls that was sweeping the nation in the late 1960s was not as revolutionary in Hawaii as expected. The gap between public plans and specific decisions intended to implement these plans is well documented (Lowry 1977, pp. 15–26). The land-use law enabled the large landowners who wished to terminate leases on land used for sugar and pineapple production to take advantage of the soaring demand for low-density housing by families with young children, by restricting the supply of urban land ready for construction elsewhere on Oahu. Developers who anticipated the seller's market in single-family housing and who had purchased their land before prices skyrocketed profited handsomely.

To disadvantaged part-Hawaiians, residing in Waianae, Waimanalo, and the north shore, "highest and best use" of land has been a cruel hoax. Suburban subdivisions like Kailua, Hawaii Kai, and Mililani have been developed for middle-class residents, many of whom were born on the U.S. mainland. Although some Hawaiians whose children attend Kamehameha School (financed by Bishop Estate) or whose jobs are located at Campbell Industrial Park (owned by the James Campbell Estate) benefit directly from such developments, many Hawaiians have been affected adversely.

Sedimentation from land development on steep hillsides and ridges has degraded reef ecosystems and shoreline fisheries. Rising land rents, higher property taxes, and lower water supplies have made it difficult for small farmers. Oahu no longer supports as wide a range of rural and urban lifestyles as it did prior to the 1960s. Although there is still a great deal of agricultural land left that might be developed for urban use, it is doubtful that further suburban growth on Oahu could be accommodated without raising the cost of agricultural land and lowering the availability of water to Oahu's small farmers, on whom the price of food in Honolulu at least indirectly depends.

The purpose of managing growth on Oahu is not merely to preserve more land for sugar and pineapple or more scenic vistas for Hawaii's visitors; it is also to preserve the variety of subcultures and lifestyles that have made Honolulu such an interesting city to visit as well as such an ideal place in which to raise children. Low-cost housing in mixed-use urban districts and small family farms are desperately needed. Private landbanking has been practiced for two decades and with a great deal of success. The overwhelming majority of Hawaii's residents believe that it is important to preserve the many different types of life-styles that exist in Hawaii (Marshall, Kaplan, Gans, Kahn, and Yamamoto 1975, 56). If rural life-styles are to be preserved, then past experience suggests that further regulation per se will not be effective. In Hawaii it is often difficult to differentiate

between the public and private interest, between the regulators and those who are being regulated, and between flexible planning and politics.

METROPOLITAN HAWAII

Proposition Six: *The problems of nonmetropolitan Hawaii are not an inherent outgrowth of urbanization; they are rooted in failures to anticipate economic changes and mitigate their ill effects through the planning process.*

The conversion of agricultural and conservation land into urban development, in many cases, creates environments that are less scenic and less preserving of a characteristic life-style. Yet, as populations increase, so does the need for housing; urbanization is inevitable if the needs of those who are or wish to become residents of an area are to be met. The "conventional wisdom" is that if we are to have urbanization, we must accept its undesirable consequences: less open space, crowded cities, changed life-styles for some, and a loss of scenic and recreational resources. Although the process of urbanization *may* lead to these consequences, it is not true that it *must*.

The resurgence of the neighbor islands during the past decade did not occur by chance. It was precipitated by longstanding state growth policies that date back to the beginning of the Burns administration during the early 1960s. Governor John Burns was a strong advocate of redistributing growth to the neighbor islands, each of which had lost population during the 1930s, 1940s, and 1950s. Huge investments were thus made in new state highways, airports, harbors, and community colleges to stimulate their development. About one-third of the land redesignated by the State Land Use Commission from agricultural to urban use from 1962 to 1977 was located on the Big Island, where large resort developments on the Kona coast had been planned. Tourism for the neighbor islands was supported by the International Longshoremen's and Warehousemen's Union (ILWU), to which most of their hotel workers belong, by major landowners who stood to make large profits from rezoning decisions, and by many a county politician whose influence in state and county planning decisions rose in value.

With the imposition of tighter local development controls in Waikiki (the Waikiki Special Design District) in 1976, which was supported by the Waikiki Improvement Association, many resort developers were finally convinced that the quarter was indeed saturated and that outer-island resorts might be more profitable investments. The State Land Use Commission had, after all, continued to favor tourism, especially for the Big Island where more land was rezoned to urban use than in any other county from 1972 to 1979.

Governor Burns promised a crowd at Hilo on the eve of his 1970 gubernatorial campaign victory that the 1970s would, like the 1960s, be a decade of sweeping changes, bringing more individualized education, better environmental planning, new transit systems, quality tourism, and new housing to all the islands (Coffman 1972, 152–153). He was for the most part correct. The neighbor islands, as he envisioned, did indeed grow faster than either urban or suburban-rural Honolulu from 1970 to 1978. The number of private single-family housing units authorized annually on the outer islands surpassed that of Oahu from 1974 to 1979. Growth on the neighbor islands accelerated as new resort communities were developed on the Kona coast of the Big Island, on the southwest shores of Maui, on West Molokai, and at Poipu and Wailua on Kauai. All three of the neighbor island counties grew faster than Oahu from 1970 to 1978. Tourism no doubt helped to repopulate the outer islands by attracting a new breed of immigrants into their communities. The industry offered seasonal, casual, part-time employment in which earnings depended heavily on gratuities and personalized services. Newcomers often wound up with jobs that many long-time residents did not want.

The growth of *pakalolo* (marijuana) also helped to diversify the rural economy. While it is probably still the leading export crop in the islands in terms of commercial value, raids by law-enforcement officials and poaching by competitors appear to have driven out many of the cultivators, who flocked to the "jungle" section of Waikiki during the late 1960s and dispersed to the outer islands by the early 1970s. As might be expected, the apostles of the counterculture were sometimes tolerated but rarely welcomed. Income from the sale of "Puna butter," "Maui wowie," and "Kona gold" pumped income into the rural economy and helped to renovate mainstreet stores and workshops, but the benefits were otherwise quite limited. Countercultural practices also undermined working class values and the spirit of *ohana*, which had held so many of these plantation and farming communities together. Dilapidated farmsteads and long-neglected company towns now support an amazing number of four-wheel-drive vehicles, health food stores, and young, self-employed entrepreneurs. The price of real estate in remote rural areas continues to climb, even where their populations have remained stable or declined; their towns have been badly neglected; the land has been phased out of sugar, pineapple, or coffee production; and prospects for resort or residential development are slim.

The viability of traditional rural lifestyles will not be decided merely by agricultural subdivision and zoning controls. It will also depend on efforts to acquire public access to the shoreline and forest, most of which is within the public domain, in the face of further urbanization and scattered resort expansion. Fishing, ocean sports, hunting, and gathering still play an important role in rural communities, where exchange and mobility are rooted in the *ohana* tradition. Opportunities to pass through plantation or ranch gates were usually open to local community residents, even though the process of gaining permission may have varied widely from place to place. Heavier traffic through rural areas, as a result of highway improvements, resort development, and *pakalolo* cultivation, has increased vandalism, littering, and disrespect for private property. The influx of new mainland residents and property owners with little respect for the traditional Hawaiian rural life-style has likewise accentuated pressure to close the shoreline and forests to local use. Keeping the countryside open and affordable for long-time residents has become increasingly difficult during the past decade, when the emphasis has been on making it more manageable and profitable for the visitor industry.

There are already signs, however, that lack of attention to the needs and values of long-time residents may be self-defeating. Tourism, unlike sugar, pineapple, and livestock, can be made or broken by local attitudes. Hawaii's violent-crime rate, which was only one-fourth of the national rate in 1959, has been growing. The past few years have seen increasing incidents of violent crime and expressions of antagonism by long-time residents against unsuspecting visitors. Mainland press coverage of violent crimes against visitors in rural Hawaii has understandably been sensational, since the industry still conveys in its advertising an image of the islands as a verdant paradise where visitors can relax, unwind, and get away from it all for a week or two. Although violent-crime rates in Honolulu are admittedly still lower than they are in many large metropolitan areas, they are nonetheless too high.

Why should the islands, whose economy is so dependent on tourism, be guided by mainland metropolitan standards? Crime is not an inherent part of urbanization. It flourishes where it is tolerated and legitimized. The benefits of mass tourism do not necessarily circulate among the residents of rural Hawaii where so many new hotels have been built during the past

decade. Most of the benefits leak immediately back to Honolulu and other metropolitan areas (Chow 1978, 357), which upsets many rural residents.

Immigrants to the plantations consisted mainly of poor foreign workers who had little to show for their labor. The affluent visitors and professional resort workers being drawn to the neighbor islands are wealthy and urbane by local standards. Yet unlike the pre–World War II era, when plantation workers could readily find better opportunities in Honolulu or in one of the outer-island towns, present rural residents have no such alternatives. Housing and food in metropolitan Honolulu and even in the smaller cities are too expensive for most of them. Relative deprivation has been heightened by tourism. Many of the young adults of rural Hawaii who cannot afford to own a house in the rural communities in which they were raised are bitter about sweeping changes over which they seem to exert little control.

Although it is true, as one would expect, that in metropolitan Oahu more residents and visitors are victimized by crimes than in rural areas, there seems to be little relationship between urbanization and crime. According to the Hawaii Commission on Crime (1978, 10), a larger proportion of those in Hawaii County than on Oahu, for example, believe that organized crime is a serious problem in the islands. A larger portion of those responding to the survey from Kauai County than from Honolulu County claim that crime or the fear of crime has affected their lives very much. Moreover, crimes in nonmetropolitan Hawaii apparently tend to be underestimated, since fewer of those responding from all of the three outer-island counties than from Oahu reported cases to the police in which they or their immediate families were victims of a crime. A strong degree of association exists between tourism and certain crimes in Hawaii (Fujii and Mak 1980, 28), despite major variations in the extent to which the state has been urbanized.

In the words of Charles Mulford Robinson (1906, 4), "When all is said, whatever development is given to Honolulu and to its surrounding country should be first of all for the comfort and enjoyment of its own citizens. . . . If we make the city more beautiful and attractive to them, adding to their contentment and happiness, we shall also make it more attractive to strangers."

REFERENCES

Armstrong, R. W. *Atlas of Hawaii.* Honolulu: University Press of Hawaii, 1973.

Bank of Hawaii. *Construction in Hawaii.* Honolulu: Bank of Hawaii, 1980.

Central Business District Consultants. *The Central Business District of Honolulu.* Prepared for the City and County of Honolulu by Harlan Bartholomew & Associates; Community Planning, Inc., of Honolulu; and Charles Bennett & Associates of Los Angeles, 1961.

Chow, W. T. "Tourism and Regional Planning: The Legend of Hawaii." *Proceedings of the Fifth Pacific Regional Science Conference, Vancouver, B.C.,* Bellingham: Western Washington University, 1978, pp. 349–368.

Coffman, T. *Catch a Wave: A Case Study of Hawaii's New Politics.* Honolulu: University Press of Hawaii, 1972.

Creighton, T. H. *The Lands of Hawaii: Their Use and Misuse.* Honolulu: University Press of Hawaii, 1978.

Fairfax, G. W. *The Architecture of Honolulu.* Norfolk Island, Australia: Island Heritage, Ltd., n.d.

Fisher, T. "Hawaii: Growing Pains in Paradise." *Population Bulletin* 29 (1973): 1–40.

Fujii, E., and Mak, J. "Tourism and Crime: Implications for Development Policy." *Regional Studies* 14 (1980): 27–36.

Glick, C. "Residential Dispersion of Urban Chinese." *Social Process in Hawaii* 2 (1936): 28–34.

Handy, E.S.C., and Pukui, M. K. *The Polynesian Family System in Ka'u, Hawai'i.* Rutland, Vt.: Charles E. Tuttle Co., 1972.

Honolulu, Department of General Planning. "Development Plan Land Use Analysis." Honolulu: City and County of Honolulu, 1980.

Honolulu, Planning Department. "General Plan for Urban and Urbanizing Areas." Honolulu: City and County of Honolulu, 1959.

———. "Vacant Residential Land on Oahu." Table 1. Honolulu: City and County of Honolulu, 1971.

Hormann, Bernard L. "The Caucasian Minority." *Social Process in Hawaii* 14 (1950): 38–50.

Judd, G. P. *Hawaii: An Informal History.* London: Collier MacMillan, 1961.

Kuykendall, R. S., and Day, A. G. *Hawaii: A History.* Englewood Cliffs, N.J.: Prentice-Hall, 1976.

Lind, A. W. *Hawaii's People.* Honolulu: University of Hawaii Press, 1967.

Loomis, A. *Grapes of Canaan: Hawaii 1820.* Honolulu: Hawaiian Mission Children's Society, 1951.

Lowry, K. et al. "Analysis of Alternative Land Use Management Techniques in Hawaii." *Growth Management Issues in Hawaii.* Honolulu: Hawaii State Department of Budget and Finance, Hawaii Institute for Management and Analysis in Government, 1977, pp. 9–94.

Lowry, K., and McElroy, M. "State Land Use Control: Some Lessons From Experience." *State Planning Issues* 1 (1976): 15–28.

Marshall, Kaplan, Gans, Kahn, and Yamamoto. *Report to the People.* Technical Report No. 2. Prepared for the Hawaii State Land Use Commission, 1975.

Meller, N., and Horowitz, R. H. "Hawaii: Themes in Land Monopoly." In *Land Tenure in the Pacific,* edited by Ron Crocombe, pp. 25–42. London: Oxford University Press, 1971.

Mumford, L. *City Development: Studies in Disintegration and Renewal.* Westport, Conn.: Greenwood Press, 1975. (Also published New York: Harcourt Brace and Co., 1945.)

———. *The City in History.* New York: Harcourt Brace and World, 1961.

Philipp, P. F. *Diversified Agriculture of Hawaii.* Honolulu: University of Hawaii Press, 1953.

Robinson, C. M. "The Improvement of Honolulu." Prepared for the Board of Supervisors of the County of Oahu, 1906.

Schmitt, R. C. *Historical Statistics of Hawaii.* Honolulu: University Press of Hawaii, 1977.

State of Hawaii, Commission on Crime. "A Survey of Crime and the Criminal Justice System." A report to the State Legislature. Honolulu: State of Hawaii, Commission on Crime, 1978.

State of Hawaii, Department of Planning and Economic Development. "County Trends in Hawaii, 1967–79." Research & Economic Analysis Division, Statistical Report 134, Table 14. Honolulu: State of Hawaii, 1980.

_____. *Data Book.* Honolulu: State of Hawaii, 1979.

Vargha, L. A. *Urban Development on Oahu, 1946–62.* Land Study Bureau Bulletin no. 2 (September). Honolulu: University of Hawaii, 1962.

CHAPTER 16

SEQUENT OCCUPANCE: TWO CENTURIES OF DUALISM

The Hawaiian economy, as it evolved from a completely subsistence agriculture to one based on capital-intensive plantations and trade, underwent a period of dualism, traces of which still exist today.

Boeke (1953, 14) defined dualism in an attempt to describe the economy and social structure of the Netherlands East Indies. In his words, "Social dualism is the clashing of a native system with an imported social system of another style." Thus dualism, which is usually thought of in its economic contexts, has social and cultural attributes as well. It is probably common, to a certain extent, in all societies where an existing culture is dominated by an imported culture characterized by a more highly developed economy.

Typically the native economy has limited needs and is essentially subsistence, while the imported economy is profit oriented and capital intensive. Boeke believed that the culture of the native system was "perfectly adapted to the environment" and that its agriculture "could hardly be improved upon" (Boeke 1953, 31). Strong words to be sure, but the idea that native agriculture is essentially adapted to the environment while the more modern agricultural styles attempt to alter the environment is basically true.

Dual societies are characterized by a labor-intensive peasant economy existing side by side with a capital-intensive economic sector, with little or no integration of the two (Geertz 1963). Geertz, too, was describing the social and economic structure of the Netherlands East Indies, but Higgins (1956) contended that some degree of dualism exists in almost all underdeveloped economies and that examples can be found in such highly developed economies as the United States and Canada as well.

THE FISH-AND-POI ECONOMY

Prior to Cook's arrival in the Hawaiian Islands in 1778 the Hawaiian people were subsisting entirely on the produce of the land and nearby waters. The economy was closed, without imports from or exports to areas outside the islands themselves, but there was some trade within the islands, particularly between Oahu and Kauai. Oahu specialized in the manufacture of tapa cloth, which was bartered for canoes built on Kauai (Morgan 1948, 48).

The population was stable at about 250,000, according to the most widely accepted estimates made by Cook's officers. The intensity of use of the land as well as the resources of the sea was indicative that the carrying capacity of the land and sea was just sufficient to sustain the population under the existing conditions of technology. Fields were irrigated and terraced, and boundaries were definitely and permanently marked. Land suitable for cultivation, the well-watered valleys, was scarce and valuable (Morgan 1948, 8, 19). Political and economic order were preserved by an elaborate system of tabus (*kapus*), which, however, produced and perpetuated great economic inefficiencies. A feudal system of land tenure had been developed; by 1778 it was highly organized and sustained by the elaborate complex of *kapus*. In theory, all land belonged to the ruler (*alii aimoku*) of each island, who apportioned this land to his supporting chiefs in exchange for their allegiance. The chiefs (*alii*) in turn allocated the land to commoners (*makaainana*) for cultivation. "Tenure was thus at the will of the king and conditional upon the faithful fulfillment of feudal responsibilities" (Lind 1938, 32).

The available land was subdivided into a number of units: *mokus, ahupuaas, ilis,* and *kihapais.* The *moku* was a large sector of an island, defined and governed by the principal *alii* of the island as an administrative unit. A smaller unit, the *ahupuaa,* was a complete estate, whenever possible extending from the mountains to the sea and thus self-sufficient: fish could be obtained from the coastal waters, while taro, yams, sugarcane, breadfruit, and bananas could be grown in the fertile lowlands. The mountain regions supplied firewood, wooden poles for houses, logs for canoes, bark for tapa cloth, oloana and other fibers for cord and rope, and bird feathers for adornment (Morgan 1948, 17). The *ahupuaa* was under the control of an important chief (*alii nui*).

The *ili*, the next smaller land section, was either part of the *ahupuaa* or a land unit ceded directly by the *alii aimoku*. The smallest parcel of land was the *kihapai*, the basic unit awarded to *makaainana* for their cultivation. The word *hapai* means "to carry"; thus the *kihapai* was the smallest parcel of land that could carry or sustain a family.

All land was held on condition of obedience and payment of taxes. Military service, an obligation of the *alii*, was seldom required of commoners (Morgan 1948, 22).

In addition to the two basic groups, *alii* and *makaainana*, there were three other classes of people: *konohikis, ilamukus,* and *kahunas.* The *konohiki* was an executive agent for the ruler and important *alii* for the purpose of managing the land and collecting the taxes. *Ilamukus* were roughly equivalent to police and sheriffs, while the *kahunas* were an important class of a semireligious nature who enforced the *kapus*. Since the *kapus* chiefly benefited the *alii*, the *kahunas* and *alii* were in a sense allies who stood to benefit most by maintenance of the established order.

Taxes were oppressive. In addition to a certain percentage of the yield of the *kihapai*, the commoner was required to contribute one day of labor per week to his *alii*. This labor was performed on special plots of land within the *ahupuaa*. The *alii* also had the unlimited right to levy additional taxes as he desired. Consequently, it has been estimated that the commoners were able to retain not more than one-third of the produce of their lands. In exchange for these taxes the *alii* were obligated to do no more than permit the commoner the use of the land and to provide him with some degree of protection (Morgan 1948, 22–28).

Since the *alii* could levy taxes at will there was little incentive for the commoner to improve his land or increase production, for additional produce raised was likely to be confiscated by the chief in the form of an additional tax (Morgan 1948, 27, 28). The *makaainana* had no beasts of burden, and farm implements were exceedingly simple and rudimentary. The *oo*, a spoon-shaped paddle, was the principal tool used to cultivate the soil; it was held by the farmer and moved back and forth in the ground.

The chief food crops were taro, from which poi was made, and sweet potatoes. Bananas, sugarcane, breadfruit, plantains, coconuts, and mountain apples were also raised or were available growing wild. Pigs, dogs, domestic fowl, and wild geese provided meat, chiefly for the *alii*, and the ocean provided oysters and a variety of species of fish. The *alii* maintained fish ponds in which mullet were raised until mature enough to eat.

Since the islands were verging on over-population and there was a shortage of usable land, commoners had the freedom to move from one *ahupuaa* to another. *Alii* had no fear of a shortage of labor, and it was not unusual for commoners to shift from one *kihapai* to another on a different *alii*'s land.

Many of the *kapus* served merely to impress the commoner with the importance of the *alii*. Thus, they served to provide the *alii* with suitable trappings of office, similar to the plush wall-to-wall carpet and expensive office furniture maintained by important business executives today. Conspicuous consumption on the part of the *alii* manifested itself in "astonishing fatness" (Morgan 1948, 52), as there were few durable goods that could be collected and displayed, and food was virtually the only mark of wealth.

THE TRADING ECONOMY

When Captain Cook made his discovery of the Hawaiian Islands in 1778 and anchored at Kealakekua Bay, Hawaii, to obtain needed provisions, Hawaii's economy changed from a closed to an open one. The Hawaiians, despite their lack of a trading tradition (the trade between Oahu and Kauai was quite small in scale and generally unimportant), readily agreed to supply the British ships with food and water in exchange for articles that sailors could provide, principally bits of iron. There are some who surmise that the Hawaiians might have considered their barter of food for iron an exchange of gifts—a measure of the Hawaiian spirit of hospitality—rather than true economic trade. Nevertheless, as ship visits increased in number after the existence of the islands and their desirability as a provisioning stop became known, a regular trade was established with prices and values determined by market principles.

Initially, it was only the *alii* who received any benefits from trade with the visiting ships. The commoners continued to cultivate their fields and pay their taxes to the chiefs. The taxes became heavier, however, as more food had to be available both for the chief's sustenance and for trade to the sailors.

Fur traders began to stop in the islands in the last decade of the eighteenth century, Hawaii being then recognized as a favorite spot to obtain "refreshments" (Morgan 1948, 58). By 1802, however, there were complaints about the high cost of provisions in the islands compared to former times. Nevertheless the fur traders kept coming, Hawaii's mid-Pacific location being valuable as a recreational and provisioning stop.

Sandalwood was discovered in the islands in the early nineteenth century; by 1809 it had become a regular trading item. The discovery of the value of sandalwood as an article of trade resulted in the most profound changes in the day-to-day life of the *makaainana*, who was then required to spend long hours, sometimes days or weeks, in the forest cutting sandalwood for his *alii*. His crops suffered, as did his health. Again it was the *alii* who benefited from the new, western economy, as they obtained additional trade goods in exchange for sandalwood. By the 1820s the chiefs had developed a more sophisticated taste for trade goods and the commoners were forced to work ever harder and longer to provide the sandalwood needed to pay for their *alii*'s expensive tastes. The economy was becoming dual; the *alii* had entered the modern trading economy while the commoners remained as subsistence farmers with the added burdens imposed by the chiefs. The economy of the commoners was increasingly more labor intensive.

Trade in sandalwood soon came to an end; in 1835 the wood taken in the islands was valued at only $26,000 compared to a peak year when the value was $300,000 (Morgan 1948,67). The trade had introduced new consumer goods of European, U.S., and Chinese manufacture to Hawaii, impoverished the commoners, and established the islands as an outpost of the U.S. mainland economy.

Although in 1823 there were fewer than 200 foreigners in Hawaii, 15 or 20 were permanent residents. A few were well-to-do businessmen, the others clerks and employees for four mercantile houses that had been established (Morgan 1948,71).

During this period there were social changes as well as economic ones. *Haoles* (foreigners) had never been required to obey the *kapus*, yet they apparently suffered no harm from their disregard of the multitude of sacred rules. Because of this the faith of the Hawaiian commoner in his gods was being undermined, and even the *alii* were beginning to find the system of *kapus* burdensome and unnecessary. While formerly many of the *kapus* had served the *alii* as marks of respect and importance, he now no longer needed these; he had real material wealth to prove his *mana* (roughly translated "divine power"). The loss of faith in the *kapus* even resulted in instances of both commoner and *alii* bartering their god images for nails (Lind 1938,143).

The *kapu* system was kept in operation by Kamehameha I, who by 1810 had conquered the islands and become king. On his death, in 1819, the *kapus* were formally abolished. They were simply no longer of value in an economy that had largely shifted from subsistence agriculture to a trade ba-

sis. The commoner, however, clung to his beliefs for many years, and there is evidence that some Hawaiians even today believe in the old gods. (At many of the *heiaus* scattered throughout the islands, Hawaiians leave food offerings, presumably to Lono, god of agriculture and fertility.)

Whaling ships began stopping in the islands in 1810 and in the 1820s were visiting Hawaii in large numbers (Morgan 1948,76). The vessels needed provisions, equipment, and repairs, all of which could be provided by the Hawaiians, albeit at the expense of their subsistence crops. Increasing amounts of labor and agricultural resources were diverted from native consumption to sales to whalers. During this period whalers spent between $800 and $1,500 per vessel during an average visit to the islands (Morgan 1948,80), and their demand for fresh meat was the chief incentive for the beginning of cattle production in Hawaii.

The whaling trade further intensified the dual nature of the Hawaiian economy and society. Whaling's golden age, from 1843 to 1860, provided an external market for Hawaii's crops and encouraged diversified agriculture. However, "farming organization was not stabilized: the kuleana (kihapai) of the native produced for the market in competition with larger farms and plantations of the nobility and foreigner" (Morgan 1948,151). Even by 1845 production techniques had not changed much. The axe and knife were used, now made of steel instead of stone, but there were no heavier tools in use—no plows, scythes, or sickles. However, metal fishhooks had been substituted for bone ones (Morgan 1948,103).

Foreigners and chiefs enjoyed a standard of living far superior to that of the commoners. It was not merely the great disparity of wealth between foreigners and *aliis*, on the one hand, and commoners, on the other, that was indicative of the dual nature of Hawaiian society—for *alii* had always enjoyed a much higher standard of living than the commoners. Much more important, there was evidence of a drastic decline in the native Hawaiian population. From an estimated 250,000 when the islands were discovered in 1778, the population was down to 134,750 in 1823. While certainly the introduction of diseases for which the Hawaiians had no natural immunity was largely responsible for a greatly increased death rate, economic factors also played an important role.

> Second, was the continuing foreign interference with the native economy and its flow of productive effort. There was an important, widespread diversion of labor from producing food for home use to producing it for consumption by visiting ships, and to collecting sandalwood. In each case the returns to the Islands were largely in the form of importations valued by the chiefs as items of conspicuous consumption, with a negligible import of goods increasing the material welfare of the people at large. (Morgan 1948,115)

The Hawaiians, who were described as being hard working, industrious, and healthy by the first white visitors to the islands, were being described as lazy, shiftless, and sickly in the 1840s. There seemed to be a clearcut collapse of native morale.

Not all of the Hawaiian commoners were excluded from enjoying the rewards associated with the new economy, however. In the 1840s the clothing, housing, utensils, and furniture of some natives had changed, and by 1844 it was reported that the habit of regular work for wages was making headway among those natives who had chosen to abandon their subsistence farms for work at the ports (Morgan 1948,114). "An increasing number of the Islanders were living on the margins of the two competing economies, deriving most of their livelihood from the cultivation of their own kuleanas but also earning some money for the purchase of trade goods from the sale of farm surplus or from an occasional day of work for the government" (Lind 1967,66).

Protestant missionaries, who reached the islands in 1820, initially had little effect on the native economy, although they were quickly successful in interesting both *alii* and commoners in the new religion and in learning to read and write. It was not until the religious and educational work of the missionaries had largely been completed that their effect on the economy became important.

> They were energetic, trained to anticipate the future, and acutely conscious of the sharp upward trend in land values in the middle and late nineteenth century. As they preached thrift to the natives, so they practiced it themselves, adding good example to good doctrine. They improved their lands, experimented in and furthered agriculture, and showed the native the way to get ahead. This seemed to them worthy work: the Puritan code gave credit to the honest and shrewd businessman. (Morgan 1948, 95)

LAND REFORM

Until 1839 it was clear that all land in the islands was owned by the king. Land holdings were at the king's pleasure and were revocable by him in the case of *ahupuaas* held by the *alii*. Likewise the *alii* had the right to expel from the land commoners who held *kihapais* in the various *ahupuaas*, although this was seldom done. In the Hawaiian Bill of Rights of 1839, however, the first changes to the Hawaiian land system became apparent. Part of the Bill of Rights reads, "Protection is hereby secured to the persons of all the people together with their lands, their building lots and all their property, and nothing whatever shall be taken from any individual except by express provision of the law" (Chinen 1958,7). The act further stated that the "landlord cannot causelessly dispossess his tenant."

Changes in the Hawaiian land system had been advocated by traders, merchants, and missionaries. In the case of the missionaries the desire for change was partially to improve the status of the tenant-commoner and partially so that they too could hold land in fee simple (Chinen 1958,7).

On December 10, 1845, a statute was enacted creating the Board of Commissioners to Quiet Land Titles "for the investigation and final ascertainment or rejection of all claims of private individuals, whether natives or foreigners, to any property acquired anterior to the passage of this Act" (Chinen 1958,8). Although most of the claims heard by the land commissioners were for leasehold interests, a few natives filed claims for land in fee simple.

The Great Mahele (land division) of 1848 assigned fee-simple ownership of land to the king (crown lands), the *alii* (*konohiki* lands), and the government of Hawaii. In 1849 the land commission was authorized to award fee-simple titles to all native tenants who occupied any portion of crown, government, or *konohiki* lands (Chinen 1958,29). These lands, referred to as *kuleana* lands, totaled only 28,000 acres (11,200 ha) compared to 1,495,000 acres (598,000 ha) of government lands, 984,000 acres (379,200 ha) of crown lands, and *konohiki* lands totaling 1,619,000 acres (647,600 ha).

On July 10, 1850, sales of land in fee simple to resident aliens were authorized, and the legal requirements for a new land system in the islands were completed. According to Morgan (1948,139), "The land reform and the social reform which accompanied it were the indispensables of economic advance." The immediate advantages to commoners were not apparent, however, and it would be a long time before they reaped any benefits from this economic advance.

The *kuleanas* were frequently too small to support a family and this, coupled with the attraction of the port towns and the booming land prices, resulted in the passing of many of the *kuleanas* into the hands of plantation owners and speculators (Morgan 1948,137). Nevertheless most of the plantation lands must have been obtained from the *alii* or from government lands,

as *kuleana* lands totaled only 28,000 acres (11,200 ha).

SUGAR

Whereas the Hawaiian commoner was precluded from obtaining economic benefits from the trading economy, because he still owed allegiance to his chief, he deliberately chose not to enter the modern agricultural economy of the sugar plantation. There are several possible explanations for the shortage of Hawaiian laborers in the early plantations. First, there were not many Hawaiians left, the population having been drastically reduced by disease and a falling birth rate. Second, Hawaiians were reputed to be lazy and incapable of sustained field work. It seems clear, however, that the Hawaiian commoner simply preferred to remain on his *kuleana* or to take a job in one of the towns. Work on a plantation for long hours with low wages just didn't appeal to him, particularly since the plantation social system seemed in many ways to duplicate the feudal system from which he was anxious to escape. "A paternalistic concern for the kanaka of the thirties and forties was necessary, both because he had little thought for the morrow, and because of the desirability of isolating him from the claims of the chief" (Morgan 1948,187).

Among the early problems of the plantation managers were the resistance of the natives to regular labor and their lack of knowledge of, and skill with, tools. An attempt to solve these two problems was made at Kohala in 1841 by an agreement between the chief and the mill owner. The chief was expected to grow and harvest the cane, using native labor, for delivery to the mill. In exchange he received a share of the profits. Planting was done with the *oo* (the native hand spade that was used to cultivate taro) (Morgan 1948,177).

In 1852 the plantations turned to foreign labor. Chinese contract laborers entered the islands, followed in turn by Portuguese,

Japanese, Puerto Ricans, Koreans, and Filipinos. From the beginning of plantation dominance in Hawaii there was almost complete dependence on immigrant labor.

The virtual exclusion of the Hawaiians from the plantations resulted in a dual economic system. The plantations utilized foreign laborers, who, after an initial period on the plantation, entered the larger trading economy of the islands. The Hawaiians, for the most part, reverted to the subsistence agriculture of their *kuleanas*.

In the 1860s Hawaiians were considered to be superior to foreign laborers, although they still were not numerous on the plantations. They still preferred the old ways, and

to a number of isolated areas and valleys the foreigner came infrequently, or hardly at all; and there the native caught his fish and grew his taro as in former days. So far as he had wants the native economy could not supply, a day's work now and then sufficed to bring in a bit of wages—work perhaps on the government road, or perhaps for another native who had some plantation money to pass on. These isolated rural retreats remained, with the ghosts of the old culture—tabus, religion, and ancient tradition—hovering over them. (Morgan 1948,202)

But the new ways were taking over and "by 1876 the haole merchants and planters and missionaries had reformed the Island economic structure especially after their own image. Their plantations, stores, steamships, churches, and weekly brass band were drowning out the traditions of the past" (Morgan 1948,206).

DUALISM TODAY

The census of the islands taken in 1866 revealed that well over half the natives were still living under a predominantly subsistence economy (Lind 1967,67). Thereafter, Hawaiians gradually drifted into the *haole* economy, and after 1870 a growing acclimatization of Hawaiians to regular work was reported.

But the old traditions died hard. Census reports as late as 1930 showed distinct enclaves of Hawaiians, unassimilated into the general economy. "The old fish and poi economy, with its accompaniment of tutelary deities, taboos, religion and magic still persists in modified form within many of these isolated communities. A small plot of taro and access to the sea and mountains are apparently all that is required for the satisfaction of their material wants" (Lind 1938,102).

There are still small groups of Hawaiians who have chosen not to take part in Hawaii's modern economy. The farmers in Waiahole and Waikane valleys on Oahu's windward coast and the fishermen on Mokauea Island, in the path of noisy jet aircraft taking off from Honolulu International Airport, prefer to preserve what they see as the Hawaiian way of life, counting on the land and the sea to sustain them.

On the island of Niihau cultural dualism and a modified system of the ancient Hawaiian feudalism still exist. The island was acquired by its current owners, the Robinson family of Kauai, in the 1870s, and for the native Hawaiians then in residence time stood still. There is still no electricity on the island and life is simple and old-fashioned. The population today is 95 percent Hawaiian, and the Hawaiian language is regularly spoken. The principal industry is the raising of cattle and sheep, and virtually all residents work for the Niihau Ranch owned by the Robinsons.

But even among those with Hawaiian blood who enjoy the fruits of the modern western economy there has been a resurgence of interest in Hawaiian culture. While the economic aspects of dualism are few and hard to find, the social and cultural aspects are becoming more common. Today's multi-ethnic population in the islands can find evidence of social dualism in the existence of Hawaiian sports, language, and music side by side with their American cultural counterparts.

Hawaiian Sports

Two of the more well-known and widely practiced athletic activities in Hawaii are surfing and canoe paddling, both sports enjoyed by Hawaiians before the coming of Captain Cook. There is evidence both in oral tradition and eyewitness accounts by early westerners that the *alii* were skilled at riding surfboards on the islands' breaking waves, and there are old Hawaiian koa surfboards preserved in museums. The modern sport of surfing is enjoyed by residents of all ethnic backgrounds in the islands, but it owes its beginnings to the ancient Hawaiian culture.

The modern team sport of canoe paddling is based on the canoe designs in use by the Hawaiians when the islands were first discovered by Westerners. Today there are dozens of teams participating in races of various lengths. The outrigger canoes of today are sometimes made of native koa wood, as well as the more modern fiberglass. The racing season culminates in the famous race from Molokai to Oahu, which draws participating teams from Tahiti and the mainland United States in addition to the numerous Hawaiian canoe paddling clubs.

Hawaiian Language

Hawaiian is taught at the University of Hawaii and at other schools throughout the islands. Although it is regularly spoken by few—chiefly the population of Niihau—there are many, including Hawaiians, Caucasians, and Orientals, who can speak a few Hawaiian words and enjoy hearing the language in the form of Hawaiian music.

Hawaiian Music

The distinctive musical forms in Hawaii are based on the contributions of many cultures. The Hawaiians had rhythmic chants and musical instruments made from materials found in the islands. Some of the early immigrant groups added to the instruments with some of their own. The ukulele, for instance, was introduced by the Portuguese. Today Hawaiian music is distinguished by its instrumentation: typically the steel guitar, bass, ukulele, and slack-key guitar (a distinctive way of tuning and playing the instrument rather than an instrument itself). Added to the instruments is a distinctive singing form: the male falsetto voice.

Two other characteristics of Hawaiian music make it unique. First, it frequently is at least partly in the Hawaiian language, and second, it is intensely geographic in its lyrics. Most Hawaiian folk songs, and many modern songs as well, are about the beauty of the islands. A classic theme in the music is a love for the land and a yearning to return to it by those who have mistakenly believed that life would be more pleasant elsewhere.

To illustrate, consider one classic folk song, "Na Moku Eha" ("The Four Islands"), and one modern song in the folk tradition, "Hele on to Kauai." In "Na Moku Eha" each of the principal islands—Hawaii, Oahu, Maui, and Kauai—is described by its most prominent mountain and the flower for which the island is best known. Thus for the island of Hawaii:

Hanohano Hawaii, la Honored Hawaii
Lei ka lehua, la With its lehua lei
Kuahiwe nani, la The beautiful
  mountain
O Mauna Kea Of Mauna Kea

The three remaining verses describe Oahu (mountain—Kaala, flower—ilima), Maui (mountain—Haleakala, flower—roselani), and Kauai (mountain—Waialeale, flower—mokihana) (Piianaia 1980, 47).

"Hele on to Kauai" can be loosely translated "Come Back to Kauai." The song's theme concerns a local Kauai boy who wants to leave home and see more of the world. After visiting a busy American city he realizes that the beauty and aloha of his island home are what he really wants, and he returns. The song's chorus describes "Hanalei by the bay, Wailua river valley, and the canyons of Waimea" and concludes with, "The magic of the Garden Isle is calling me back home."[1]

There are a number of other modern songs in the folk tradition with similar themes. Among them are: "Paniolo Country," "Honolulu I Am Coming Back Again," and "The Beauty of Mauna Kea."

The *hapa haole* ("half white") music of an earlier era, made famous by such singers as Alfred Apaka and Gabby Pahinui, was also full of geographic description, with songs such as "Beyond the Reef," "Blue Hawaiian Moonlight," "Magic Island," and "Blue Hawaii."

Hawaii's Religions

To the ancient Hawaiian religion were added Christianity, Buddhism, Shinto, and the Chinese religions by the successive waves of immigrants to the islands. Although the ancient Hawaiian faith is no longer practiced as an organized religion, elements of it have found their way into other faiths, and there are certainly some in the islands who subscribe to one or more of the ancient beliefs.

Religion has left its mark on the land in the form of religious architecture, which in Hawaii is unique. There are Protestant churches in distinctly oriental styles, as well as the traditional New England forms of the missionaries' homeland. Buddhist temples and Shinto shrines are common, and there are many old Hawaiian *heiaus* scattered throughout the islands.

Dualism and the Landscape

Economic, social, and cultural dualism have left their diverse influences on the land. The cultural landscape has resulted from 200 or more years of Polynesian, European, American, and Oriental occupation. The resulting economy, which has at various times included subsistence and plantation agriculture, quaint "mom and pop" neighborhood stores and modern supermarkets, and barter trade for agricultural products as well as modern business and banking housed in concrete skyscrapers, is extremely interesting and diverse.

REFERENCES

Boeke, J. H. *Economics and Economic Policy of Dual Societies.* Haarlem: H. D., 1953.

Chinen, J. J. *The Great Mahele: Hawaii's Land Division of 1848.* Honolulu: University of Hawaii Press, 1958.

Cox, J. H. with Stasack, E. *Hawaiian Petroglyphs.* Honolulu: Bishop Museum Press, 1970.

Daws, G. *Shoal of Time: A History of the Hawaiian Islands.* New York: Macmillan Co., 1968.

De Francis, J. *Things Japanese in Hawaii.* Honolulu: University Press of Hawaii, 1973.

Gallagher, C. F., and Levy, D. *Hawaii and its Gods.* New York: Weatherhill/Kapa, 1975.

Geertz, C. *Agricultural Involution: The Process of Ecological Change in Indonesia.* Berkeley: University of California Press, 1963.

Higgins, B. "The Dualistic Theory of Underdeveloped Areas." *Economic Development and Cultural Change* 4(1956): 99–115.

Lind, A. W. *Hawaii's People.* 3rd ed. Honolulu: University of Hawaii Press, 1967.

Lind, A. W. *An Island Community: Ecological Succession in Hawaii.* Chicago: University of Chicago Press, 1938.

Morgan, T. *Hawaii, A Century of Economic Change 1778–1876.* Cambridge, Mass.: Harvard University Press, 1948.

Mulholland, J. F. *Hawaii's Religions.* Tokyo: Charles E. Tuttle Co., 1970.

Nordyke, E. C. *The Peopling of Hawaii.* Honolulu: University Press of Hawaii, 1977.

Piianaia, I. A. "Place in Hawaiian Folk Songs," *Mana: A South Pacific Journal of Language and Literature* 5, no. 2 (1980): 43–52.

1. Excerpts from "Hele on to Kauai" by Al Nobriga are reprinted with permission of Mauna Kea Publishing.

CHAPTER 17

THE CULTURAL LANDSCAPE: A PICTORIAL ESSAY

FIGURE 17.1. The old Hawaiian culture lives on in sport. Canoe races, such as this one in Honolulu harbor, are popular in the islands; the Molokai-to-Oahu race attracts contestants from the mainland and from Pacific island nations.

FIGURE 17.2. Ancient Hawaiian petroglyphs carved in a rock in Moanalua Valley, Oahu. The presence of the petroglyphs resulted in a court ruling that the valley was "historic" and that the planned H-3 freeway would have to be rerouted.

FIGURE 17.3.   Old Hawaiian fish pond in Kaneohe Bay, at Heeia, windward Oahu.

FIGURE 17.4.   The ancient Hawaiian religion left its marks on the landscape. *Heiaus,* large stone platforms used as temples, dot the islands. The Ulupo Heiau, shown here, is located in Kailua, Oahu.

FIGURE 17.5. Two Congregational (United Church of Christ) churches in the classic New England architectural style. *Above,* Kawaiahao Church, built in 1842 on the site of an old thatched-hut church used by the first company of missionaries. *Below,* Central Union Church, built early in the twentieth century. Both churches are prominent features of the cultural landscape of Honolulu.

FIGURE 17.6. Congregational churches come in all building styles to accommodate the variety of ethnic groups in Hawaii who are adherents to the faith. *Above,* Makiki Christian Church is patterned after a Japanese castle. *Below,* the First Chinese Church of Christ.

202

FIGURE 17.7.   Kuan Yin Temple, Honolulu, where the Chinese religions are practiced.

FIGURE 17.8.   St. Luke's Episcopal Church, Honolulu. Although the religion is distinctly western, the architecture is not.

FIGURE 17.9.   A Shinto shrine, complete with tori, or Japanese ceremonial gate. Located in the Chinatown district of Honolulu, it is typical of a large number of small Shinto shrines that contribute to the religious landscape of the islands.

FIGURE 17.10. Buddhist landscapes on Oahu. *Upper left,* Byodo-in, in windward Oahu, an exact replica of a Buddhist temple in Kyoto, Japan. It was built in 1968 to commemorate the 100th anniversary of the arrival of the Japanese in Hawaii. *Upper right,* a statue of Buddha in the Byodo-in. *Lower right,* a Zen Buddhist temple in downtown Honolulu.

FIGURE 17.11. The agricultural landscape. *Above,* taro patches on the Keanae Peninsula, east Maui; *below,* a pineapple field in central Oahu.

FIGURE 17.12. The landscape of tourism. The giant Sheraton Waikiki hotel (*left*) with 1,100 rooms, dwarfs the historic Royal Hawaiian (*center*). At the extreme right is the Moana, oldest of Waikiki Beach hotels.

FIGURE 17.13. Now used for weekly performances of the Royal Hawaiian band, the bandstand on the Iolani Palace grounds was originally built for the coronation of King Kalakaua in 1883, nine years after he actually acceded to the throne.

FIGURE 17.14. C. Brewer and Co., one of Hawaii's "Big Five" and now a multimillion-dollar conglomerate, has its corporate headquarters in this handsome building in downtown Honolulu. The structure is dwarfed by high-rise buildings that surround it.

FIGURE 17.15. Merchant Square, in downtown Honolulu, preserves old buildings. Built in the first two decades of the twentieth century, their architectural style decidedly is not tropical.

FIGURE 17.16. The Korean Studies Center on the campus of the University of Hawaii in Manoa, Honolulu. An exact replica of an old castle in Seoul, Korea, it was built with funds provided jointly by the governments of the Republic of Korea and the state of Hawaii.

FIGURE 17.17. The Chinese community in Hawaii has fraternal organizations, such as the Lum Sai Ho Tong, shown here in Chinatown, Honolulu.

FIGURE 17.18. The old company store has become the more modern Shopping Basket in the sugar plantation town of Ewa, Oahu. When the sugar workers unionized, the characteristic paternalism of the plantations diminished.

FIGURE 17.19. Two views of modern Honolulu. *Above,* the plantation village at Poamoho; *below,* the masses of concrete high-rise apartments and hotels that some environmentalists refer to as the "concrete jungle."

FIGURE 17.20 (*above and right*). Shoppers at Ala Moana Shopping Center, Honolulu.

FIGURE 17.21 (*left*). Cliffs of eroded tuff on the southeast coast of Oahu and a pretty girl enjoying the sunshine and scenery form a cultural landscape typical of the natural beauty of Hawaii.

PART 4

THE ISLANDS

PART 2

CHAPTER 18

OAHU

The most remarkable of the Hawaiian Islands is Oahu (Fig. 18.1). With an area of 607.7 sq mi (1,573.9 sq km) it is only the third largest; yet its population of 760,926 is almost 80 percent of the population of the state. Despite the crowding of a large number of people onto a small land mass, many parts of the island are devoted to plantation agriculture, and the magnificent scenery for which the Hawaiian Islands are noted is clearly evident on Oahu.

PHYSICAL GEOGRAPHY

The basic geological structure of the island is simple; it consists of four main geologic provinces: the Koolau Range, the Wainanae Range, the Schofield Plateau, and the coastal plain.

The Koolau and Waianae mountains are greatly eroded shield volcanoes. The Waianae is the older of the two, having appeared 3.4 to 2.7 million years ago, according to potassium-argon dating methods (Stearns 1966, 75). The same methodology has dated the Koolau shield at 2.5 to 2.2 million years ago. Both shield volcanoes have undergone seven of the eight stages described in Chapter 3, so classic shield-volcanic features such as calderas are not clearly evident. However, the caldera complex of the Waianae Range seems to be near Kolekole Pass at the head of Lualualei Valley, based on the appearance of numerous dikes in the area through

which lava once issued. The Koolau caldera is even less evident, but eroded rocks at the base of the pali behind Lanikai indicate an ancient caldera complex (Stearns 1966, 93).

The Schofield Plateau was formed from Koolau lavas that ponded up against the older Waianae shield. The coastal plain also lies mostly on ponded lavas of the Koolau volcano both north and south of the Schofield Plateau, but here the lavas have been covered with a broad, elevated coral reef (Macdonald and Abbott 1970, 355). The plain is most extensive in the Ewa district, but portions of it are clearly recognizable as the Honolulu, Waialua-Haleiwa, and Kahuku plains.

A unique feature of the geology of Oahu is the large number of tuff cones, formed in the last of the volcanic stages that the island has undergone. The most well known of the tuff cones is Diamond Head, which formed about 150,000 years ago as a crack opened through the emerged reef. After a series of violent phreatomagmatic eruptions, the resultant ash solidified into tuff with embedded limestone (Stearns 1966, 85–87). Other tuff cones—Punchbowl, Makalapa, Salt Lake, Hanauma Bay, Koko Head, and Rabbit Island (Manana)—were formed in the same way.

Oahu has the spectacular erosional landforms for which the islands are famous. There are numerous amphitheater-headed valleys in both the Koolau and Waianae ranges, and the Nuuanu Pali is one of the

216

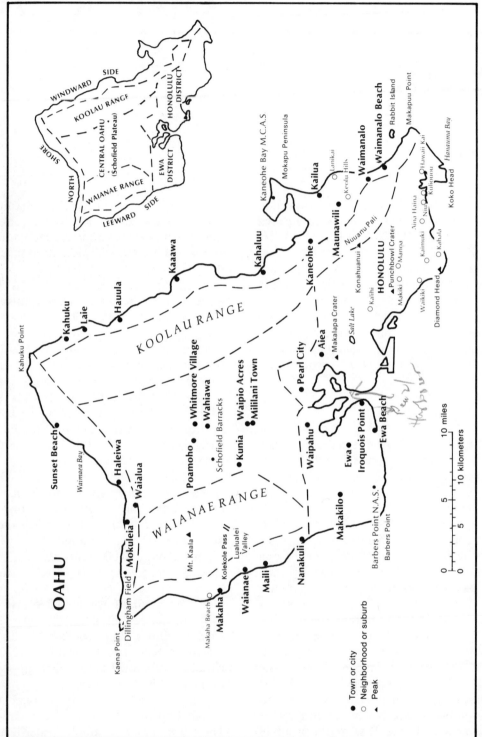

OAHU

Town or city
Neighborhood or suburb
Peak

WINDWARD SIDE
KOOLAU RANGE
CENTRAL OAHU
(Schofield Plateau)
WAIANAE RANGE
NORTH SHORE
LEEWARD SIDE
HONOLULU DISTRICT
EWA DISTRICT

Kaneohe Bay M.C.A.S
Mokapu Peninsula
Waimanalo Beach
Rabbit Island
Makapuu Point
Waimanalo
Lanikai
Kailua
Olomana Hills
Makapuu Point
Hawaii Kai
Koko Head
Hanauma Bay
Kuliouou
Niu
Aina Haina
Maunawili
Nuuanu Pali
Punchbowl Crater
Kahala
Konahuanui
HONOLULU
Kaimuki
Manoa
Kahaluu
Kaneohe
Waikiki
Makiki
Diamond Head
Kalihi
Salt Lake
Makalapa Crater
Aiea
Pearl City
Kahuku Point
KOOLAU RANGE
Kaaawa
Hauula
Laie
Kahuku
Whitmore Village
Wahiawa
Waipio Acres
Mililani Town
Schofield Barracks
Poamoho
Kunia
Waipahu
Ewa
Iroquois Point
Ewa Beach
Sunset Beach
Waimaea Bay
Haleiwa
Waialua
WAIANAE RANGE
Makakilo
Barbers Point N.A.S.
Barbers Point
Kaena Point
Dillingham Field
Mokuleia
Mt. Kaala
Kolekole Pass
Lualualei Valley
Nanakuli
Makaha Beach
Makaha
Waianae
Maili

0   5   10 miles
0   5   10 kilometers

FIGURE 18.1.

FIGURE 18.2. Diamond Head, Oahu's world-famous tuff cone, in a view from Maunalani Heights, Honolulu. In the left foreground is the residential district of Kaimuki. (Photo courtesy David Kornhauser.)

scenic wonders of the state. Its formation was complex: stream erosion, alluviation of valley floors, and the battering back of headlands by the force of the sea all played a part. The prominent fluting is due to waterfalls, which have worn plunge pools in many areas (Stearns 1966, 81).

Also complex is the origin of Pearl Harbor, essentially a drowned river system affected by a number of changes in sea level (Stearns 1966, 82).

Although the Waianae and Koolau ranges rise abruptly from the intervening Schofield Plateau, their elevations are modest. The highest peak in the Waianaes is Kaala at 4,020 ft (1,225 m). Konahuanui in the Koolau range has an elevation of 3,150 ft (960 m).

The climate of Oahu displays most of the climatic types described in Chapter 6. It lacks only the distinctive climate of the Kona coast of the island of Hawaii and the effects of genuinely high mountains such as those on the Big Island. Remarkable variations in rainfall over short distances

on Oahu are evident in the great variety of vegetation types. Windward and leeward sides are distinctly different in their rainfall characteristics and to a lesser degree in temperature.

ECONOMIC AND CULTURAL REGIONS

Superimposed on the physical geography of Oahu is the work of both the early Polynesian settlers and later immigrants, who changed landscapes as they put the land to use. Six distinct economic and cultural regions have evolved from the long history of human occupation of the island: Honolulu, the Ewa district, the windward side, the leeward side, the central district, and the north shore.

Honolulu

Honolulu, as discussed here, consists not only of the city as defined in the 1980 census (population 365,083) but some neighboring related communities as well.

These are Pearl City (population 42,535) and Aiea (32,616), which are clearly "bedroom suburbs" of the city. Honolulu has other identities as well; it is the state's principal link with the outside world, the center of its commerce and government, and the place where the greatest variety of life-styles and economic activities come together. Honolulu dominates the economic and cultural geography of Oahu and the state of Hawaii. It is by all definitions a primate city.

Early Hawaiians living in the area called the place Kou; it was a small, undistinguished settlement, no more important than dozens of similar coastal villages. Things began to change, however, in 1792 when Captain William Brown of the trading vessel *Butterworth* discovered the harbor and named it Fair Haven. Hawaiians apparently adopted this name and translated it into the Hawaiian *Honolulu* (literally "sheltered bay").

The utility of Honolulu as a refuge for ships was enhanced by the production of the first known chart of the harbor by Captain William R. Broughton of the British ship *Providence* in 1796.

Archibald Campbell, an English seaman who traveled around the world from 1806 to 1812 and spent a year in the Hawaiian Islands, described the island of "Wahoo" as the most important island in the Hawaiian group because it possessed "the only secure harbour to be met with in the Sandwich Islands." His description of the harbor went a long way toward making Honolulu famous:

> Three miles to the west of Whyteete [Waikiki] is the town of Hanaroora [Honolulu], now the capital of the island, and the residence of the King. The harbour is formed by the reef, which shelters it from the sea, and ships can ride within in safety in any weather, upon a fine sandy bottom. There is a good channel through the reef, with three or four fathoms water. . . . The best anchorage is in five fathoms of water about two cables from the shore, directly in front of the village. (Campbell 1967, 112–113)

FIGURE 18.3.   The *Falls of Clyde*, an early Matson ship, has been refurbished and is now a museum on the Honolulu waterfront.

Today the city of Honolulu can be subdivided into a number of individual neighborhoods. There is the downtown area (central business district) close to the waterfront, a characteristic of many port cities. Nearby is famed, colorful Chinatown. Residential neighborhoods include Kalihi, Makiki, Manoa, Nuuanu, Palolo, Kaimuki, Kahala, and the more distant suburbs of Aina Haina, Niu, Kuliouou, and Hawaii Kai.

The city has grown, expanding mauka into the valleys and ridges of the Koolau Range, as well as to the east and west. Constrained by its physical geography to the southeastern corner of Oahu, Honolulu has grown upward as high-rise condominium apartments have been built.

Waikiki, in many respects Honolulu's most important neighborhood, is the primary site of the state's tremendously important tourist industry. It is a city within

FIGURE 18.4.   Chinatown, Honolulu. The pseudo-Chinese architecture of Wo Fat's, a well-known Chinese restaurant, is a landmark in the area.

FIGURE 18.5.   Iolani Palace, Honolulu. This recently restored building once served as the palace for King Kalakaua and his successor, Queen Liliuokalani. Construction on the palace began in 1879 and took almost four years to complete.

FIGURE 18.6. The sugar mill at Waipahu, which dominates the older part of the town, is one of two on the island of Oahu.

a city and a center for entertainment, shopping, and fine restaurants. Waikiki Beach and its view of Diamond Head is world famous.

In the downtown area are evidences of Hawaii's history. Kawaiahao Church and the Mission Houses are relics of the missionary era, while Iolani Palace, Iolani Barracks, and the palace grounds bandstand evoke the monarchy period.

Nearby are both the state capitol building and the city hall (Honolulu Hale), as well as the high-rise office buildings that house Hawaii's business community.

The Ewa District

Extending southwestward from Waipahu (population 29,288) lies the Ewa district of the island. Waipahu grew up as a sugar town, and the sugar mill dominates the landscape of this small city. Sugar is still important in the district although one of the mills, that at the town of Ewa, has been closed for several years. Ewa (2,555) is a former plantation town, which is showing some distinct signs of decay since the nearby mill closed.

The principal economic activities of the district, other than sugar, are heavy industry, located at Campbell Industrial Park, and the Barbers Point Naval Air Station. The air station, with a resident population of 1,388 in addition to its daily employment force living outside the base, and a naval housing area at Iroquois Point (3,878) are important population centers. The second-most-important population center in the district is Ewa Beach (14,155). It and Makakilo (7,714) provide housing for employees at Campbell Industrial Park and Barbers Point Naval Air Station and in the service sectors of the various communities.

FIGURE 18.7.   The manager's house in the former plantation town of Ewa, Oahu. Although the mill is closed, the area is still growing sugarcane, which is processed at Waipahu.

Campbell Industrial Park has a cattle feedlot and both of Hawaii's oil refineries, as well as a number of other industrial tenants. It is the only area in the state zoned for heavy industry.

The character of the Ewa district will undoubtedly change if plans for the development of tourist facilities come to fruition. There are plans for a resort area with as many as ten tourist hotels in a coastal strip extending north from a small barge harbor to Kahe Point. The harbor itself may be greatly enlarged to become Oahu's second deep-draft port. The combination of a tourist industry and the increased activity associated with a new harbor would inevitably change the Ewa district from its quiet, semirural condition to one with the elements of a boom town, unless careful planning is associated with the developments.

The Windward Side

Separated from Honolulu and the rest of the island of Oahu by the Koolau Mountains is the windward side, a cultural and economic entity.

The largest communities, Kailua (population 35,873) and Kaneohe (29,500), developed rapidly as bedroom suburbs of Honolulu after tunnels and modern high-

ways across the Koolau Range were built. They have now taken on distinct urban characteristics of their own. Waimanalo (3,555) and Waimanalo Beach (4,119), both located in the southern part of the windward area, have retained more of a semi-rural atmosphere, although both have grown considerably in the past ten years.

North of the large communities of Kailua and Kaneohe the general character of the windward side remains rural. Small towns appear on the mauka side of the highway: Kahaluu (2,919), Kaaawa (961), Hauula (2,993), Laie (4,640), and Kahuku (936). There are also the dispersed farming communities of Waiahole and Waikane.

The principal economic activities are small-scale diversified agriculture and the military. The Mokapu Peninsula is the site of the Marine Corps Air Station Kaneohe Bay, with a resident population of 6,470. The cities of Kaneohe and Kailua have many military families in residence; Kailua has grown so much that it has spawned a number of suburbs of its own: Maunawili (5,217) and Keolu Hills, for example.

The largest community in the northern part of the windward side, Laie, is the focal point for activities of the Mormon church in the islands. The Polynesian Cultural Center, a thriving tourist attraction; the

FIGURE 18.8.   A tunnel through the Koolau Range forms part of the Pali Highway, which links windward Oahu to Honolulu. The road near the top of the picture is the Old Pali Road, which, without tunnels, tortuously followed the contours of the mountain.

Mormon Temple; the Hawaiian campus of Brigham Young University; and the town of Laie itself are all owned by the Mormon church.

Further north, Kahuku has been declining in economic activity since the closing of the Kahuku sugar mill. The mill subsequently reopened as a tourist attraction, providing some employment for local residents. Sugar lands have been converted to diversified agriculture, particularly the growing of corn. The Kahuku area is notoriously windy, and an experimental windmill for generating electrical power has shown promise for the area. There are now plans to build a complex of windmills in the region.

The Leeward Side

North of the Ewa district and extending to Kaena Point, the northwestern extremity of the island, is the leeward side. It is warmer and drier than the rest of Oahu and has some truly spectacular beaches, including Makaha Beach, where the winter surfing waves attract surfers from outside the state to participate in world-class surfing meets.

North of the town of Makaha there is little urban development, and the coastal highway becomes a jeep trail for the last two or three mi (3.2 or 4.8 km) to Kaena Point. The Kaena area is a rugged lava coast with examples of classic erosional features caused by the powerful breaking surf. There are a number of blowholes, spouting horns, arches, and stacks, as well as evidence of ancient shorelines. At Kaena Point itself the lava gives way to sand dunes, which are stabilized by vegetation, some of it endemic to the islands.

The principal urban communities are

Nanakuli (population 8,183), Maili (5,044), Waianae (7,968), and Makaha (6,594). The only tourist development in the region is at Makaha, where the Makaha Resort is sited in scenic Makaha Valley. The resort has had mixed success, however, and has changed ownership several times.

The leeward side has been the scene of some well-publicized crimes against tourists and visitors from other parts of the islands. That, coupled with activism by some members of the ethnic Hawaiian community, has made the area one that Oahu residents and visitors tend to avoid. The unfortunate reputation acquired by the leeward-side communities is being actively countered by a number of public-spirited local groups.

The Central District

In the Schofield Plateau between the Koolau and Waianae ranges lies the principal agricultural area of Oahu, with large tracts of land devoted to sugar and pineapple. The central district also has rapidly growing urban centers and a sizable military installation.

Mililani Town, which now has a population of 21,273, had but 2,035 people in 1970. The growth of the town has been lateral, at the expense of agricultural land. Nearby Waipio Acres (population 3,991) has made further inroads into plantation lands. Other urban centers are Schofield Barracks (18,949) and Wahiawa (16,653); the population of both has remained relatively constant in the past decade. Wahiawa has long been the center of pineapple growing in Oahu, and many residents are employed by Dole and Del Monte companies. The town also provides some housing, shopping, and recreational facilities for service personnel at Schofield Barracks. There are two small plantation villages, Kunia and Poamoho, both providing housing for pineapple workers and their families. Whitmore Village (2,320), which started as a plantation camp, has grown into a town in its own right, although many of its residents still work in the pineapple fields.

FIGURE 18.9.   The lighthouse at Kaena Point, northwesternmost point of Oahu. The sand dunes on which the lighthouse is built are stabilized by beach naupaka, a native coastal plant.

The central district has prime agricultural land and good soils. But it is also desirable land for urban development to house commuters to Honolulu. The battle lines between agriculture and urbanization are most clearly drawn in this region. Urbanization seems to be slowly winning, but it will be a long war.

The North Shore

From Kaena Point to Kahuku Point the influence of the ocean is paramount. This is Oahu's north shore, well known to surfing enthusiasts worldwide.

From Kaena Point to Waialua the coast trends east-west, and much of the shore is fronted by Mokuleia Beach. The small community of Mokuleia and Dillingham Field, an Air Force base that has been largely turned over to civilian use by glider and parachuting enthusiasts, are the only developed areas. An interesting feature of the Mokuleia area is the nearby polo field, where Sunday matches are attended by Oahuans, complete with tailgate picnics.

Past Waialua the coastal trend is northeast, and from Haleiwa to Kahuku Point the winter surf is spectacular. Ehukai Beach Park and Sunset Beach form the most well-known continuous surfing area and beach on the north coast and are the site of international surfing events. Waimea Bay is another area noted for good surf, particularly when there are intense winter storms north of the islands. At Kuilima Point, just west of Kahuku Point, there is a tourist hotel, complete with golf course and vacation condominiums.

The plantation town of Waialua (4,051), site of the Waialua Sugar Company mill, has undergone growth and modernization, but the sounding of the sugar-mill whistle morning and night are still features of life in the town. Haleiwa (2,414), although it has less population than Waialua, is the recognized "capital" of the north shore. It has changed rapidly in the past few years, with new shopping centers and commercial establishments seeming to appear overnight. Other communities, Pupukea and Sunset Beach, are small but prominent along the coast.

SUMMARY

Virtually everything characteristic of the Hawaiian Islands can be found on Oahu. All of the islands' ethnic groups and their life-styles are represented on this small island—and Oahu has some things the neighbor islands lack. It has the University of Hawaii at Manoa and four community colleges. It has two interstate freeways (an anachronism for an island state) and may one day have a third. It has rush-hour traffic the equal of most mainland cities, as well as quiet rural villages. The variety of churches, restaurants, architectural styles, holidays, and languages is bewildering. And it has problems.

Land and housing prices have put home ownership outside the reach of most local residents. The crime rate is increasing. The island badly needs a second airport to relieve congestion at Honolulu International and to cure the dangerous mix of small, propeller-driven planes and the large commercial and military jet airplanes. But nobody wants an airport in the neighborhood, and the only available land would also remove hundreds of acres from sugar production. Waikiki, site of the islands' all-important visitor industry, is showing signs of shabbiness. There have been some well-publicized crimes against tourists, and airline strikes and economic conditions in the United States have combined to cause the first drop in visitor-arrival figures since the tourist industry began its spectacular growth after statehood.

Despite these and other problems Oahu is a fascinating place to live and visit. It has something for everyone.

REFERENCES

Campbell, A. *A Voyage Round the World From 1806 to 1812.* Honolulu: University of Hawaii Press, 1967. (Facsimile reproduction of the 3rd American edition of 1822.)

Macdonald, G. A., and Abbott, A. T. *Volcanoes in the Sea.* Honolulu: University of Hawaii Press, 1970.

Macdonald, G. A., and Kyselka, W. *Anatomy of an Island: A Geological History of Oahu.* Honolulu: Bishop Museum Press, 1967.

Morgan, J. R., and Street, J. M. *Oahu Environments.* Honolulu: Oriental Publishing Co., 1979.

Stearns, H. T. *Geology of the State of Hawaii.* Palo Alto, Calif.: Pacific Books, 1966.

State of Hawaii, Department of Planning and Economic Development. *Data Book.* Honolulu: State of Hawaii, Department of Planning and Economic Development, 1980.

CHAPTER 19

HAWAII

THE BIG ISLAND

The island of Hawaii (Fig. 19.1), with an area of 4,038 sq mi (10,458 sq km), is truly deserving of the name Big Island. It dwarfs the other Hawaiian Islands, both in geographic area and in the immensity of its volcanic landforms. Its mountain peaks, two of which tower more than 13,000 ft (4,000 m), are far taller than the greatest elevations on Oahu, Kauai, Molokai, and Lanai. Only Haleakala on Maui approaches the heights of the Big Island's mountains, and it falls short by more than 3,000 feet (914 m).

PHYSICAL GEOGRAPHY

Of the five shield volcanoes that make up the land mass of the Big Island, Mauna Loa and Mauna Kea are the largest, with Mauna Loa making up 50.5 percent of the area of the island and Mauna Kea 22.8 percent. Of the two, Mauna Kea is a little higher peak, with an elevation of 13,796 ft (4,205 m); Mauna Loa is 13,677 ft (4,167 m) high. Hualalai, 8,271 ft (2,521 m), Kohala, 5,480 ft (1,670 m); and Kilauea, 4,093 ft (1,248 m) follow in that order. The latter nestles on the slope of the more massive Mauna Loa, but is a volcano in its own right, erupting independently of Mauna Loa.

Both Mauna Loa and Kilauea are live. Hualalai has erupted in historic times; Mauna Kea and Kohala are much older. Mauna Kea lavas have been dated by the potassium-argon method at about 0.6 million years old, while the Kohala shield is slightly less than 1 million years old.

Mauna Loa has been one of the most prolific lava producers on earth. There are only a few cinder cones on its slopes, most eruptions having produced copious amounts of pahoehoe and aa lavas. Its caldera, Mokuaweoweo, is growing via coalescence of adjacent pit craters. In addition to summit eruptions there are well-defined southwest and northeast rift zones, which alternate with the summit in producing lava flows.

Kilauea, on the southeast slope of Mauna Loa, has a summit caldera with an active pit crater, Halemaumau. A chain of smaller craters extends along a southeast rift zone. The formation of lava lakes and lava tubes are characteristic features of Kilauea-type eruptions. Although most eruptions have been comparatively mild, in 1959 an eruption in Kilauea Iki, a crater in the summit area, produced fountains 1,900 ft (570 m) high. The following year the Hawaiian village of Kapoho was buried and destroyed by wet, black ash. Fortunately, evacuation of the residents was carried out in time, and there were no casualties. From 1969 to 1974 virtually continuous eruptions produced Mauna Ulu, a small shield volcano. The name appropriately means "growing mountain" (Pukui, Elbert, and Mookini 1974).

Mauna Kea, which is the highest insular peak on earth, is studded with cinder cones. It became extinct in Recent geological time.

FIGURE 19.1

FIGURE 19.2.   Big Island shield volcanoes, Mauna Loa and Mauna Kea, are faintly visible from the summit of Haleakala, east Maui.

The high plains of the Waimea region of the Big Island are blanketed with tan-colored ash deposits from the many Mauna Kea cinder cones.

The most symmetrical of the Hawaiian volcanic peaks is Hualalai. It is studded with approximately 120 cinder cones and spatter cones and has a number of craters near the summit. Puu Waawaa, on the north slope of Hualalai, is a cinder cone 1,220 ft (366 m) high.

Despite the abundant rainfall in the windward regions of the island, no perennial streams enter the ocean in the entire stretch from the Wailuku River, near Hilo, clockwise around the coast to Upolu Point, the northern extremity of Kohala. Kilauea, Mauna Loa, Hualalai, and the western slopes of Kohala have produced such porous lavas that there are no rivers. Only the east coast of the island, north of Hilo—the Hamakua coast—has rivers. While the western slope of Kohala shows little erosion, the eastern slope has canyons more than 2,000 ft (600 m) deep, with walls so sheer that the slopes are unsurpassed anywhere in the islands.

With its wide range of elevations and large size the island of Hawaii has all the climate types characteristic of the Hawaiian Islands. The climate of the Kona coast, with its summer rainfall maximum, and the cold climate of the summits of Mauna Kea and Mauna Loa are unique in the islands. The clarity of the air at the Mauna Kea summit makes it ideal for astronomical observations, and a number of observatories have been established to capitalize on these conditions.

In general, steep sea cliffs are characteristic of the Big Island, and only the Kona coast has very many beaches or offshore coral reef formations.

ECONOMIC GEOGRAPHY

Sugar, cattle ranching, and tourism are the island's biggest industries. A unique feature of the sugar industry is the large acreage on the wet Hamakua coast, where the cane is not irrigated. Because of the lack of abundant sunshine in the region, yields are somewhat less than in other areas of the Hawaiian Islands. Much of the sugarcane grown without irrigation is produced by small land owners who have formed a cooperative and sell their cane to the Hilo Coast Processing Company, which mills it.

FIGURE 19.3.   Mauna Kea viewed from north Hilo.

The Parker Ranch headquarters at the town of Waimea (population 1,179) is the home of the *paniolos* (Hawaiian cowboys) who work on the ranch. It is the site of a popular restaurant and inn.

The tourist industry is based on the allure of the active volcano at Kilauea, about 30 mi (48 km) from Hilo, as well as the abundant sunshine and warm, clear ocean waters along the Kona coast. There are a number of hotels in Hilo, but occupancy rates have been low in recent years. Undoubtedly Hilo's abundant rainfall is part of the problem. At the Hawaii Volcanoes National Park there is only one hotel, the venerable Volcano House, with thirty-eight rooms. Kona coast tourism is more successful, and one of the finest hotels in the islands is the Mauna Kea Beach Hotel in the South Kohala district.

In addition to the main economic activities there is diversified agriculture, with papayas, macadamia nuts, Kona coffee, flowers, and nursery products important. There is some military activity at Pohakuloa, in the saddle area between Mauna Loa and Mauna Kea, but the region is used for training, including live firing, and there is little contribution to the island's economy.

There are two deep-water ports: Hilo and Kawaihae. The latter was developed recently primarily to serve the sugar industry, but the closing of the Kohala plantation made the facilities superfluous. Hence the port is little used. The port at Hilo serves the entire island, and has facilities for handling bulk sugar shipments and roll-on–roll-off container ships, as well as tugs and barges.

REGIONS AND DISTRICTS

The Big Island is divided into the following districts: South Hilo, North Hilo, Hamakua, North Kohala, South Kohala, North Kona, South Kona, Kau, and Puna. The districts, which serve as judicial districts and once were part of the old Hawaiian land system, have their individual characteristics, in part due to differences in physical geography (See Figure 19.1).

South Hilo

The city of Hilo (population 35,303) dominates the South Hilo district and the island of Hawaii. Its population is more than one-third the entire population of the Big Island, and its importance as a port and economic center is uncontested. Located at the head of Hilo Bay, the city unfortunately has been subject to destructive tsunamis; those of 1946 and 1960 were particularly devastating.

FIGURE 19.4.   The waterfront area of Hilo, Hawaii. Disastrous tsunamis in 1946 and 1960 damaged the town severely, and authorities rezoned the area for open-space and park use.

North of Hilo is the suburb of Papaikou (1,565), the site of a sugar mill. The coastal cliffs are steep from Papaikou north; this is the southern end of the Hamakua coast, noted for its high rainfall and sugar plantations.

North Hilo

The coastal highway in this district passes through the tiny communities of Honohina, Ninole, and Laupahoehoe. The latter is famous because nearby Laupahoehoe Point was badly hit by the tsunami of 1946. There is a tsunami memorial marker on the site of the former Laupahoehoe Elementary School, where most of the loss of life occurred.

Hamakua

Honokaa (1,944) is the largest town in the Hamakua district, which extends well inland from the coast and contains the summit of Mauna Kea, part of the caldera of Mauna Loa, and the military camp at Pohakuloa. The coastal strip is planted in sugar.

Waipio Bay and Waipio Valley, a flat-floored valley in which taro is grown, are important physical features on the Hamakua coast. The valley is at the southern end of a stretch of coast that is very steep—steepness believed by some geologists to be the result of faulting.

North Kohala

At the northern end of the Hamakua coast lies Pololu Valley, which has the same general physical features as Waipio Valley. The greatest tsunami wave heights in the islands were recorded here, 55 ft (17 m) against the steep sea cliffs.

Sugar formerly was grown in North Kohala, but the plantation closed in the early 1970s, creating a good deal of unemployment. The state of Hawaii formed the Kohala Task Force, designed to provide state financial assistance to a number of small industries that would provide employment to those who lost their jobs when the sugar plantation closed. The task force has not been a success; most of the businesses failed, and those still in operation

FIGURE 19.5.   The Hamakua coast near Po-lolu Valley, island of Hawaii.

have not provided many jobs.

The village of Hawi (798) is the only settlement of consequence in the district. Despite the loss of jobs in the sugar industry, the town maintained the same population between the 1970 and 1980 censuses. A number of residents commute to jobs at the Mauna Kea Beach Hotel.

North Kohala is steeped in Hawaiian history. Kamehameha the Great, first ruler of the islands, was born here, near Upolu Point. The important Mookini *heiau*, which was built about A.D. 1250, is nearby. At Kapaau, just east of Hawi, is a statue of Kamehameha; one copy is in downtown Honolulu and another at the Capitol in Washington, D.C.

South Kohala

The deep-draft port of Kawaihae and the Mauna Kea Beach Hotel are the important economic features of the South Kohala coast. Inland is the town of Waimea (1,179) and the grazing lands of the Parker Ranch. Waimea (also called Kamuela) has an airport with daily service to Honolulu; it is a tourist attraction for those who want to see the high-plateau ranch lands.

Near Kawaihae is the Puu o Kohola Heiau, built by Kamehameha as a temple to the war god Ku.

North Kona

The volcano Hualalai is the dominant geological feature of the North Kona district. Its lava flows dominate the coastal and inland landscape.

Tourism is the dominant industry in this district with the town of Kailua (Kona) (4,763) an important center. In the 1970 census there were only 365 residents of the village, which has grown with the growing visitor industry. North of Kailua (Kona) is the airport at Keahole Point. Tourists usually fly into the Big Island via the Kona Airport and leave via the Hilo Airport.

Kailua (Kona) also has its history. There are two *heiaus*; the Hulihee Palace, a summer home for Hawaiian royalty; and the Mokuaikaua Church, which dates from 1837.

South Kona

At Kealakekua Bay, in South Kona, Captain Cook made a landing in the islands and in 1779 met his death at the hands of Hawaiians. There is an important *heiau* at Napoopoo and the Captain Cook monument. The towns of Captain Cook (2,025) and Kealakekua (1,039) are small but important population centers in the region.

On the coast south of Kealakekua Bay is the Puuhonua o Honaunau, officially the City of Refuge National Historical Park. The area has been restored as it appeared in the late 1770s, when it was a refuge for those who broke the laws (*kapus*) of the Hawaiian way of life. If they reached the refuge they were cleansed of their transgressions by a ceremony of absolution performed by the *kahuna* (priest). Thereafter, they could return in safety to their homes.

FIGURE 19.6.   Hulihee Palace, Kailua (Kona), Hawaii. The structure was built in 1838 by Kuakini, then governor of the island of Hawaii and a brother of Kaahumanu, a favorite wife of Kamehameha I and a powerful political figure in the islands. King Kalakaua used it as a summer palace and changed its name to Hikulai Hale ("seventh ruler house"). The "palace" later belonged to Jonah Kuhio Kalanianaole, first delegate of the Territory of Hawaii to the U.S. Congress.

South of Honaunau, lava flows from Mauna Loa are prevalent in the district.

Kau

The Kau district includes most of the Hawaii Volcanoes National Park, including the summit calderas of both Mauna Loa and Kilauea. The coastal portions of the district lie in a rain shadow, and southwest of the Kilauea summit is the Kau Desert. The southwest rift zones of both Kilauea and Mauna Loa are the chief geological features.

Sugar is an important economic crop in the district, and the towns of Pahala (1,631) and Naalehu (1,161) are former plantation camps.

The southernmost point in the United States, Ka Lae, has ancient canoe moorings and a *heiau*, indicating that this area was an important center of Hawaiian life and culture.

Tsunamis of local origin have been important natural hazards; in 1975 a local tsunami was the cause of two deaths in a campsite at Halape and more than $1 million in property damage at Punaluu.

Puna

The East Rift Zone of the Kilauea volcano is an important geological feature of Puna, for a number of geothermal wells have been drilled in the area. Geothermal energy is a controversial issue among residents of the Puna District (see Chapter 24). The Chain of Craters Road in the Hawaii Volcanoes National Park runs through the Puna district, and the legends associated with Pele have always been important to Puna residents.

The village of Kapoho was destroyed in 1960, and lava flows came perilously close to the lighthouse at Cape Kumukahi.

Pahoa (925) is the principal urban center

FIGURE 19.7.   Street scene in Pahoa (Puna district).

in Puna, but there are a number of residential developments planned for nearby areas. These have names such as Fern Forest Vacation Estates, Orchid Estates, and Hawaiian Paradise Park—uncharacteristic names for Hawaii.

The well-known Black Sand Beach, at Kaimu, and the Hawaii Volcanoes National Park visitor center and museum are located on the highway that skirts the southeast coast. The beach has suffered from much erosion, in part caused by the local earthquake and tsunami in 1975. In addition to the quake there was serious subsidence of the land on this stretch of coast.

Keaau, Kurtistown, and Mountain View, bedroom suburbs of Hilo, are located in the Puna district.

THE FUTURE?

The Big Island's population increased from 63,468 in 1970 to 92,206 in 1980, with both Hilo and the Kona coast showing substantial gains. But the island is still sparsely populated and there is room for development. The question is: do the island's residents want development?

Development of geothermal energy in the Puna district and ocean thermal energy off Keahole point in north Kona could bring additional industry to the island, a prospect feared by many but anticipated with pleasure by others.

Low occupancy rates at Hilo hotels and the ups and downs of sugar prices are causes for concern. Diversified agriculture has shown gains, despite the ailing Kona coffee industry, but a sustained drought in 1980 resulted in some reduced yields. The giant Parker Ranch has been less than entirely successful as an economic enterprise.

REFERENCES

Decker, R., and Decker B. *Volcano Watching.* Honolulu: Hawaii Natural History Association, 1980.

Macdonald, G. A., and Abbott, A. T. *Volcanoes in the Sea.* Honolulu: University of Hawaii Press, 1970.

Pukui, M. K.; Elbert, S. H.; and Mookini, E. T. *Place Names of Hawaii.* Honolulu: University Press of Hawaii, 1974.

State of Hawaii, Department of Planning and Economic Development. *Data Book.* Honolulu: State of Hawaii, Department of Planning and Economic Development, 1980.

Stearns, H. T. *Geology of the State of Hawaii.* Palo Alto, Calif.: Pacific Books, 1966.

CHAPTER 20

MAUI

The second largest of the Hawaiian Islands (Figure 20.1), Maui has an area of 728.8 sq mi (1,887.6 sq km), but its population is still small. Its general geological structure is similar to that of Oahu, with two shield volcanoes and an interior plain, but it lacks the extensive coral plain that is so prominent on Oahu. Development on Maui has been very rapid during the period 1970 to 1980 and the population growth of the island, from 38,691 to 63,136 during the ten-year period, has been the greatest of any island in the state. Maui has great variety in its landforms, climate, and economic geography. It is a fascinating island for both tourists and *kamaainas* (Hawaiian-born residents).

PHYSICAL GEOGRAPHY

The West Maui shield volcano has been dated as 1.3 to 1.15 million years old (Stearns 1966, 75), while the huge dome of Haleakala, which constitutes the eastern three-fourths of the island, is much younger. The intervening isthmus has been formed from lava flows from Haleakala that filled the depression between the two shields.

West Maui has a maximum elevation of 5,788 ft (1,764 m) at Puu Kukui, while the much more massive Haleakala rises to 10,025 ft (3,055 m) at Red Hill. West Maui is greatly eroded and has the characteristic deep amphitheater-headed valleys associated with the older, wetter Hawaiian Is-

lands. The West Maui volcano went through the caldera stage; the old caldera can now be identified in Iao Valley, site of the remarkable Iao Needle, an erosional remnant.

Haleakala still has the classic shield-volcano silhouette, but the summit depression is the result of erosion by Kaupo and Keanae streams and the coalescence of their large amphitheater valleys (Stearns 1966, 165). The floor of the depression is covered with bare lava flows and large cinder cones, some caused by the most recent eruption, believed to be in the year 1790 (Stearns 1966, 61).

Maui's climate shows the great variability in rainfall characteristic of volcanic islands where the orographic effect is important. Puu Kukui in West Maui gets 400 in. (1,016 cm) of annual rainfall, while south of Kihei less than 10 in. (25.4 cm) of rain falls in an average year. In general the northern and eastern slopes of Haleakala are wet, as are the summit and higher elevations in West Maui. Leeward areas are dry.

Lava flows that make up the isthmus have weathered into soils ideally suited to sugar and pineapple production. With its abundant sunshine and good soils, the isthmus needed only water to make it productive. This was provided in the development of the sugar plantations by 160 mi (256 km) of tunnels that brought water from east Maui to the cane fields.

233

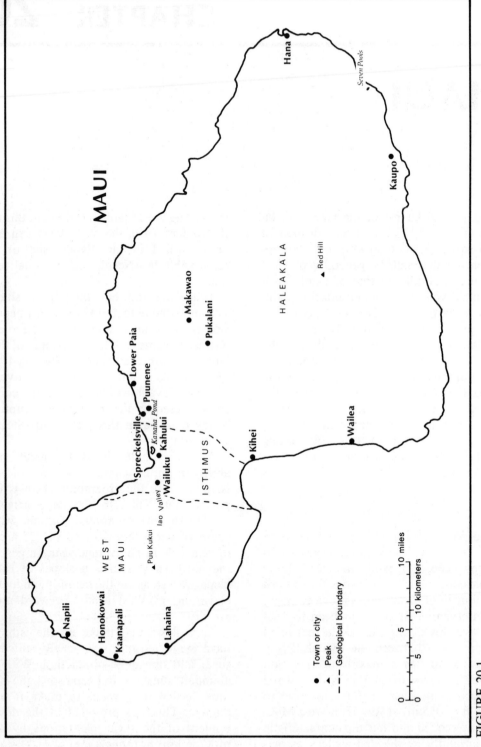

FIGURE 20.1

FIGURE 20.2.   Haleakala Crater, Maui. *Upper view*: In late morning and early afternoon the sun heats the black cinder and rock of this great eroded pit. *Lower view*: Clouds begin to form and obscure the otherwise prominent cinder cones.

FIGURE 20.3. Waterfalls on the north coast of east Maui, typical of many seen on the Hana Highway that links the urban centers of Wailuku and Kahului with the small settlement at Hana.

ECONOMIC GEOGRAPHY

Maui is the only Hawaiian island that grows both sugar and pineapple. The pineapple industry is small, with only one company, Maui Land and Pineapple; the large growers, Dole and Del Monte, do not have plantations on the island. Pineapple is grown on the lower slopes of Haleakala, in the isthmus area, and in the northwest portion of West Maui. Sugar is grown in both the isthmus region and near the coast of West Maui. In both areas the fields are irrigated. The yields of the Hawaiian Commercial and Sugar Company plantation at Puunene are the second highest in the islands. Two other companies, Pioneer Mill Company at Lahaina and Wailuku Sugar Company at Wailuku, are also getting good yields.

Cattle ranching and diversified crops are also important to the agricultural economy. Haleakala Ranch Company and Ulupala Kua Ranch, Inc., are two of the biggest landowners in the islands. Maui onions are famous for their high quality and delicate flavor; locally grown potatoes are used in Maui potato chips, which are popular on all the islands.

Sugar is shipped in bulk from the port of Kahului, which has facilities for receiving roll-on–roll-off vessels, as well as tugs and barges. It is the principal port for the island. A much smaller port at Maalaea is used mostly by commercial and recreational fishing craft.

The visitor industry is extremely important on Maui, with hotels in the Lahaina-Kaanapali area and on the coast south of Kihei. Development of new facilities has been rapid in both regions, which have ample sunshine and very little rain, and the coastal strip south of Kihei is now lined with condominium apartments. Attractions of particular interest to visitors are the Haleakala summit, Iao Needle, and the winding, narrow road to the Seven Pools in the Hana district. The town of Lahaina capitalizes on its history. It was once the capital of the islands and

an important center for the whaling industry. Nearby is the famous old school at Lahaina Luna, established by the early missionaries for the education of the native Hawaiian population and now a unit of the state's public education system.

URBAN PLACES

The small cities of Kahului (population 12,972) and Wailuku (8,270) at the northern end of the isthmus have coalesced to become one urban center, by far the largest on the island. Wailuku is the county seat; Kahului has both the harbor and the airport. Both cities have shown considerable growth since 1970, when the combined total population was about 16,000. Surprisingly, however, the Kahului suburb of Puunene declined in population from 1,132 in 1970 to 571 in 1980. The pineapple cannery is located in Kahului, as is Kanaha Pond, an important bird sanctuary. The sugar mill is located in Wailuku. Both cities have their high schools: Maui High in Kahului and Baldwin High in Wailuku.

Southeast of Kahului are Pukalani (3,963) and Makawao (2,912). In some respects both can be considered to be bedroom suburbs of Kahului, but Makawao is a *paniolo* town for the Haleakala Ranch lands nearby and seems to have a more distinct identity of its own. Changes in the character of the community, with the down-to-earth *paniolo* influence diminishing and more sophisticated restaurants and boutiques increasing, have caused dissatisfaction among some of the local residents.

The third-largest community on Maui is Lahaina (6,105) on the West Maui coast. The booming tourist industry in the area has resulted in growth from 3,718 in 1970 to the present population. Lahaina is full of historical buildings as well as more modern housing areas and shopping centers; the older residential areas are evolutions of the plantation camp for workers at Pioneer Mill. The residence of Maui's most famous missionary family, the Baldwins, is located on Front Street, and close

FIGURE 20.4. Two views of Lahaina, Maui. *Above*, the refurbished Pioneer Inn is a popular tourist attraction. *Below*, the "real" Lahaina, a small village where local people live and work.

FIGURE 20.5.   Buddhist temple near Lower Paia, Maui. The small structure near the palm tree houses the bell. When rung, it is supposed to bring good luck to the ringer.

by the harbor is the *Carthaginian,* a refurbished whaling ship. A small boat-and-yacht harbor has replaced the old Lahaina Roads, home port of the whaling fleet, as the principal waterfront facility. Mauka of Lahaina are the sugar fields of Pioneer Mill Company.

On the coastal strip north of Lahaina and extending through Kaanapali to the Napili-Honokowai settlement (2,455) is the most highly developed tourist hotel district on the island. Napili-Honokowai did not exist as a census unit in 1970, but now has a population of more than 2,000. North of Napili the coastal highway becomes narrow and difficult, and there is little in the way of settlements on the north and northeast coasts of the West Maui mountain.

East of Kahului the famous (or perhaps infamous) Hana Highway winds its way past Spreckelsville (named for Clause Spreckels, who controlled much of the sugar industry of the islands during the reign of King Kalakaua) and Lower Paia (1,516) to Hana (640) and the Seven Pools, an important tourist attraction. The road is narrow, winding, and in a poor state of repair. But it has its charms as it passes through tropical rain forests and coastal sections with marvelous views. Hana is famous as the location of the Hasegawa Store, a general store with a myriad of items for sale, and as the birthplace of Kaahumanu, said to be the favorite wife of King Kamehameha I.

From Kihei (5,644) to Wailea (1,111) urban growth has been intense; neither community appeared in the 1970 census. Urbanization has been in the form of uniformly new and expensive condominium communities.

GEOGRAPHIC IMPRESSIONS

Maui is an enigma. On the one hand, development has been intense. The tourism that has grown by leaps and bounds north of Lahaina on the west coast shows signs of producing another Waikiki, with all its problems. The new "boom town" on the western coastal strip of Haleakala seems to please few local residents, but it makes real estate salespeople and speculators happy. On the other hand, there is still the old Maui: cattle ranches; diversified farms; tiny settlements reached only by poor, narrow roads or jeep trails; sugar plantations and the ever present mills; pineapple fields; and the magnificent Haleakala summit crater.

One gets the impression that there are two Mauis, one that visitors and new residents from the mainland are familiar with and one that they may never see. The Maui that the visitor rarely sees has the appeal of the old Hawaii that *kamaainas* know and love.

REFERENCES

Kyselka, W., and Lanerman, R. *Maui: How It Came to Be.* Honolulu: University Press of Hawaii, 1980.

Macdonald, G. A., and Abbott, A. T. *Volcanoes in the Sea.* Honolulu: University of Hawaii Press, 1970.

State of Hawaii, Department of Planning and Economic Development. *Data Book.* Honolulu: State of Hawaii, Department of Planning and Economic Development, 1980.

Stearns, H. T. *Geology of the State of Hawaii.* Palo Alto, Calif.: Pacific Books, 1966.

CHAPTER 21

KAUAI AND NIIHAU

Kauai and Niihau, collectively Kauai County, are remarkable islands. The former has spectacular features in its physical geography, while Niihau, an economic satellite of Kauai, has a unique cultural geography (Figure 21.1).

KAUAI

The northernmost of the main group of Hawaiian Islands, Kauai is also the oldest. It is a single, greatly eroded shield volcano whose rocks have been dated by the potassium-argon method as 5.6 to 3.8 million years old (Stearns 1966, 75).

Physical Geography

Perhaps the most remarkable feature of the physical geography of Kauai is its climate, particularly the great rainfall at Mount Waialeale, at 5,148 ft (1,569 m) the second-highest peak on the island. Average rainfall has been measured at 485 in. (1,232 cm) per year, highest of any location in the world. The island is farther north than the other inhabited Hawaiian Islands and is in the path of a greater number of cold-front storms that traverse the Pacific Ocean. Its location also puts it in the path of the prevailing trade winds that produce most of the summer rainfall in the islands, so that it is subject to frontal and orographic precipitation to an exceptional degree. Nevertheless, the southwestern coast has less than 20 in. (51 cm) of rain per year; it is in a pronounced rain shadow of the higher elevations at the center of the island.

The great rains are responsible for the Alakai Swamp, which extends for almost 10 mi (16 km) northwest of Waialeale and the island's highest peak, nearby Mount Kawaikini, 5,243 ft (1,598 m). Native vegetation adapted to the moisture thrives in the swamp as do some species of native Hawaiian birds that are endangered elsewhere in the islands.

Despite the great rainfall the longest river on the island, Waimea River, has a length of only 19.7 mi (31.7 km). It has carved the spectacular Waimea Canyon, 14.5 mi (23.3 km) long and 2,750 ft (838 m) deep. An equally spectacular gorge, Wainiha Gorge, is 11 mi (17.6 km) long and 2,000 to 3,000 ft (610 to 914 m) deep. It is not nearly as well known, however, since it is out of sight of the ordinary visitor.

The Wailua River, much shorter than the Waimea, is nevertheless well known since it is navigable by small boats and is a popular tourist attraction. It is fed by two beautiful waterfalls, Opaekaa and Wailua. The falls are of modest height but are visible and highly photogenic. Hinalele, Kapaka nui, and Manawaiopuna falls are all much higher but not as well known.

The famed Na Pali coast, in the northwestern part of the island, has intricately eroded sea cliffs towering to heights of as much as 2,700 ft (823 m). A number of amphitheater-headed valleys are part of the Na Pali coast. The most well known is

242

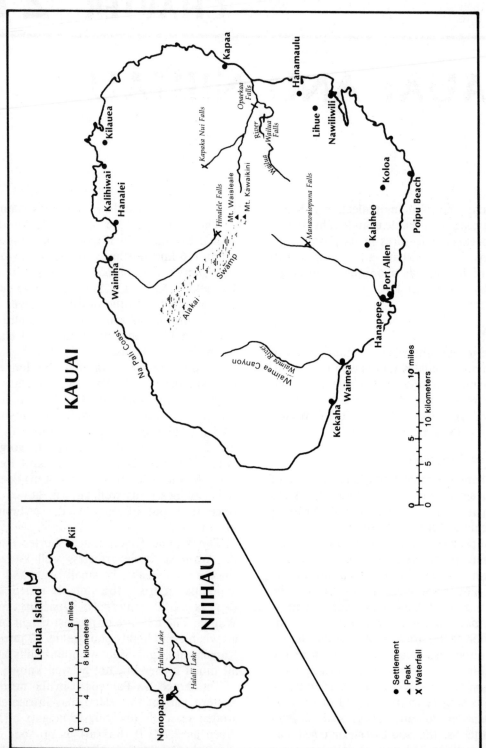

FIGURE 21.1

FIGURE 21.2 (*above*). Waimea Canyon, Kauai.
FIGURE 21.3 (*right*). Opaekaa Falls, Kauai.

Kalalau Valley, which can be reached by
a rugged, 12-mile (19.3-kilometer) hike or
seen more easily and conveniently from
above from a lookout point reachable by
automobile.

The north coast of Kauai is susceptible
to tsunamis, particularly those originating
in the Aleutians region. It is the most
vulnerable Hawaiian coast. Tsunami waves
have reached heights greater than 50 ft (15
m) at Wainiha, and there has been considerable property damage at Kalihiwai.

Settlement Patterns

Kauai's population of 38,891 (1980 census) is scattered throughout a number of
small towns. The largest population centers
are Kapaa (population 4,491) and the county
seat, Lihue (4,001). On the southwest coast
are Kekaha (3,261) and Waimea (1,565).
The latter is the site of Captain Cook's

FIGURE 21.4.   The Wainiha General Store on the north shore of Kauai. *Below*, the sign reminds residents that tsunamis are a hazard in the area. Wainiha was hit badly by tsunamis in 1946 and 1957.

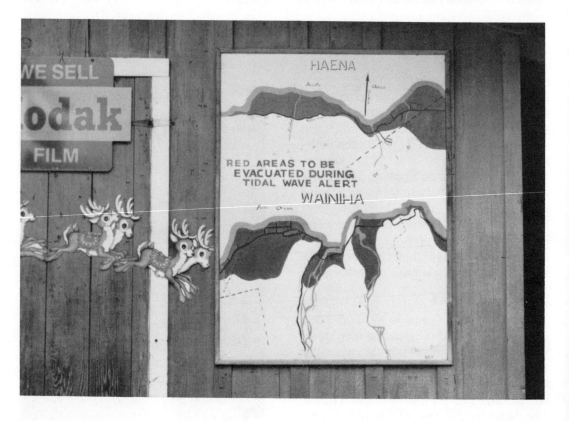

first landing in the islands, and there is a monument to this event in the town.

Hanamaulu (3,231), north of Lihue, is the island's fourth-largest town. In the southern part of the island are Kalaheo (2,499), Koloa (1,461), and Hanapepe (1,420). The north coast is less populated. Hanalei, sited on a beautiful semicircular bay and close to a picturesque valley where taro is still grown, has 482 residents. The largest of the north-shore communities is Kilauea (891).

Economy

Sugar and tourism are the mainstays of the island's economy. There are four plantations, with sugar planted extensively on the east and south coasts. The Koloa area, in the southeastern part of the island, was the site of the first successful plantation in the islands, and sugar is still grown there.

Tourist hotels are concentrated on the east coast near Kapaa and at Poipu Beach on the southeast coast. A hotel development at Hanalei Bay has not been successful, but there are plans for resorts on the north coast at other locations. A serious problem in planning developments in the area is the tsunami hazard.

Kauai has two ports: Nawiliwili near Lihue and Port Allen on the south coast near Hanapepe. Nawiliwili gets most of the shipping; it is equipped to load sugar in bulk and to receive Matson's small self-contained container ship *Mauna Kea*. Both Nawiliwili and Port Allen are provided with tug and barge service on a regular schedule.

NIIHAU

The island of Niihau is privately owned by the Robinson family of Kauai, who operate their land under the Niihau Ranch Company.

Physical Geography

The eroded remnant of the shield volcano that formed the island is only 73 sq mi (189 sq km) in area and 1,281 ft (390 m) in elevation, at Paniau. Niihau sits in the lee of the much larger Kauai and is shielded from the prevailing trade-wind orographic showers. Precipitation varies from an estimated 40 in. (102 cm) per year on the east coast to less than 20 in. (51 cm) in the extreme south. Despite the low rainfall the island has the largest natural lake in the state, 182-acre (74-hectare) Halulu Lake. A much larger, though intermittent, lake is Halalii, 840 acres (340 ha).

Cultural and Economic Geography

At the time of its discovery by Westerners Niihau had a subsistence agricultural economy based primarily on yams, which were noted by early ship captains for their high quality. The most reliable estimate of the population was by William Bayly, an astronomer on Cook's ship, who believed that the population numbered about 500.

There were 1,047 Niihauans in 1831, the date of the first accurate census. When the island was purchased from King Kamehameha V on January 23, 1864, for $10,000, the population was about 650. It was 164 in 1896 and 226 in 1980.

In 1970, 95 percent of the residents were pure Hawaiians, and the Hawaiian language is regularly spoken on the island, although English is taught in the elementary school.

No changes have been made to the Hawaiian life-style since the purchase of the island. There is no electricity, no hospital or clinic, no police force, no firearms, and no paved roads. There are a few trucks for the ranching operations. A number of the old Hawaiian fish ponds are still in operation.

While ranching has been the principal economic use since 1864, at one time Niihau exported turkeys, honey from kiawe trees, and charcoal. The yams for which the island was famous are still grown.

No visitors are permitted, except guests of the residents. Transportation from Kauai by means of a World War II vintage landing craft is provided by the owners. The craft makes weekly runs from Makaweli, Kauai,

FIGURE 21.5. Hanalei Valley on the north coast of Kauai. The Hanalei River provides irrigation water for taro fields, one of the few locations in the islands where Hawaii's first food crop is still grown.

FIGURE 21.6. Waioli Mission, Hanalei, Kauai. The home of the first Congregational missionaries has been refurbished and is open for visitors.

FIGURE 21.7.   From a broad sand beach on the west coast of Kauai, the island of Niihau is faintly visible on the horizon.

to one of three landings: Kii, on the northeast coast; Lehua, on the northwest coast; and Nonopapa, on the west coast (the appropriate landing is chosen based on prevailing wind and sea conditions). The island's cattle are taken off and food and necessities for the islanders landed.

Niihau is only 17 mi (27 km) from Kauai and 152 mi (245 km) from Honolulu. The sense of isolation experienced by the residents is entirely voluntary on their part. They are free to leave for visits to other islands or permanently. Most choose to stay, preferring their old Hawaiian lifestyle.

REFERENCES

Piianaia, A. "Niihau." Mimeographed. Honolulu: University of Hawaii, Hawaiian Studies Program.

State of Hawaii, Department of Planning and Economic Development. *Data Book*. Honolulu: State of Hawaii, Department of Planning and Economic Development, 1980.

Stearns, H. T. *Geology of the State of Hawaii*. Palo Alto, Calif.: Pacific Books, 1966.

CHAPTER 22

MOLOKAI AND LANAI

The islands of Molokai and Lanai (Figure 22.1) are discussed in a single chapter because both are small islands with relatively small populations and are of approximately the same degree of importance in the economic geography of the state. They are both in Maui County. There are nevertheless some interesting differences between the two in both physical and cultural geography.

MOLOKAI

This island is only 261 sq mi (676 sq km) in area but has an extremely varied geology and physical geography. In many respects it is the least economically developed of the main group of Hawaiian Islands.

Physical Geography

Molokai is made up of three principal geologic provinces: three separate shield volcanoes form the island. East Molokai, with a maximum elevation of 4,970 ft (1,515 m) at Kamakou, has the lush, heavily eroded, spectacular scenery of other windward island locations. The shield measures 27 mi (43 km) east to west and 8 mi (12.8 km) north to south.

The West Molokai shield rises to only 1,381 ft (421 m) at Puu Nana and has an east-to-west extent of approximately 12 mi (19.3 km). It is considerably older than

East Molokai and has few of the typical features (amphitheater-headed valleys, for instance) commonly associated with Hawaiian physical landscapes. It has a flatter dome than most Hawaiian shield volcanoes; the dome is made up almost exclusively of thin pahoehoe and aa lava flows, with only a few well-eroded and weathered cinder and spatter cones in evidence. The Hoolehua plain was formed when East Molokai lavas ponded against the older West Molokai shield, in a manner similar to the formation of the Schofield Plateau of Oahu and the isthmus area of Maui.

A much smaller shield volcano formed the 4-square-mile (10.4-square-kilometer) Kalaupapa Peninsula, whose maximum elevation is only 405 ft (123 m). A crater 400 ft (122 m) deep indents the summit of the shield. A steep pali separates the Kalaupapa Peninsula from the remainder of the island.

Molokai's north coast has spectacular sea cliffs, some as much as 3,600 ft (1,097 m) high, and three great amphitheater-headed valleys—Wailau, Pelekunu, and Halawa—east of the Kalaupapa Peninsula.

The south shore of Molokai is a coastal plain with a wide fringing coral reef. According to Stearns (1966, 177), "Introduction of livestock and agricultural development caused great quantities of red soil to be eroded from the uplands, partly filling

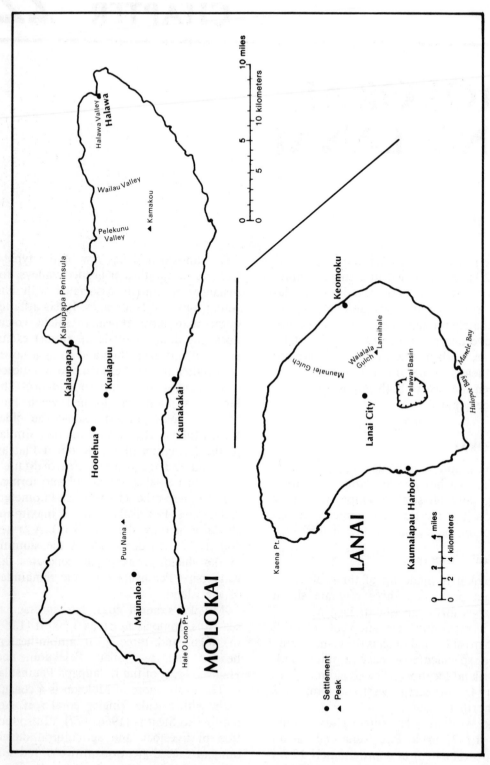

FIGURE 22.1

FIGURE 22.2.   Kalaupapa Peninsula, north Molokai. Kauhako Crater is visible near the water on the far side of the peninsula and the settlement of Kalaupapa on the near side. The steep palis separating Kalaupapa from the rest of the island of Molokai provided the isolation deemed necessary for establishment of a colony for victims of leprosy.

53 fishponds along the south coast now being invaded by mangrove trees."

East Molokai is generally wet, with maximum rainfall exceeding 250 in. (635 cm) per year northeast of the summit. West Molokai is decidedly dry; precipitation ranges from 40 in. (102 cm) per year to less than 15 in. (38 cm). The Kalaupapa Peninsula receives 40 to 50 in. (102 to 127 cm) of annual rainfall. Vegetation patterns follow climatic types: the eastern part of the island has tropical rain forests; West Molokai consists mainly of pineapple fields and overgrazed grasslands.

Cultural and Economic Geography

The island's population of 6,076 (1980) is scattered among a number of small com-

FIGURE 22.3.   Moaula Falls, Halawa Valley, Molokai, cascades 250 ft (75 m) down the head of the amphitheater-headed valley.

munities. The largest town, Kaunakakai, has a population of 2,249, up considerably from the 1,070 counted in the 1970 census. The second-largest community is Maunaloa, whose population decreased from 872 to 636 in the period 1970 to 1980. The decrease can be related to the closing of the Dole Pineapple plantation, which had been operating with only moderate success during the early years of the 1970s. Kualapuu, with a 1980 population of 502, is third largest. It was the plantation village for the Del Monte pineapple operation and the population of the town increased from 441 in 1970. Since the closing of the Del Monte plantation in January 1983 the village has no real economic base. As in Maunaloa, we might predict that the population will decrease.

Molokai's economy is based chiefly on ranching and tourism. The closing of the Dole plantation resulted in considerable

unemployment, some of which was alleviated by the opening of the Sheraton Molokai hotel on the western end of the island. The recent loss of employment due to the demise of the Del Monte pineapple operations may not be as easily compensated for since there are no current plans for additional development of tourist facilities.

Virtually all of western Molokai is either owned by Molokai Ranch, Ltd. (73,975 acres or 29,960 ha) or is Hawaiian Home Lands. These are lands provided as farmsteads to native Hawaiians, but the residents are raising few crops. Some of the Hawaiian Home Lands were previously leased to Dole Pineapple, but with the closing of the plantation they have reverted to their Hawaiian occupants.

Kaunakakai is the principal retail center of the island; there are two small tourist hotels nearby. It is also the island's chief

FIGURE 22.4.   Puu o Hoku Ranch, Molokai. The ranch is one of the island's largest land holdings. The much larger Molokai Ranch occupies almost all of central and western Molokai.

FIGURE 22.5. *Left*, the statue of Father Damien, the famous leper priest of Molokai, is on the grounds of the state capitol building in Honolulu, but tiny St. Joseph's Church (*right*), built by Damien before he took up his ministry at Kalaupapa, is on Molokai's south coast.

port and is provided with biweekly tug-and-barge service. Smaller barge harbors are at Kalaupapa, site of the colony for victims of leprosy, and Hale O Lono.

Most of eastern Molokai is conservation land, but there is some agriculture in the south coastal plain. The Puu O Hoku Ranch covering 14,262 acres (5,776 ha) is the largest agricultural enterprise.

The island of Molokai is most famous for Father Damien, who was the "leper priest" of the colony at Kalawao on the Kalaupapa Peninsula. He established churches, some of which are still in operation, both on the peninsula and "topside" on Molokai as well. The original colony at Kalawao was moved to the village of Kalaupapa where it remains today.

In 1979 unemployment on Molokai was 11.3 percent, highest of any of the Hawaiian Islands.

LANAI

Across the Kalohi Channel from Molokai lies the 139.5-square-mile (361.3-square-kilometer) island of Lanai. Unlike its neighbor to the north it has a rather simple physical and cultural geography, but its history is fascinating.

Physical Geography

Lanai is a single dome-shaped shield volcano with a maximum elevation of 3,370

FIGURE 22.6.   A tiny church with a big name, Ka Ekalesia O Jerusalem Hou-Hoomana O Ke Alii Ona Alii Ka Haku Ona Haku ("Jerusalem Hou, Congregational Church of the King of Kings and the Lord of Lords") in Halawa Valley, Molokai. Built in 1948, it is in the classic style of small churches on the island.

ft (1,027 m) at Lanaihale. According to Emory (1969, 4) the name means "a swelling or hump," presumably due to its regular shape when viewed from nearby Maui. Pukui, Elbert, and Mookini (1974), generally considered to be authoritative regarding Hawaiian place-names and their meanings, give a meaning of "conquest day," however (128, 262).

The lee provided by Maui makes Lanai dry, with annual rainfall ranging from 35 in. (89 cm) near the summit to less than 10 in. (25 cm) in the southwest. The island has no perennial stream or lake. The Maunalei-Waialala Gulch, now mostly dry, is 12.9 mi (20.7 km) long and is the longest stream feature.

Historical Geography

Captain James King of Cook's expedition provides us with the first description of the island: "The country to the south [Lanai] is high and craggy; but the other parts of the island had a better aspect and appeared to be well inhabited. We were told that it produced very few plantains, and bread-fruit trees; but that it abounds in roots such as yams, sweet potatoes, and tarrow" (King 1785, 115).

The next sighting of the island was by Nathaniel Portlock on May 30, 1786, and, coincidentally, by Jean Francoise de G. LaPerouse on the same night. Neither included much in the way of a description, but Portlock (1789, 66) reported that a few canoes came out to his ship but "brought nothing of any consequence to barter."

A more complete description of Lanai was provided by Archibald Menzies, the surgeon on George Vancouver's ship. He wrote:

Early next morning we passed to the southward of Kahoolawe and was [sic] at noon off the south end of Lanai. . . . the south point of which appearing a steep, sandy precipice bore N 20 E about 4 miles off. The wind being light and variable, with clear weather in the middle of the day, gave us an opportunity of observing the state and naked appearance of the island, which seemed thinly covered with shrivelled grass in a scorched state. No hamlets or plantations were to be seen, no trees or bushes adorned the face of the country, which swelled out gradually to a moderate height, so that we have reason to think that the island is but very thinly inhabited. A few canoes came off to us with two or three men in each, which we conjectured were a fishing party or led merely by curiosity, as they brought nothing to dispose of and had no women with them. (Menzies 1920, 22)

Estimates of the island's population could not have been very accurate, since the early explorers did not make landings. In 1823 Reverend William Ellis described the island as he passed it on an interisland schooner. He thought "the inhabitants are few, probably not exceeding 2,000" (Ellis 1969, 23). The 1838 census counted 1,200 on Lanai, while the census of 1846 numbered but 616. The reason for the drastic reduction

FIGURE 22.7.   The island of Lanai as seen across the Auau Channel from Lahaina, Maui.

in population can only be a matter of speculation. Emory (1969, 8) believes that there was large-scale emigration to Lahaina, Maui, which then was an important community in the islands. There was no evidence of deaths from epidemics of measles or smallpox, which were affecting the populations of some of the other islands.

Missionaries reached Lanai by 1837, when it was reported that a church and schools had been built. The northwest point of Lanai (Kaena Point) had been established as an exile colony for women who had committed theft or adultery. Men guilty of the same crimes were sent to Kahoolawe.

In 1855 a colony of Mormons arrived and established a community in Palawai Basin on land leased from native chiefs (*alii*). The colony did not succeed and the population dropped from 600 to 378 between 1863 and 1866, due to the exodus of the Mormons. There were further declines to 348 in 1872 and to 177 six years later.

Frederick H. Hayselden, son-in-law of Walter Murry Gibson, the Mormon leader on the island, established a sugar plantation in 1882 on land his wife inherited from Gibson. The Maunalei Sugar Co. Ltd. at Keomuku brought in Japanese laborers and made a number of improvements to the land, but the enterprise failed in 1901.

In 1922 the Lanai Ranch Company owned most of the island, except for some ranch lands owned by Charles Gay and approximately 500 acres (203 ha) in native land titles. In December 1922 the Hawaiian Pineapple Co., Ltd., acquired the Lanai Ranch Company lands. Castle and Cooke, Inc., which subsequently acquired Dole Pineapple (originally Hawaiian Pineapple Co.), now owns 98.3 percent of Lanai. The remaining acreage is either in small private plots or is state owned.

Economic Geography Today

Pineapple is virtually the only economic activity on the island and provides employment for most of the island's residents. Lanai City (1980 population of 2,097) has all but 28 of the entire population of Lanai. It is the state's largest and most sophisticated plantation "camp."

A barge harbor has been built at Kaumalapau, on the southwest coast, to provide shipping facilities so that the island's pineapple crop can reach the cannery at Honolulu and consumer goods can be provided for island residents. The best road on Lanai links Lanai City with Kaumalapau Harbor. An adequate road provides transportation to Manele and Hulopoe bays on the south coast. Manele Bay is the site of a small-boat harbor and marina, and Hulopoe Bay has an excellent county beach park.

Lanai Airport is served by both major

airlines in Hawaii; a number of smaller airlines also fly to Lanai. The only hotel on the island is the Lanai Lodge, which has twelve rooms for guests—its bar and dining room are the chief meeting place for both island residents and visitors.

There is a public school with grades from kindergarten through twelfth and a public library.

Lanai had the largest percentage of residents of Filipino extraction of any census district in the islands in 1980, with 51.3 percent so classified. In the summer months, however, large numbers of Caucasian youths from the U.S. mainland come to the island to work in the pineapple harvest. They swell the population of the island and reduce the percentage of Filipinos considerably.

REFERENCES

Ellis, W. *Polynesian Researches: Hawaii.* Tokyo: Charles E. Tuttle Co., 1969.

Emory, K. P. *The Island of Lanai: A Survey of Native Culture.* Honolulu: Bishop Museum Press, 1969.

King, J. *A Voyage to the Pacific Ocean.* vol. 3, 2nd ed. London: H. Hughes for C. Nicol and T. Dell, 1785.

LaPerouse, J.F. de G. *A Voyage Around the World.* vol. 1. London: Printed for G. G. and J. Robonson, 1799.

Menzies, A. *Hawaii Nei 128 Years Ago.* Honolulu: The New Freedom Press, 1920.

Portlock, N. *Portlock's Voyage Around the World.* London: Printed for J. Stockdale, 1789.

Pukui, M. K.; Elbert, S. H.; and Mookini, E. T. *Place Names of Hawaii.* Rev. and exp. ed. Honolulu: University Press of Hawaii, 1974.

State of Hawaii, Department of Planning and Economic Development. *Data Book.* Honolulu: State of Hawaii, Department of Planning and Economic Development, 1980.

Stearns, H. T. *Geology of the State of Hawaii.* Palo Alto, Calif.: Pacific Books, 1966.

Vancouver, G. *A Voyage of Discovery in the North Pacific Ocean.* vol. 2. London: Printed for G. G. and J. Robonson, 1798.

CHAPTER 23

THE PROBLEM OF KAHOOLAWE

The smallest of the islands in the main Hawaiian group is Kahoolawe, containing but 45 sq mi (116 sq km). The island is uninhabited and has been used as a military firing range since the beginning of World War II. What, then, is the problem? It is simply that there are many in the state who want the island returned to what they consider more suitable uses.

PHYSICAL GEOGRAPHY

The island is formed from a single volcanic dome and is one of the older of the main group of islands. Its location, in the lee of the massive shield of Haleakala on Maui, prevents Kahoolawe from receiving much in the way of orographic, trade-wind precipitation. Consequently it is a relatively dry island with an estimated 25 in. (63 cm) rain per year on its eastern slopes and a good deal less in the southwestern area. The island has no perennial stream.

Wind erosion has been a factor on the island. Following overgrazing and deforestation, great quantities of soil have blown away. In windy weather dust clouds of red soil have been noted downwind, as well as dunes of the same red soil.

Maximum elevation is 1,477 ft (450 m) at Lau Makika in the northeastern sector of the island. Kahoolawe is separated from Maui by the Alalakeiki Channel, 6.9 mi (11.1 km) wide, and from Lanai by the Kealaikahiki Channel, 17.5 mi (28.1 km) in width.

HISTORICAL LAND USE

At the time it was appropriated by the U.S. government, the island was being used as a cattle ranch, but ranching operations were becoming increasingly difficult. Workers were able to remain on the island for only about one week at a time due to the scarcity of water.

Recent surveys have revealed a large number of archaeological sites indicating that the island was inhabited by ancient Hawaiians. The extent of habitation is conjectural, however, and Stearns (1966, 186) believed that "only a few families have lived on the island at one time, even in ancient days."

CURRENT LAND USE: THE NAVY VIEW

The U.S. Navy—specifically the Commander Third Fleet, with headquarters at Pearl Harbor—administers the island and schedules its use for military exercises, including firing of live ammunition. As there are units of all the armed forces stationed in Hawaii and all require realistic training in order to maintain an acceptable degree of combat readiness, the Navy view is that current use of the island for military purposes is amply justified. Kahoolawe is large enough to provide realistic targets, and it cannot be economically used for any other purpose. Moreover, if target islands such as Kahoolawe were not available near Hawaii, some units of the military forces in the state might be better located elsewhere.

THE HAWAIIAN VIEW:
ALOHA AINA

Aloha Aina ("love of the land") is the rallying cry of groups trying to retain the natural character of the land. Many part-Hawaiians feel that land is sacred and should not be abused by such activities as firing of live ammunition. The Protect Kahoolawe Ohana (*ohana* means family) is one such group. Initially some members of the ohana were activists who without permission occupied the island, thus preventing its use by the military. More recently, however, the ohana has chosen to fight its battle in the courts, with some degree of success. The Navy has been required to write an environmental impact statement justifying its use of the island, and the entire island has recently been declared to be worthy of inclusion on the National Register of Historic Sites. This designation alone does not preclude military use, but does place additional administrative controls over Navy activities.

THE SOLUTION:
IS THERE A MIDDLE GROUND?

The Navy has participated in archaeological surveys of Kahoolawe and has permitted visits to the island by members of the ohana and other interested groups. Such a cooperative attitude on the part of the military establishment is encouraging to those who would like to see the island returned to the state, possibly for park use. But there is still need for training exercises that utilize live ammunition.

Is joint use possible? Under current conditions it is not, since there is too much danger from unexploded ordnance to permit civilian use except under very carefully controlled conditions. In the future it might be possible to clean up a portion of the island and make it safe, but the effort is bound to be expensive and might in itself be dangerous.

A ready solution to the controversy is not in sight, but as long as both groups maintain their current cooperative attitudes, perhaps something can be worked out to provide each one with what it needs. Considerable progress has been made. Initially the Navy seemed to have no understanding of the largely spiritual views of the ohana, but continued dialogue has brought the two sides closer together. There is hope for the future. The problem cannot be viewed as one of right or wrong; there is virtue on both sides.

REFERENCES

Department of Geography, University of Hawaii. *Atlas of Hawaii.* Honolulu: University Press of Hawaii, 1973.

Stearns, H. T. *Geology of the State of Hawaii.* Palo Alto, Calif.: Pacific Books, 1966.

PART 5

CONCLUSIONS

CHAPTER 24

THE GEOGRAPHIC FUTURE: PROSPECTS AND PROBLEMS

Can we forecast the geographic future? Perhaps. In Hawaii a number of trends have become evident, and these can be used to make educated guesses about some aspects of the future geography of the islands. Some of these trends have been mentioned in previous chapters and will receive little or no elaboration here. Others are discussed for the first time and at greater length.

POPULATION

Hawaii's rate of population increase has been greater than the average for the United States as a whole, not surprising since the islands are part of the U.S. Sun Belt, which is attracting new residents throughout the nation. Other aspects of population affect Hawaii to a greater degree than other states. The small size of the islands and the scarcity of usable land makes a population increase more consequential in Hawaii than in most of the other states. Hawaii will certainly become more crowded, and there are many residents who will deplore this.

More important than the actual number of people is the ethnic mix. If most of the

newcomers are from the U.S. mainland, there will be a slow increase in the proportion of Caucasians to other ethnic groups. Inevitably, as the islands become more Americanized, the charm of Hawaii will be lost. There are many in the state who already deplore the proliferation of typical fast-food restaurants and the demise of local establishments specializing in ethnic dishes.

HOUSING

The average price of a single-family house or condominium apartment in Hawaii far exceeds that for the United States as a whole. Exceptionally high housing costs are a consequence of a shortage of land, the high cost of building materials, and the undeniable fact that Hawaii is a desirable place to live. Local residents who bought their houses when prices were lower and mortgage interest rates more reasonable can enjoy Hawaiian living. Those who are in the market for housing now in most cases cannot afford it. There is an increasing trend for high-priced homes to be bought by wealthy mainlanders who can afford to live in Hawaii and for local residents, who were born here and have families here, to migrate to the mainland.

ECONOMY

In the early years of the islands' history the Hawaiian economy was based successively on subsistence agriculture, trade with visiting ships, sandalwood, whaling, and plantation agriculture. The modern economy is more diversified, although it is still dominated by four industries: tourism, military activities, sugar, and pineapple.

The most important industry, tourism, has grown rapidly and steadily since statehood. But recent trends are disquieting. High air fares, airline strikes, inflation, and some changes in the local sentiment toward visitors have combined to cause a drop in visitor arrivals for the first time in many years. Whether this is a true trend or merely a dip in the ever-rising growth curve of this important industry remains to be seen.

Even if tourism continues as an important element of the state's economy for years to come, it may not retain its dominance. There will probably be no single industry that will take its place; the economy will become more diversified. Some of this diversification is already in evidence; there have been increases in manufacturing, retail sales, and service industries. A small but growing part of the economy is based on the utilization of Hawaii's exceptionally clear air and high mountains for scientific observations. A number of astronomical observatories have been built, most at the summit of Mauna Kea.

The plantation industries, sugar and pineapple, will become less important as land is shifted from agriculture to more remunerative urban uses.

ENERGY

The islands are still largely dependent on imported petroleum for the production of electrical power. But this is changing. Bagasse (sugarcane waste) is providing bio-mass energy for plantations, and in many cases the excess electrical power produced is being sold to the utility companies. Solar hot-water heating is in wide use in Hawaiian homes; more than 19,000 houses are equipped with solar systems. The regular trade winds make wind power a possibility, and some experimental windmills are already in operation. Ocean thermal energy shows some promise, but its development depends on outside funding from the federal government. Geothermal steam is more than just a promising source of electrical power, its development is already underway. Its development in the Puna district of the island of Hawaii has not been without controversy and problems.

Geothermal Steam
In Puna, Hawaii:
Cultural and Social Impacts

Extensive geothermal exploration and testing conducted by the Hawaii Institute of Geophysics (HIG) in the early 1970s resulted in the discovery of varying degrees of potential for geothermal power development on four islands: Oahu, Maui, Molokai, and Hawaii. By far the greatest potential source was found to be the Puna district of Hawaii, where recent volcanic activity associated with the summit craters of Kilauea and the East Rift Zone of the volcano demonstrates the presence of molten magma close to the surface.

After the extensive testing in the 1970s the HIG selected a site along the East Rift Zone, southwest of Pahoa in Puna, for a test well. Drilling was initiated in December 1975 and continued until April 1976, when the well had been drilled to a depth of 6,450 ft (1,966 m) (or 5,800 feet [1,768 m] below sea level) and geothermal water under pressure was reached (Thomas 1980). Temperatures measured at the well bottom were 676° F (358° C), well above those needed to make geothermal power generation feasible (Hawaii Institute of Geophysics 1978, iii). Six weeks of continuous flashing, from March to May 1977, verified

FIGURE 24.1.   A windmill near Kahuku Point, Oahu, is an experimental installation designed to test the feasibility of using wind power as an alternate energy source for the islands.

the existence of a significant geothermal reservoir.

This geothermal test well, when in operation, will generate a constant 3.5 megawatts of electricity, and plans have been made to sell power from the well to the Hawaiian Electric Company. Design work and testing continue to solve problems related to the corrosive properties of the steam, fluid disposal, noise abatement, and other matters associated with extensive development of the resource. Members of the HIG project estimate that the field could produce as much as 400 megawatts of power for 100 years (Thomas 1980). This amount substantially exceeds the 85.8 megawatts that is the current electricity usage on the island of Hawaii (Lee 1980). Thus there is the potential to generate far more power than the island of Hawaii currently needs, and there are interesting alternatives for industrial and economic expansion. However, concrete plans for development of the resource depend upon the solution of various problems relating to ownership and development rights and

FIGURE 24.2.   Geothermal steam facility (Puna district, Hawaii).

an evaluation of the environmental, socio-economic, and cultural aspects of various development alternatives.

Socioeconomic and Cultural Impacts of Development Alternatives

Since the geothermal reservoir is capable of producing substantially more power than the Big Island currently needs, several alternatives for development have been proposed:

- develop only enough of the geothermal resource to supply island power needs
- develop the resource more fully and encourage industries with high power needs to settle on the island
- develop the full potential of the resource and export power to other islands

Developing only enough of the geothermal resource to supply island needs would have a moderate and largely beneficial impact on the Puna district. Potential benefits are an increase in energy self-sufficiency, stimulation and diversification of the economy, and a decrease or stabilization of electrical power rates.

Potential negative consequences other than environmental concerns might be "domination of resource development by large integrated companies at the exclusion of small firms, . . . local population growth, change in land use, loss of traditional values of some cultural groups, . . . decreased scenic beauty by necessary transmission lines, . . . and population relocation to accommodate installation" (Austin 1979, 180).

Rapid full development of the geothermal resource, if great care is not taken to preserve local character, could cause substantial socioeconomic and cultural distress to local residents.

The possibility of transmitting excess electrical power to other islands has also been considered. Although the deep-sea cable technology to accomplish this is not currently available, it seems to be a strong possibility for the future. The state's interest is to make Hawaii energy self-sufficient, but the residents of Puna see this merely as an extension of a recurring state government trend to divert money and resources from the neighbor islands for use in Honolulu (Kinney 1980).

The State of Hawaii is growing and developing at a rapid rate, and it is unrealistic to expect the Puna district to remain unchanged in the face of overwhelming forces of population growth, modernization, and economic expansion. There are many potential benefits to be realized by a rational development of the geothermal resource, both locally and statewide. However, any development should be planned carefully to maximize benefits and minimize negative effects on the local communities involved. Thus in evaluating development alternatives, substantial statewide economic benefits must be balanced against the desirability of preserving local character, culture, and the environment.

A decision to proceed with full-scale geothermal power development, despite the arguments of the local Puna community, has been made. The prodevelopment forces have won this battle, but there are a number of others throughout the state.

PROBLEMS: DEVELOPMENT OR A UNIQUE HAWAII

The Puna district's controversy over geothermal power is just one of many in the state. On Oahu a battle has raged for many years between those favoring and opposing the building of a new interstate freeway (H-3). The fight to save agricultural lands in the Waiahole and Waikane valleys on the windward side of Oahu also had its vocal contestants, and the supporters of the rural life-style have temporarily won out. Development of a resort at Nukolii on the island of Kauai was also controversial. In this case the resort was approved

despite overwhelmingly negative opinion expressed in a local referendum. There have been similar disagreements on the islands of Maui, Hawaii, and Molokai. Although those who support the preservation of conservation and agricultural land and the unique Hawaiian rural life-style have won some battles, it seems clear that they eventually will lose the war.

PROSPECTS

Hawaii is bound to lose some of its uniqueness as it becomes increasingly just like the other forty-nine states. This is cause for sadness among some island residents. But some of the things that are so wonderful about the islands will never change. The trade winds will continue to blow, and the palis and magnificent amphitheater-headed valleys will be as spectacular as ever. Kilauea will continue to provide occasional shows for visitors and residents alike, the great summit crater of Haleakala will continue to awe spectators, and the Na Pali coast of Kauai will remain one of the scenic wonders of the world. Most important, the people of Hawaii will retain their unique spirit of Aloha for many years to come.

REFERENCES

Austin, P. C. *An Environmental Overview of Geothermal Development in Hawaii: Socio-Economic Issues.* Honolulu: Department of Planning and Economic Development, 1979.

Bostwick, B. E., Jr., and Murton, B., eds. *Puna Studies: Preliminary Research in Human Ecology, 1971.* Honolulu: Department of Geography, University of Hawaii, 1967.

Hawaii Institute of Geophysics. *Hydrology and Geochemistry of a Hawaiian Geothermal System: HGP-A.* Honolulu: Hawaii Institute of Geophysics, 1978.

Kamins, R. M. *Revised Environmental Impact Statement for Hawaii Geothermal Research Station Utilizing the HGP-A Well at Puna, Island of Hawaii.* Honolulu: Department of Planning and Economic Development, 1978.

Kamins, R. M., and Kornreich, D. *Legal and*

Public Policy Setting for Geothermal Resource Development in Hawaii. Honolulu: Department of Planning and Economic Development, 1976.

Kinney, E. Coordinator of Puna Hui Ohana. Conversation on January 15, 1980.

Lee, N. Hawaii Public Utilities Commission. Conversation on April 9, 1980.

Ripperton, J. C., and Hosaka, E. Y. *Vegetation Zones of Hawaii.* Bulletin 89. Honolulu:

Hawaii Agricultural Experiment Station, 1942.

State of Hawaii, Department of Planning and Economic Development. *Alternate Energy Sources for Hawaii.* Honolulu: Hawaii Natural Energy Institute and Department of Planning and Economic Development, 1975.

Stearns, H. T. *Geology of the State of Hawaii.* Palo Alto, Calif.: Pacific Books, 1966.

Thomas, D. M. Hawaii Institute of Geophysics. Conversation on January 15, 1980.

HAWAIIAN PLACE-NAMES

Common Name	Hawaiian Name	Meaning
Aiea	'Aiea	*Nothocestrum* tree
Aina Haina	'Āina Haina	Hind's land
Alakai	Alaka'i	to lead
Alalakeiki	'Alalākeiki	child's wail
Ala Moana		ocean street
Ala Wai		freshwater way
Alenuihaha	'Alenuihāhā	great billows smashing
Aliamanu	Āliamanu	bird salt-pond
Auau	'Au'au	bathe
Ehukai	'Ehukai	sea spray
Ewa	'Ewa	crooked
Haiku	Ha'ikū	speak abruptly or sharp break
Halalii	Hālāli'i	
Halape	Halapē	buried and missing
Halawa	Hālawa	curve
Haleakala	Haleakalā	house [used] by the sun
Haleiwa	Hale'iwa	house [of] frigate bird
Hale Koa		soldiers' house
Halemaumau	Halema'uma'u	fern house

Common Name	Hawaiian Name	Meaning
Hale O Lono		house of Lono
Halona	Hālona	peering place
Halulu		
Hamakua	Hāmākua	poetic: kuhi loa . . . long corner
Hana		poetic: rainy land, low-lying sky
Hanalei		crescent bay
Hanamaulu	Hanamā'ulu	tired [as from walking] bay
Hanapepe	Hanapēpē	crushed bay (due to landslides)
Hanauma		curved bay or hand-wrestling bay
Haupu	Hā'upu	recollection
Hauula	Hau'ula	red hau tree
Hawaii	Hawai'i	
Hawaii kai	Hawai'i kai	sea Hawai'i
Hawi	Hāwī	
Heeia	He'eia	
Hiilawe	Hi'ilawe	lift [and] carry
Hikulai Hale		
Hilo		
Hinalele		Hina's leap
Honaunau	Hōnaunau	
Honohina		gray bay or Hina's bay
Honokaa	Honoka'a	rolling [as stones] bay
Honokahua		sites bay
Honokowai	Honokōwai	bay drawing water
Honolulu		protected bay
Hoolehua	Ho'olehua	acting the expert
Hualalai	Hualālai	
Huialoha		meeting [of] compassion
Hulihee	Hulihe'e	turn and flee
Hulopoe	Hulopo'e	
Iao	'Īao	cloud supreme
Iolani	'Iolani	royal hawk
Iwilei		collarbone or a unit of measurement

Common Name	Hawaiian Name	Meaning
Kaaawa	Ka'a'awa	the wrasse fish
Kaala	Ka'ala	
Kaanapali	Kā'anapali	division cliff
Kaena	Ka'ena	the heat
Kahala	Kāhala	amberjack fish
Kahaluu	Kahalu'u	diving place
Kahana		cutting
Kahe		flow
Kaheana		
Kahoolawe	Kaho'olawe	the carrying away
Kahuku		the projection
Kahului		the winning
Kailua		two seas
Kaimu	Kaimū	gathering [at the] sea
Kaimuki	Kaimukī	the *ti* oven
Kaiwi		the bone
Kakaako	Kaka'ako	
Ka Lae		the point (cape)
Kalaheo	Kalāheo	the proud day
Kalalau		the straying
Kalapana		announce noted place
Kalaupapa		the flat plain
Kalawao		announce mountain area
Kalihi		the edge
Kalihi-Uka		inland kalihi
Kalihiwai		kalihi [with] stream
Kalohi		the slowness
Kaluanui		the big pit
Kamakou		the *Peucedanum* herb
Kamehameha		the lonely one
Kamuela		Samuel
Kanaha	Kanahā	the shattered [thing]
Kaneohe	Kāne'ohe	bamboo husband

Common Name	Hawaiian Name	Meaning
Kapaa	Kapa'a	the solid or the closing
Kapaau	Kapa'au	elevated portion of heiau (temple)
Kapahulu		the worn out soil
Kapaka Nui		large kapaka (raindrop)
Kapoho		the depression
Kau	Ka'ū	
Kauai	Kaua'i	
Kauhako	Kauhakō	the dragged large intestines
Kaukonahua		
Kaulakahi		the single flame (streak of color)
Kaumakani		place [in] wind
Kaumalapau		soot [from burning] placed [in] gardens
Kaumana	Kaūmana	
Kaunakakai		beach landing
Kaupo	Kaupō	landing [of canoes] at night
Kawaiahao	Kawaiaha'o	the water [used] by Ha'o (a chiefess)
Kawaihae		the water [of] wrath
Kawaikini		the multitudinous water
Kawailoa		the long water
Keaau	Kea'au	
Keahole	Keāhole	the *āhole* fish
Kealaikahiki		the way to foreign lands
Kealakekua		pathway [of] the god
Keanae	Ke'anae	the mullet
Kekaha		the place
Keolu		
Keomuku	Keōmuku	the shortened sand
Kihei	Kīhei	cape, cloak
Kii	Ki'i	image
Kikoa		
Kilauea	Kīlauea	spewing, much spreading
Kohala		
Koko		

Common Name	Hawaiian Name	Meaning
Kolekole		raw, scarred
Koloa	Kōloa	
Kona		leeward
Konahuanui	Kōnāhua'nui	large, fat innards
Koolau	Ko'olau	windward
Kou		Kou tree
Kualapuu	Kualapu'u	hill overturned
Kuilima		joining hands
Kukui		candlenut lamp, light of any kind
Kula		plain
Kuliouou	Kuli'ou'ou	sounding knee
Kumukahi		first beginning
Kunia		burned
Lahaina	Lāhainā	cruel sun
Lahaina Luna		upper Lahaina
Laie	Lā'ie	*'ie* leaf
Lanai	Lāna'i	day [of] conquest
Lanaihale	Lāna'ihale	house [of] Lāna'i
Lanikai		sea heaven, marine heaven
Laupahoehoe	Laupāhoehoe	smooth lava flat
Lawai	Lāwa'i	
Lehua		*lehua* flower
Lihue	Līhu'e	cold chill
Lualualei		
Lua Makika		mosquito pit
Maalaea	Mā'alaea	
Maili	Mā'ili	pebbly
Makaha	Mākaha	fierce
Makakilo		observing eyes
Makalapa		ridge features
Makapuu	Makapu'u	hill beginning or bulging eye
Makawao		forest beginning
Makaweli		fearful features

Common Name	Hawaiian Name	Meaning
Makiki		
Makua	Mākua	parents
Manawaiopuna		
Manele	Mānele	sedan chair
Manoa	Mānoa	vast
Maui		
Mauna Kea		white mountain
Maunalani		heavenly mountain
Maunalei		*lei* mountain
Maunaloa (also Mauna Loa)		long mountain
Mauna Ulu		growing mountain
Maunawili		twisted mountain
Mililani		beloved place [of] chiefs
Moanaloa		
Moiliili	Mō'ili'ili	pebble lizard
Mokapu	Mōkapu	taboo district
Mokauea		
Mokuaikaua	Moku'aikaua	section won [during] war
Mokuaweoweo	Moku'āweoweo	*āweoweo* fish section
Mokuleia	Mokulē'ia	isle [of] abundance
Molokai	Moloka'i	
Mookini	Mo'okini	many *mo'o* or many lineages
Naalehu	Nā'ālehu	the volcanic ashes
Nanakuli	Nānākuli	look at knee or look deaf
Na Pali		the cliffs
Napili	Nāpili	the joinings or *pili* grass
Napoopoo	Nāpō'opo'o	the holes
Nawiliwili	Nāwiliwili	the *wiliwili* trees
Niihau	Ni'ihau	
Ninole	Nīnole	bending
Niu		coconut
Nonopapa		invalid
Nukolii		

Common Name	Hawaiian Name	Meaning
Nuuanu	Nu'uanu	cool height
Oahu	O'ahu	
Olomana		forked hill
Onomea		
Ookala	O'okala	sharp digging stick
Opaekaa	'Ōpaeka'a	rolling shrimp
Pahala	Pāhala	cultivation by burning mulch
Pahoa	Pāhoa	
Paia	Pā'ia	noisy
Palama	Pālama	*lama*-wood enclosure
Palawai	Pālāwai	
Pali		cliff
Palolo	Pālolo	clay
Paniau	Pānī'au	touch midrib
Papaikou	Pāpa'ikou	
Pauoa		
Pelekunu		smelly (for lack of sunshine)
Pepeekeo	Pepe'ekeo	
Poamoho		
Pohakuloa	Pōhakuloa	long stone
Poipu	Po'ipū	completely overcast or crashing (as waves)
Pokai	Pōka'i	night [of] the supreme one
Pololu	Pololū	long spear
Puako	Puakō	sugarcane blossom
Pukalani		heavenly gate
Puna		
Punaluu	Punalu'u	coral dived for
Pupukea	Pūpūkea	white shell
Puuhonua O Honaunau	Pu'uhonua O Hōnaunau	
Puu Kukui	Pu'u Kukui	candlenut hill
Puunana	Pu'unānā	observation hill
Puunene	Pu'unēnē	goose hill

Common Name	Hawaiian Name	Meaning
Puu O Hoku	Pu'u O Hoku	hill of Hoku (night of the full moon)
Puu O Kohala		
Puu Puai	Pu'u Pua'i	gushing hill
Puu Waawaa	Pu'u Wa'awa'a	furrowed hill
Ulupalakua	'Ulupalakua	breadfruit ripening [on] back [of carriers]
Upolu	'Upolu	
Wahiawa	Wahiawā	place of noise
Waiahole	Waiāhole	mature *āhole* (a fish) water
Waialae	Wai'alae	mudhen water
Waialala	Wai'alalā	screaming water
Waialeale	Wai'ale'ale	overflowing water or rippling water
Waialua		
Waialua-Haleiwa		
Waianae	Wai'anae	mullet water
Waiawa		milkfish water
Waihee	Waihe'e	squid liquid
Waikane	Waikāne	Kāne's water
Waikapu	Waikapū	water [of] the conch
Waikiki	Waikīkī	spouting water
Wailau		many waters
Wailea		water of Lea (canoe-maker's goddess)
Wailua		two waters
Wailuku		water [of] destruction
Wailupe		kite water
Waimanalo	Waimānalo	potable water
Waimea		reddish water
Wainiha		unfriendly water
Waiohinu	Wai'ōhinu	shiny water
Waioli	Wai'oli	joyful water
Waipahu		bursting water
Waipio	Waipi'o	curved water

INDEX